Kierkegaard and Possibility

Also available from Bloomsbury

Kierkegaard and Philosophical Eros, by Ulrika Carlsson
The Selected Writings of Jan Patočka, by Erin Plunkett
Kierkegaard, Alastair Hannay

Kierkegaard and Possibility

Erin Plunkett

BLOOMSBURY ACADEMIC
LONDON • NEW YORK • OXFORD • NEW DELHI • SYDNEY

BLOOMSBURY ACADEMIC
Bloomsbury Publishing Plc
50 Bedford Square, London, WC1B 3DP, UK
1385 Broadway, New York, NY 10018, USA
29 Earlsfort Terrace, Dublin 2, Ireland

BLOOMSBURY, BLOOMSBURY ACADEMIC and the Diana logo are trademarks of
Bloomsbury Publishing Plc

First published in Great Britain 2023
This paperback edition published in 2025

Copyright Erin Plunkett and contributors, 2023

Erin Plunkett has asserted her right under the Copyright, Designs and Patents Act, 1988, to be identified as Editor of this work.

For legal purposes the Acknowledgements on p. xiii constitute an extension of this copyright page.

Cover image:
Sketch, c. 1959–61
oil and pencil on paper, from spiral-bound sketch book
10⅝ × 13⅜. (27 × 34 cm)
Tate, T07360
© The Estate of Francis Bacon. All rights reserved. DACS 2022
Series design by Charlotte Daniels

All rights reserved. No part of this publication may be reproduced or transmitted in any form or by any means, electronic or mechanical, including photocopying, recording, or any information storage or retrieval system, without prior permission in writing from the publishers.

Bloomsbury Publishing Plc does not have any control over, or responsibility for, any third-party websites referred to or in this book. All internet addresses given in this book were correct at the time of going to press. The author and publisher regret any inconvenience caused if addresses have changed or sites have ceased to exist, but can accept no responsibility for any such changes.

A catalogue record for this book is available from the British Library.

A catalog record for this book is available from the Library of Congress.

ISBN: HB: 978-1-3502-9898-9
PB: 978-1-3502-9902-3
ePDF: 978-1-3502-9899-6
eBook: 978-1-3502-9900-9

Typeset by Deanta Global Publishing Services, Chennai, India

To find out more about our authors and books visit www.bloomsbury.com and sign up for our newsletters.

Contents

List of contributors	vii
Foreword	x
Acknowledgements	xiii
List of abbreviations	xiv
Introduction: Existence and possibility *Erin Plunkett*	1

I Possibility and the philosophical tradition

1. From possibility to actuality and back again: Kierkegaard's ontology of the possible and the actually ideal *Jeffrey Hanson* 23
2. 'What our age needs most': Kierkegaard's metaphysics of *Virkelighed* and the crisis of identity of philosophy *Gabriel Ferreira* 42

II Possibility and experience

3. Possibility, meaning and truth: Kierkegaardian themes in Proust *Rick Anthony Furtak* 63
4. The secrecy of possibility in Kierkegaard's 'pattern' *Frances Maughan-Brown* 78
5. Kierkegaard and Deleuze: Anxiety, possibility and a world without others *Henry Somers-Hall* 99

III Possibility and freedom

6. On being educated for the possibility by *The Concept of Anxiety* *Jakub Marek* 125
7. Isaac I cannot understand: Sacrifice and the possibility of radical intersubjectivity *Tatiana Chavalková Badurová* 145

IV Possibility and hope

8. Just a glance! Kierkegaard's eschatology of the possible *Saitya Brata Das* 167

9 Climate despair from a Kierkegaardian perspective: Asceticism, possibility and eschatological hope *Hjördis Becker-Lindenthal*   184
10 Hope in the task of forgiveness *John Lippitt*   204

Bibliography   223
Index   238

Contributors

Hjördis Becker-Lindenthal is Affiliated Lecturer at the Faculty of Divinity at the University of Cambridge, UK. She is the author of the book *Die Wiederholung der Philosophie. Kierkegaards Kulturkritik und ihre Folgen* (2015), and co-editor with Andrew Sackin-Poll of *Kierkegaard in France* (2023). Her research interests are eco-theology, mysticism and philosophy of religion.

Saitya Brata Das teaches literature and philosophy at Jawaharlal Nehru University, New Delhi. He is the author of *The Political Theology of Schelling* (2016) and *The Political Theology of Kierkegaard* (2020).

Tatiana Chavalková Badurová is a PhD student at Charles University in Prague. Her doctoral thesis is an analysis of the philosophical and anthropological aspects of gift and sacrifice. She has written several articles on Kierkegaard, Derrida, Patočka, Girard and Nietzsche. She is currently finishing the first French-to-Czech translation of Derrida's *Gift of Death*.

Gabriel Ferreira is Assistant Professor of Philosophy at Unisinos University, Brazil, and former president of the Brazilian Kierkegaard Society. He is the author of *Esculpir em Argila: Albert Camus – uma estética da existência* (2014), as well as several papers on Kierkegaard and nineteenth-century philosophy. His research interests are metaphysics and epistemology, and the origins of contemporary philosophy.

Rick Anthony Furtak is Associate Professor of Philosophy at Colorado College, and past president of the Søren Kierkegaard Society (USA). His books include *Wisdom in Love: Kierkegaard and the Ancient Quest for Emotional Integrity* (2005), the edited volume *Kierkegaard's* Concluding Unscientific Postscript: *A Critical Guide* (2010), *Knowing Emotions: Truthfulness and Recognition in Affective Experience* (2018), *The Sonnets of Rainer Maria Rilke* (2022) and *Love, Subjectivity, and Truth: Existential Themes in Proust* (2023). Along with James D. Reid, he is Book Series Editor for *Bloomsbury Studies in Philosophy and Poetry*.

Jeffrey Hanson is Senior Philosopher at Harvard University's Human Flourishing Program. He is the author of *Kierkegaard and the Life of Faith: The Aesthetic, the Ethical, and the Religious in* Fear and Trembling (2017) and *Philosophies of Work in the Platonic Tradition: A History of Labor and Human Flourishing*. He is co-editor with Sharon Krishek of *Kierkegaard's* The Sickness unto Death: *A Critical Guide* (2022), co-editor with Michael R. Kelly and Brian Harding of *Michel Henry's Practical Philosophy* (2022), co-editor with Michael R. Kelly of *Michel Henry: The Affects of Thought* and editor of *Kierkegaard as Phenomenologist: An Experiment* (2010).

John Lippitt is Professor of Philosophy and Director of the Institute for Ethics & Society at the University of Notre Dame Australia. He is the author of *Love's Forgiveness: Kierkegaard, Resentment, Humility, and Hope* (2020), *The Routledge Guidebook to Kierkegaard's* Fear and Trembling (2nd edition, 2016), *Kierkegaard and the Problem of Self-Love* (2013) and *Humour and Irony in Kierkegaard's Thought* (2000). He has also co-edited several books, including (with George Pattison) *The Oxford Handbook of Kierkegaard* (2013). His current research interests focus mostly on ethical and intellectual virtues and vices, including self-righteousness as a vice of the digital age.

Jakub Marek is Assistant Professor in Philosophy at the Faculty of Humanities, Charles University, Czechia. He is the author of *Kierkegaard: Nepřímý prorok existence* [Kierkegaard. The Indirect Prophet of Existence] (2010) and *Leporello, A Philosophical Interpretation of Mozart's Don Giovanni* (2016). He has written numerous articles and book chapters on Kierkegaard, Jaspers, Nietzsche and philosophical anthropology.

Frances Maughan-Brown is Lecturer in Philosophy and the First Year Program at the College of the Holy Cross, Massachusetts. Her research interests are at the intersection of aesthetics and the political, especially feminism. She is the author of *The Lily's Tongue: Figure and Authority in Kierkegaard's Lily Discourses* (2019).

Erin Plunkett is Senior Lecturer in Philosophy and Religious Studies at the University of Hertfordshire, UK. Her research interests are phenomenology, existentialism and philosophical poetics. She is the author of *A Philosophy of the Essay: Scepticism, Experience and Style* (2018) and the co-editor (with Ivan Chvatík) of *The Selected Writings of Jan Patočka: Care for the Soul* (2022).

Henry Somers-Hall is Reader in Philosophy at Royal Holloway, University of London. He is the author of *Hegel, Deleuze and the Critique of Representation* (2012), *Deleuze's* Difference and Repetition (2013) and *Judgement and Sense in Modern French Philosophy* (2022). He is also co-editor of the *Cambridge Companion to Deleuze* (2012) and *A Thousand Plateaus and Philosophy* (2018).

Foreword

'Possibility' runs through Kierkegaard's writings from beginning to end; it is a term that he variously defines, deploys, applies, critiques, hints at and triumphantly affirms. As the chapters in this volume demonstrate, it is therefore not a term that can be given a single, simple and unequivocal meaning. 'Don't ask for the meaning, ask for the use', counselled Wittgenstein, and Kierkegaard uses, warns against and recommends possibility in sometimes bewildering but nevertheless arguably consistent ways. To follow the manifold of these uses, we need to be alert to the often-simultaneous presence of the philosophical, theological, literary, political and biographical dimensions in Kierkegaard's writings – and, again, the different viewpoints from which the subject is approached in the chapters that follow help us get some sense for this.

Among Kierkegaard's earliest writings is his 'Gilleleie Journal', a semi-fictional, semi-autobiographical account of a journey he took to northern Zealand, aged twenty-two, where he brooded over the multiple bereavements he had recently suffered and thought about what to do with his life. Standing on the sandy cliff-tops overlooking the Sound, he depicts himself as someone possessed of a manifold of possibilities – but which should he choose as the one possibility that will define his life? The question is personal and is expressed in literary form, but Kierkegaard already knows that it is loaded with philosophical and religious implications.

Each of the dimensions of possibility is taken up by one or more of the pseudonyms and fictional characters through whom Kierkegaard further developed his own intellectual persona. Assessor Vilhelm (also known in English as Judge William) depicts the aesthete of *Either/Or* as someone who has become lost to the world and alienated from himself through his absorption in aesthetic possibilities and consequent lack of concern for the real-world impacts of both his actions and inaction. Vigilius Haufniensis, author of *The Concept of Anxiety*, complicates the picture, showing how possibility is involved in human beings' original fall from the innocence of paradise, but is also a means of recovery from the debilitating effects of this fall. Johannes Climacus will be the one through whom Kierkegaard most systematically attends to philosophical treatments of possibility, turning the critique of possibility onto Hegelian (and some other) versions of philosophy and showing that they suffer from confusing what is only possible or ideal with actuality. This, he argues, is not something that can be arrived at through thinking alone but demands existential decision and action. Yet, as a later pseudonym, Anti-Climacus will explain, possibility is not merely to be discarded since it is integral to the very structure of being human. Without possibility, we would be slaves of necessity, unable to rise above the givens of our situation and move towards our future in freedom and hope.

Nor is Kierkegaard himself, writing in his own name as the author of a series of devotional or 'upbuilding' works, silent. The very first of these discourses urges us always to expect victory in facing the uncertainties and dark nights of our existential situation. Such a victory is only one possibility, but it is the possibility we must grasp and hold to if we are to live up to our own true potential. In *Works of Love*, he writes that it is through possibility that eternity 'entices and attracts a person onwards, from the cradle to the grave – if only we choose to hope'. But it is the pseudonym Anti-Climacus, who provides the most radical formulation, climaxing a meditation on the biblical saying that 'For God, all things are possible' with the startling and controversial assertion that 'God is: that all things are possible'. To know possibility in the right way or, better, to exist with a right relation to possibility, would be to know and to live with God.

To think this claim through to its logical conclusion would thoroughly recast the kinds of debates about the existence of God that have dominated the philosophy of religion and Christian apologetics for so long. The issue would no longer be whether God 'existed' in abstraction from human beings' existential struggles but whether, versus the Sartrean counsel of despair, those struggles – our struggles – allow us to see hope as the ultimate horizon of our existence. An impossible possibility beyond all possibility, perhaps – and certainly beyond any calculus of probabilities. Putting it like this, of course, suggests that the question of God, thus conceived, is at the same time a question about what it is to be human. We cannot therefore be surprised that Kierkegaard was (in Heidegger's own words) 'philosophically essential' for the godless philosophy of human existence developed in *Being and Time* – a philosophy in which the issue of existential possibility plays a central role. Whether it is the divine or the human or the relationship between divine and human, possibility is inescapable.

It is not the task of a foreword such as this to anticipate the contents of the book that follows. My aim here is simply to underline – three times in red, if possible – that 'possibility' is absolutely central to Kierkegaard's own path of thinking across the whole span of his writings and that it is also decisive with regard to the questions and insights that he bequeathed to his intellectual and spiritual (read, the German: *geistig*) posterity. Remarkably, this importance has scarcely been reflected in the secondary literature to date. We may therefore hope that this volume will not only be read and debated in its own right but will also stimulate a wider engagement – existential *and* intellectual – with the issues that are focussed in the deceptively simple concept that the contributors so illuminatingly address.

George Pattison
St Monan's, Fife

Acknowledgements

Several of the chapters in this collection began as conference papers for the three-day conference 'Living in Uncertainty: Kierkegaard and Possibility' at Senate House in London in November 2019. I am grateful to the Kierkegaard Society of the UK, the Danish Embassy of the UK, Iben Damgaard and Joakim Garff at the Søren Kierkegaard Research Centre, Graham Henderson of the Rimbaud and Verlaine Association, the Institute for Modern Language Research, the University of London School of Advanced Study and the University of Hertfordshire for their support with this event.

Chapter 11 is a revised version of chapter 8 from John Lippitt's book *Love's Forgiveness*[1] and is reproduced with the kind permission of the Licensor through PLSclear.

Thank you to Rick Anthony Furtak, John Lippitt, Maria Balaska, Daniel Conway and George Pattison for their generous advice during the conception of this volume, and warmest thanks to all the contributors.

Note

1 John Lippitt, *Love's Forgiveness* (Oxford: Oxford University Press, 2020).

Abbreviations

The following are conventional abbreviations for references to Kierkegaard's published works.

SKS   *Søren Kierkegaards Skrifter*, 28 vols, edited by Niels Jørgen Cappelørn, Joakim Garff, et al. Copenhagen: Gads, 1997–2013. (Citations give volume and page number)

KJN   ___. *Journals and Notebooks*, 11 vols., edited by Niels Jørgen Cappelørn, Alistair Hannay, David Kangas, Bruce H. Kirmmse, George Pattison, Vanessa Rumble and K. Brian Söderquist. Princeton, NJ: Princeton University Press, 2007–2020.

JP   ___. *Søren Kierkegaard's Journals and Papers*, 7 vols., edited and translated Howard V. Hong and Edna H. Hong, assisted by Gregor Malantschuk. Bloomington, IN: Indiana University Press, 1967–1978. (Citations give entry number rather than page number)

Pap.   *Papirer*, 16 vols., edited by P. A. Heiberg, V. Kuhr and R. Torsting. Copenhagen: Gyldendal, 1909–48. (Citations are to volume and tome number, entry category (A, B, or C), entry number and page number)

Introduction

Existence and possibility

Erin Plunkett

The term 'possibility' (*Mulighed*)[1] and its variants occur with curious frequency across Kierkegaard's writings. Key to Kierkegaard's ontology of the self, possibility, is linked to imagination, anxiety, despair, temporality, transition, the moment and a number of other core ideas in his works. The term is also central to Kierkegaard's critique of Hegelian logic, in which the underlying questions seem to be: What does freedom have to do with history? How is change possible? What does it mean to begin? Yet, it is a term that has not received sustained critical attention in studies of Kierkegaard. In what follows, I will attempt to establish a philosophical context for Kierkegaard's modal categories, to explain the reception of these categories within Kierkegaard scholarship and to sketch an outline of the meaning and significance of possibility in Kierkegaard's works.

In contemporary philosophy, the categories of 'possibility' and 'necessity' are most often discussed as part of modal logic, a subfield of analytic philosophy that deals with categories of propositions or judgements. The rather narrow logical understanding of these terms does not encompass the sense that they had for Kierkegaard, nor the sense in which these terms have been understood in the history of philosophy and theology, from which Kierkegaard draws. In this wider tradition, the logical use of these terms is grounded in a more fundamental ontology, that is, the modalities of possibility, actuality and necessity are modes of being; they are attempts to think about the nature of what is and about how things come to be. Kierkegaard, as a thinker of existence, movement and beginnings, could not help but be drawn to such questions.

It is Kierkegaard's ontological thought that, to my mind, grounds the different themes and approaches to Kierkegaardian possibility that are represented in this collection, even where ontology is not the explicit concern. Some basic historical context in this area will therefore help to lay the groundwork for an understanding of Kierkegaard's use of possibility and related terms.

Senses of being

Aristotle's recognition in the *Metaphysics* of a diversity of senses of being, particularly his distinction between 'what a thing is' and 'that a thing is' is a seminal moment in the thinking of being.

> There are several senses in which a thing may be said to 'be', . . . for in one sense the 'being' meant is 'what a thing is' or a 'this', and in another sense it means that a thing is of a certain quality or quantity or has some such predicate asserted of it. While 'being' has all these senses, obviously that which is primarily is the 'what', which indicates the substance of the thing.[2]

On the one hand, *what* a thing is, or essence, accounts for our ability to know the world and our experience of continuity through time and change. On the other hand, *that* a thing is, or existence, refers to the sheer contingency of factual being, that there is being (or some particular being) rather than nothing.

Two strands of thinking about these terms emerge in the history of philosophy, existing side by side and forming something of the soul of philosophy, the impulses that drive philosophical enquiry.[3] The first strand is broadly Platonic, affording to 'essence', that which makes a thing what it is or ensures its stable identity. Particular entities are granted shares of being in proportion to their contact with or participation in essence or idea. Full being is that which is eternal, unchanging and universal. Conceiving of essence as being in the fullest sense, and as that to which thought properly relates, ensures the intelligibility of being, or, in other words, seeks to guarantee the identity of being with our thought. This sort of approach is taken up by various scholastic and idealist figures and reaffirmed in Hegel, who, although does not share the details of Plato's ontology, follows the broad strokes of identifying being with the universal or the whole, rather than the particular. This is evident in Hegel's analysis of language at the beginning of the *Phenomenology of Spirit*, in which the ontological 'truth' of language lies in universal concepts or essences, such that even when one appears to be referring to some particular, the actual referent is a universal.[4] In this broadly Platonic or idealist picture, the temporal and contingent character of existence is rendered obscure or occluded by the focus on being as essence.

The second strand, following Aristotle and Aquinas, denies the move to give priority to 'what is' or 'essence', recognizing that essence tells us nothing about whether a thing exists or how it came to be. The latter question will become central for Kierkegaard, as a thinker of possibility. In Aristotle, that which turns a possibility into an actuality is movement (κίνησις). Existence in this framework is an act, the coming to be of that which was not, of that which was merely possible being. As Kierkegaard's pseudonym Johannes Climacus describes it in *Fragments*: 'it is the change from not being to being' (*ikke at være til at være*).[5] There is thus no gradation of being; a thing either is or is not, and essence alone does not entail factual existence.[6] Climacus makes the point elegantly: existence is subject to the dialectic of Hamlet – to be or not to be.[7] Thus the need, in this broadly existential strand of ontological thinking, to keep existence and essence radically distinct from one another, while acknowledging that both are present for any actually existing being.

The Platonic–Hegelian approach tends to fold existence into essence as a way of preserving intelligibility, yet at the expense of recognizing the peculiar character of existence as becoming. Kierkegaard relates these difficulties as well as any reader of this tradition. What of beginnings? What of possibility in a radical sense, not some particular possibility or set of possibilities but of possibility as such, of coming into existence? While the idealist strand of metaphysics offers a world that conforms to our thinking of it through our grasping of essences, the second strand profoundly questions this identity between being and thought by acknowledging the diversity of being and confronting existence (likewise movement, beginning, possibility) as that which cannot be rendered fully intelligible. In his own thinking, Kierkegaard seizes on the sense of being as existence, and it is on the grounds of forgetting what it means to exist that Kierkegaard attacks Hegel and other idealist projects. As Climacus describes in *Concluding Unscientific Postscript*, existence is the gulf that separates being from thought.[8] And attending to existence, as a philosophical matter or as a matter of existential commitment, requires accepting that being always exceeds our conceptions of it. The category of existence becomes, in Kierkegaard's hands, a way of positioning himself against what he perceives to be a dangerous tendency in idealist thought to ignore the ontological reality of contingency and, consequently, of freedom. In order to understand these existential phenomena, Kierkegaard calls for a different mode of enquiry, one that emphasizes rather than attempts to eliminate contingency, that attends to moods, affective states and regions of experience typically left out of the frame.

The contingency (*Tilfældighed*) of existence is a consistent theme across Kierkegaard's writings and is intertwined with the notion of possibility.[9] The fact that in life we encounter determinate beings with particular qualities, beings that, to use the traditional conceptual vocabulary, have both an essence and an existence, tells us nothing about how or why a being came to exist. Climacus in *Fragments* associates the 'thatness' of existence, the fact that anything exists at all, with the feeling of wonder. He describes wonder (*Beundring*) as 'the passionate sense for coming into existence', for 'wherever coming into existence is involved [. . .] there the uncertainty (which is the uncertainty of coming into existence) of the most certain coming into existence can express itself only in this passion [wonder] worthy of and necessary to the philosopher (Plato–Aristotle)'.[10] Climacus here points to the fact that a being which comes into existence never does so necessarily; its coming into existence is rather contingent, that is, a matter of uncertainty, of possibility. While for the Greeks, philosophy begins with 'a passionate sense for coming into existence', for Kierkegaard, in a certain manner, it ends there too – provided that this 'passion' is turned towards the coming into existence of oneself.

In Kierkegaard's reading, Hegel attempts, illicitly, to appropriate existence into the realm of logic, effectively eliminating contingency, and therefore existence in finitude, altogether. As Kierkegaard's pseudonym Vigilius Haufniensis argues in *The Concept of Anxiety*, logic is the realm of necessity; it concerns *what* there is but cannot account for factual existence and how it came to be.

> Neither logic nor actuality is served by placing actuality in the Logic. Actuality is not served thereby, for contingency, which is an essential part of the actual, cannot be admitted within the realm of logic. Logic is not served thereby, for if logic has thought actuality, it has included something that it cannot assimilate, it has appropriated at the beginning what is should only *praedisponere* [presuppose]. The penalty is obvious. Every deliberation about the nature of actuality is rendered difficult, and for a long time perhaps made impossible, since the word 'actuality' must first have time to collect itself, time to forget the mistake.[11]

One way to understand the claim that logic can give no account of existence (or 'that there is') is that existence is a presupposition for logical statements rather than a predicate or a concept that can be added to something. This was the import of Kant's remark that one hundred actual thalers do not contain anything more than one hundred possible thalers.[12] In other words, the actualization of a possibility, the bringing of a thing into existence, cannot be a predicate of a thing, in the same manner as being gold or being heavy.[13] A thing may exist or not, but its coming into existence (its change from 'possible' to 'actual' being) has no part in any logical statements we might make about it. Kierkegaard adopts this point for his own purposes, since, on the other hand, he wishes to maintain that 'there is all the difference in the world between the mere idea of something and its actually existing. Precisely for that reason he rejected what he understood to be the Hegelian claim that existence can be derived from a purely logical analysis of pure thought'.[14]

To give another example of where Kierkegaard understands his own sense of possibility as a departure from the Hegelian, the 'Interlude' of *Philosophical Fragments* offers an extended understanding of possible and actual being, of the 'transition' or 'movement' by which what is not comes into being.[15] The traditional wisdom, to which Hegel adheres but which is not unique to him, is that possibility is entailed in actuality. If a thing is, if it exists, then it is de facto possible; otherwise it could not have come to be, since its coming to be would be impossible. 'Possible' here is used in the logical sense of the opposite of impossible, and the possible is seen as a precondition for actuality. If something is, then it either must necessarily be, in which case it must also be possible for it to be, or it must have come into existence contingently, in which case it must have been possible for it to come to be.[16] Possibility means, strictly speaking, that a state of affairs is not logically impossible. Kierkegaard departs from this understanding, citing two senses of being: necessary being (broadly equivalent to essence or ideality) and actual or factual being, which is contingent. Climacus insists that necessary being cannot be said either to be possible or to have been possible. In Kierkegaard's ontology, the necessary and the possible are opposite terms, since any necessary being must always be and must always have been, whereas, on the contrary, a factually existing being could either be or not be.

Ultimately, for Kierkegaard, the only sense in which the necessary and the possible may be held together is existentially, rather than logically, and this is because Kierkegaard's model of selfhood involves the relation of incommensurable elements. As Haufniensis describes in *The Concept of Anxiety*, the activity that comprises self is a holding together of incommensurables: possibility and necessity, temporality and eternity, finitude and infinitude. The self as this activity of holding together polarities is an existential achievement, a movement of freedom.[17] If it were instead a logical movement, the synthesis of apparent polarities would merely erase any real difference between them, whereas an existential act, by virtue of Kierkegaard's model of the self, is capable of maintaining difference in identity.

Reception of Kierkegaard as ontological thinker

Despite the evident ontological considerations in Kierkegaard's work, modern Kierkegaard studies do not tend to treat Kierkegaard as an ontological thinker responding to the long tradition of ontological thinking within philosophy and theology. But there was a period in the early to mid-twentieth century when questions about Kierkegaard's ontology appeared vital and urgent, and some of the most significant European thinkers of the century were profoundly impacted by Kierkegaard's understanding of existence.

There are primarily two strains of thought during this period that deal with Kierkegaard's ontology and his discussion of possibility as a modality of being: the first is Catholic theology, particularly neo-Thomist thought, and the second is phenomenology and existentialism. These strains often overlap, and both rely on a common Greek and scholastic heritage, particularly Aristotle's accounts of existence, possibility and motion. The Catholic strain is shaped by early twentieth-century *ressourcement* theology, a movement of theological renewal that began in Italy in the mid-nineteenth century and was spurred by Pope Leo XIII's (1810–1903) interest in reviving Catholic theology – especially the writings of Aquinas – for modernity. This movement spread outside of Italy and led to a blossoming of 'new theology' across several European countries. Theologians returned to the Church Fathers for inspiration and reinvigoration of the Catholic imagination, yet, rather than a simple return to the past, this gaze backward formed part of an investment in their own immediate intellectual, religious and political environment. As Joshua Furnal has shown, the Catholic engagement with Protestant sources at this time was more significant than has been previously thought, and many Catholic thinkers were influenced by Kierkegaard's writings. Cornelio Fabro is a central figure, not only as the principal translator of Kierkegaard's works into Italian but also as the author of numerous works of Kierkegaard exegesis, linking the philosopher to key ideas in Aristotle and Aquinas. Other prominent voices in neo-Thomist theology include Karl Rahner in Germany, and Étienne Gilson and Jacques Maritain in France, all of whom also engaged with Kierkegaard's ideas. In reading Kierkegaard, they saw echoes of an Aristotelian understanding of existence and motion – and of Aquinas's reworking of these ideas, specifically in his notion of being (existence) as act, in distinction from essence. Though Kierkegaard is a far cry from Thomism, particularly in its more formalist aspects, there are compelling reasons to read him within this framework, as we have already seen.[18]

Catholic thought of the period engaged extensively with early phenomenology and existentialism, motivated by a desire both to combat the atheist strands of existentialism and to use existentialist and phenomenological ideas to develop a more vital ontology, one that could compete with the nihilistic framework of modernity. They contended in particular with the ideas of Heidegger, who likewise sought to develop an ontology that would transcend the enframing (*Gestell*) of modernity. Whether in the Cartesian divide between subject and object or in the homogenization of different kinds and modes of being onto a single plane, Heidegger held that the framework of modern metaphysics did not allow for being as such, the proper object of ontological inquiry, to come into view. It was in part Kierkegaard's focus on existence that offered Heidegger a new way into the problem of being, one that he carried into his exploration of pre-Socratic sources.

Heidegger's debt to Kierkegaard is widely acknowledged in scholarship, if not by Heidegger himself. This debt is evident not only in his discussion of obvious Kierkegaardian themes, such as existence and mood, but in the whole of his philosophical undertaking.[19] George Pattison notes that Werner Brock, one of Heidegger's teaching assistants, attributes to Kierkegaard 'the distinctive and modern sense of existence'.[20] It is Heidegger's appropriation of Kierkegaard for an explicit ontology that leads many others in the early to mid-twentieth century to read Kierkegaard as an ontological thinker as well as the father of *Existenzphilosophie*.[21] In the early 1930s, Jean Wahl published an article-length study of 'Heidegger and Kierkegaard: An Investigation into the Original Elements of Heidegger's Philosophy'[22] that characterized Heidegger as an ontologization and secularization of Kierkegaard's thought. Wahl's study helped, along with the Lev Shestov's *Kierkegaard and Existential Philosophy* (1936), to launch Kierkegaard studies in France and had an enormous influence on French existentialism.[23] Jean-Paul Sartre, Simone de Beauvoir, Michel Henry and others, were, of course, readers of both Kierkegaard and Heidegger.

Heidegger's thematization of the underlying ontological schema in Kierkegaard's work was thus a significant factor in the reading of Kierkegaard as an ontological thinker, with attentiveness to his treatment of modalities – particularly possibility. Michael Wyschogrod's 1954 study, one of the few book-length treatments of Kierkegaard's ontology, is in fact a comparative study of Kierkegaard and Heidegger, and was the first English-language book on Heidegger.[24] While Kierkegaard's own ontology serves as a ground for discussions of the development of the self within an ethical and theological framework, in Heidegger the question of Being serves as the singular point of orientation, and this provides the space to fully explicate ontological structures, especially of existence and time. Likewise, Sartre takes Kierkegaard's innovative thinking of existence to heart in the development of his own analysis of essence and existence, being and nothingness.

With existentialism and Heideggerian phenomenology largely falling out of intellectual favour, and with the growth of Kierkegaard studies as a field, especially within analytic ethics and aesthetics, these ontologically grounded analyses of Kierkegaard's work also fell away. Perhaps such discussions grew to be regarded as a matter for intellectual history or simply no longer seemed capable of yielding any interesting insights. Whatever the reasons, there is a dearth of contemporary scholarship around this topic, and this is especially true of the concept of possibility. There are exceptions, most notably David Kangas's *Kierkegaard's Instant: On beginnings* (2007) which is a profound reading of the Kierkegaardian ontology of possibility in conversation with German Idealism. His analysis develops Kierkegaard's account of authentic repetition or 'repetition forwards' along with Kierkegaard's notion of the instant or the moment, offering an ontology of what he calls 'anarchic' or indeterminate beginnings in Kierkegaard's thinking.[25] Kangas focuses on Kierkegaard's rejection of the Hegelian understanding of beginning, which sees the realization and meaning of the beginning in its teleological fulfilment, in its end, rather than in the contingent act of coming to be. Such a reading makes sense of many of Kierkegaard's claims about possibility and actuality, including Kierkegaard's rejection of the notion, discussed earlier, that actuality (logically) entails possibility. In *God and Being* (2011) George Pattison considers the impact of Kierkegaard's ontology alongside other readings in scholastic and continental thought, including Heidegger and Derrida. Clare Carlisle deals with the sources for Kierkegaard's ontology and relevant themes in her book *Kierkegaard's Philosophy of Becoming: Movements and Positions*.[26] The present study aims to build on these efforts and make explicit the discussion of possibility in Kierkegaard's work, exploring the question from a number of different angles. Chapters have been organized under four general topics: (1) possibility and the philosophical tradition, (2) possibility and experience, (3) possibility and freedom and (4) possibility and hope. Within these, readers will find familiar themes in Kierkegaard's work: anxiety, despair, aesthetic experience, temporality, repetition and faith.

Beyond calculation

One common thread across these chapters is the understanding of Kierkegaardian possibility as radical, transcending the mundane. This is exemplified by Anti-Climacus's formulation in *The Sickness Unto Death*, that 'God is that *all* things are possible and that all things are possible is the existence of God'.[27] Possibility in Kierkegaard's sense involves a departure from probability or mere practical possibility. At the level of self, the possibility of coming into existence, or the movement whereby a possibility becomes actualized, is a movement of freedom and therefore outside of the realm of 'how things must go'. The attitudes of love, hope and sacrifice (the 'gift of death') are examples of possibility for human being that are not rooted in the immanent possibilities of finitude. Each goes beyond the sphere of practical expediency.

The importance of such a movement can be deduced from several themes in Kierkegaard's works, but particularly in his many scathing remarks about probability, calculation and accounting across his pseudonymous and signed authorship. A calculation of probabilities, while it may appear to be a mature means of reckoning with actuality, is for Kierkegaard an evasion of the anxious responsibility of possibility, a rejection of what he calls in *The Concept of Anxiety* the 'possibility of possibility'. The language of calculation and probability is prominent in Kierkegaard's descriptions of the 'despair of finitude' and the related 'despair of necessity' in *Sickness*, both of which are characterized by having a deficient sense of possibility. One suffering from a despair of this kind 'finds being himself too risky' and so follows the habits of the crowd and becomes 'as exchangeable as a coin of the realm', making only 'prudent calculations'.[28] This is the despair of the 'bourgeois philistine', the conformist, who 'is absorbed in the probable' and is unaware of being in despair.

The self in the despair of necessity loses itself in the habitual, in the 'dank air of the probable', with a false understanding that what is or what has been must, of necessity, continue to be in the future. 'Devoid of imagination . . . he lives within a certain orbit of trivial experience as to how things come about, what is possible, what usually happens, no matter whether he is a tapster or a prime minister.'[29] Such a position continually narrows the circle of freedom, since to view choices as necessary in this sense removes the possibility of an original or authentic relationship to my own actions, my own possibilities. To repeat the same choices again and again out of either habit or conformity, whether they are apparently virtuous or poor choices, likewise removes their value, since they are no longer free in any meaningful sense. To the extent that a self exists in and as possibility, always oriented towards what is not yet, attempts to evade the risk and anxiety that accompany this ontological reality are a kind of absent-mindedness or self-absence. As Richard Purkarthofer describes, such selves are 'undead', for they 'do not exist in the strict sense of the word'.[30]

In *The Concept of Anxiety*, Haufniensis writes that 'When origineity (*Oprindeligheden*) in earnestness is acquired and preserved, then there is succession and repetition, but as soon as origineity is lacking in repetition, there is habit (*Vanen*)'.³¹ 'Repetition' is Kierkegaard's term for the genuine achievement of self-identity or self-continuity in time. It is the holding together of the eternal and the finite, essence and existence, an activity that is an ongoing and never finished. True repetition, in this sense, is a generative 'repetition forwards'. Kierkegaard's ontology of self as a being-toward-the-future means that the activity of becoming oneself, of becoming present to oneself, must be tended to and cared for, held in the balance, or it collapses. In *Sickness*, 'Yet a self, every moment it exists, is in a process of becoming, for the self *kata dynamin* [potentially] is not present actually, it is merely what is to come into existence'.³² The despair of necessity, the embrace of actions that seek to limit and close off the riskiness of life by sheltering in the probable, thus amount to a death of the self.

When Kierkegaard refers in *The Concept of Anxiety* to being 'educated by possibility' or, in *Sickness*, seeing oneself 'in the mirror of possibility' he suggests something much more radical than plotting out possible outcomes or adapting oneself to the practical limits of one's situation.³³ *Do not even the tax collectors do so?* Kierkegaard asks instead for a transformation of vision: of how one sees oneself and the world. There is an art to seeing possibility, to seeing oneself in the mirror of possibility. In Chapter 11, John Lippitt points to one striking instance of this in *Works of Love*, where Kierkegaard contrasts possibility, specifically the possibility of the good, with 'the "tough slime" of "practical sagacity" or shrewdness [*Klogskab*]'.³⁴ Here, to hold on to calculated shrewdness is the opposite of the hopeful expectancy of love.

Possibility in (aesthetic) experience

Another theme that unites several chapters is the importance of aesthetic experience to the understanding of possibility. Because aesthetic possibility is sometimes described negatively by Kierkegaard, it is worth taking a moment to argue for its importance to the whole of his thought, even in the explicitly religious conception of repetition as the actualization of the self's possibility. It is also worthwhile to consider the role of possibility in the structure of experience more generally, in order to sketch the outline of a phenomenology of possibility, developed more fully in chapters 3–5.

As Rick Anthony Furtak argues in Chapter 2, there is much to be learned from the aesthetic experience of possibility and the rich affective life of those who, like

Proust's narrator in *À la recherche du temps perdu* and Kierkegaard's aesthetes, revel in possibility – imagining possible lovers, possible selves, relating to the world and others in myriad ways (usually, in Kierkegaard's telling, amorously).

The pseudonymous author 'A' from *Either/Or* describes the aim of the aesthetic life as the cultivation of the interesting, which is a means of evading the yawning abyss of boredom that lurks beneath every endeavour. One of the tips given by 'A' in 'On the Rotation of Crops' is to avoid becoming overly invested in any particular person, activity or project, since to give too much interest to any particular would lead to dissipation and eventually to a confrontation with boredom. The aesthete, as 'A' recommends, treats every experience, no matter how engrossing or mundane, as an occasion for imaginative reflection or 'recollection'. Such an outlook, in one sense, puts the subject in the role of spectator (or artistic director), not just for events as they unfold but even in relation to one's own life. 'A' remarks that it is a 'singular feeling when in the midst of enjoyment one looks at it in order to recollect it'.[35] The suggestion is that life must be experienced at a certain remove in order to consistently cultivate the interesting; this is a version of the Romantic principle of aesthetic distance or irony.

While Kierkegaard has plenty of criticisms of this principle, he recognizes in the figure of the aesthete a capacity that is essential for the development of spirit, namely the ability to put oneself at a remove, in the broadest sense, to entertain possibilities that do not belong to the realm of the expedient or ready-to-hand. In the 'Crop Rotation' essay, 'A' refers to this ability as the art of 'arbitrariness' whereby one can, for example, upset an expected trajectory, such as a love affair, or find amusement in the most mundane of circumstances (e.g. enjoying a boring lecture by attending closely to the bead of sweat dripping from the lecturer's nose). To adopt such a position, to distance oneself from the immediate in this way, offers perspective beyond the economic relationships or relations of exchange that dominate finite life. Of course, putting oneself at a remove also exacts a price, and those familiar with Kierkegaard will recognize that his model of self-development does not end with a departure from the finite but with a return.

What may be overlooked or lost in viewing life at a remove? As George Stack writes of aesthetically grasped possibility: 'It is the constant process of reflecting upon only hypothetical possibilities which are apprehended contemplatively or in a disinterested manner which is one of the stultifying traits of the romantic aesthete. For an individual unable to commit himself to anything except the pursuit of sensual pleasure or aesthetic pleasures, there are no concernful possibilities.'[36] The contemplation of possibility in a disinterested mode, at a remove from questions of meaning in a deeper sense, risks becoming a kind of 'stupefaction'[37] and despair. Such an attitude is characterized in *The Sickness Unto Death* as the 'despair of possibility'. It is a form of misalignment of self that is characterized by a deficient sense of necessity, urgency or responsibility, wherein possibilities proliferate in imaginative reflection but are not fully one's own. A lack of what Kierkegaard calls interest (*interesse*) in relation to what is or what may be, can prevent one from ever engaging with 'actuality' in a meaningful way, that is, a way that concerns oneself. In *The Concept of Irony*, Kierkegaard offers the example of Friedrich Schlegel's novella *Lucinde*, especially the character of (Julius's lover) Lisette, as a warning against existing in an aesthetic relation to possibility. Kierkegaard remarks that Lisette would 'write her whole story as if it were that of someone else'.[38] This mode of engagement with possibility, as merely hypothetical or general, rather than one's ownmost possibility, amounts to a kind of arrest or withering of self[39] even as it appears to be the artistic creation of self and world. At the limit of such a character, the self remains unactualized, having spent all its energies in daydreaming of possible futures and becoming exhausted at the task of realizing any particular one of them.[40] These critiques are familiar, and they must be borne in mind in any reading of what Kierkegaard means by possibility.

But all of Kierkegaard's warnings about the danger of 'floundering about'[41] in possibility and ignoring the actual, it is clear that he regards the ability to recognize possibility, and the exercise of imagination that enables such recognition, as crucial to spiritual development. In *Practice in Christianity*, Anti-Climacus reminds readers that the imagination is the 'first condition for what becomes of a person' while the will is the second and 'decisive' condition, since it is required for taking possession of possibilities as possibilities *for oneself*.[42] Imagination is the faculty that allows for engagement with possibility, with what may be. In *Sickness*, Kierkegaard refers to the imagination as the 'infinitising reflection', speaking approvingly of Fichte's grounding of the categories in imagination.[43] Furthermore, 'the imagination is the whole of reflection's possibility; and the intensity of this medium is the possibility of the self's intensity.[44] There are a number of ways to understand imagination or a sense for possibility as the first condition for an authentic way of existing. In a basic sense, the ability to entertain even 'hypothetical, abstract, conceptual possibilities'[45] is, as discussed earlier, a movement beyond the realm of the probable or expedient.

A second meaning concerns the way the world opens up to us through possibility. It is not merely that the aesthete entertains possibilities as an intellectual or conceptual exercise, but that he *sees* these possibilities in the world. In other words, it is not quite true, though Kierkegaard sometimes formulates it in this way (especially in *The Concept of Irony*) that the aesthete simply hovers above life and fails to engage with actuality. Kierkegaard is critical in many places of what he views as the hermeticism of the aesthetic life, the aesthetic tendency to approach life as the artistic production of the subject and so to be, in Augustine's words, *incurvatus in se* (curved in on itself). However, he also acknowledges the dimension of receptivity in the aesthete, which is at odds with the picture of a self-enclosed existence. The passivity associated with aestheticism is not only a penchant for idleness, as in 'On the Rotation of Crops', or a lack of decisive and consistent action, but also a sensitivity or openness to the world. One notes this dimension at moments in the Seducer's Diary, for example, when Johannes, rather than aggressively pursuing Cordelia, awaits the 'occasion' for her to emerge from the home of her aunt, offering up his prayer to chance: 'Surprise me, I am ready.'[46] In this reliance on the occasion, the aesthete recognizes something ontologically important, and something that goes against the more prevailing wisdom in Kierkegaard that the aesthetic life is prone to a self-enclosedness. Likewise, the aesthete's attunement to moods (e.g. boredom), cannot be understood as a relation to a merely subjective state. Moods such as boredom, anxiety and despair are, for Kierkegaard, not subjective emotions but ontological in nature, that is, revelatory of ontological structures. Boredom is a relation to 'the nothing that interlaces existence',[47] and anxiety is an awareness of the 'possibility of possibility'.[48] This ontological dimension of mood is of course further developed by Heidegger, especially in *Being and Time* and in *The Fundamental Concepts of Metaphysics*. Heidegger makes clear that moods and what they disclose do not issue from the consciousness of the subject but *present themselves to* the subject. The same must be said for possibilities.

To think of possibilities as imaginatively projected upon the world by a subject is to mistake the 'location' of the possible as interior to consciousness and to misunderstand the fundamental nature of imagination in all experience. Such a picture tends to have, as a corollary, a neutral and indifferent external world, a world that is not essentially related to 'subjective' possibilities. But Kierkegaard's account of possibility does not simply reinscribe this modern metaphysics of subject and object, nor does it seek to overcome it by privileging one or other of the terms. As later phenomenologists, particularly Heidegger and Jan Patočka, argue, to accept the terms of subject and object as they are given means to accept the nihilism that accompanies such a metaphysics and to deny the unique position of human being in relation to being. Deleuze too, with a different set of concerns, diagnoses the philosophical errors that proliferate from this metaphysics.

Speaking in theological terms that are more germane to Kierkegaard's thought, the modern metaphysics of subject and object denies the reality of our creatureliness and our relationship to the author of being. For possibilities to present themselves to the subject, in the way that experience says they do, or for human beings to have an affective sense for ontological reality, as Kierkegaard insists that we do, suggests our intimate link between our own existence and that of being as such. While there is qualitative difference in Kierkegaard between finite existence and infinite being, his model of self as a holding together of incommensurate poles offers a fundamental sense of relation through difference.

Following a long history of theological thinking, Kierkegaard in *Fragments* conceives of only eternal being as necessary, in relation to which all other beings are contingent. To be necessary, as discussed before, means that it is not possible not to be, and that it is therefore impossible to come into existence, since coming into existence would imply a non-being that precedes existence.[49] In Kierkegaard's understanding, Hegel errs in making the being of nature and of humanity part of the self-realization of divine being. The unfolding of being in immanence, as a self-development, removes the diversity of being and the fundamental incommensurability between Being and beings that Kierkegaard seeks to preserve. The stakes for Kierkegaard could not be higher, since it is central to his understanding of freedom that this incommensurability be maintained.[50]

Possibilities, then, are not projected onto the world as moving images upon a screen. Possibility is rather the space of emergence or becoming, the coming into being of that which need not be, and imagination, as a feeling for what is not or not yet, is required to recognize possibilities. Kierkegaard follows Kant in seeing imagination, in its productive and reproductive capacity, as crucial to the experience of a sensible world. It is 'not a faculty like the other faculties . . . it is the faculty *instar omnium* [for all faculties]'.[51] Imagination plays a foundational role in our phenomenal experience of the world, namely as that which discloses 'a world' at all. The world *offers itself* as rich with possibility, and this is especially true of our engagement with real or imagined others, who, as Somers-Hall argues in Chapter 5, represent for us possible ways of being. Furtak shows, further, how our affective moods allow us to experience the world in different lights, disclosing different possibilities to be actualized.

Of course, there is much more to say about possibility than is disclosed in the aesthetic life or in phenomenal experience in general. As with all of Kierkegaard's conceptual categories, the meaning of possibility evolves and has distinctive meanings in his religious texts. In their contributions to this volume, Marek, Das, Lippitt and Becker-Lindenthal explore the distinctively religious import of possibility. Even so, the aesthetic feeling for possibility through imaginative activity remains important. In chapters 1 and 4 of this collection, Hanson and Maughan-Brown discuss the sense in which the religious understanding of actualizing one's ownmost possibilities relies on imaginative activity and involves a parallel dynamic to what is seen in the aesthetic: between receptivity and creativity, inheritance and originality.[52] As Hanson argues, 'the religious thus in [Kierkegaard's pseudonym Frater] Taciturnus's words "plays the same role as the aesthetic, but as the superior"'.[53] In faith, as Kierkegaard understands it, there is a shift from a recognition of or awareness of possibility as such to the distinctly existential question: Is it possible for me? Do I will this possibility for myself?[54]

Postscript

I was drawn to the question of possibility in Kierkegaard's work, in part, because it seemed to answer to a growing sense of cultural anxiety and instability. The germ for this book came in 2019, just before the global pandemic that was to upend life for the next two years. A series of economic and political crises had already preceded the pandemic, while the climate crisis and the inability of existing infrastructure to respond meaningfully to it was becoming impossible to ignore. In such moments of crisis, our anxiety naturally awakens us to what Kierkegaard calls 'the possibility of possibility'.

What does it mean to think about possibility now, when our own possibilities seem at the same time impossible to predict and more and more circumscribed to a narrow circle of probability? On the one hand, the pace of technological development in the twenty-first century is without historical antecedent; it is nearly impossible to have foresight about what this development enables and what problems it creates, problems which more than ever are planetary. Viewed from this angle, it must be admitted that current feelings of uncertainty, instability and anxiety, however perennial such feelings may be, have a solid material foundation. But in another sense, it is equally true that the possibilities for human life have shrunk with the homogenizing forces of global capitalism and the adoption of probabilistic models in ever more areas of human activity. Seen from this vantage, as Heidegger pointed out, the possibilities for being and for human beings have narrowed, and being is seen as little more than a standing reserve of forces or resources.

It is in this spiritual atmosphere of generalized anxiety that Kierkegaard's remarks about possibility began to stand out to me and demand consideration. Whether or not readers share my sense of the current landscape, there is much to be learned from Kierkegaard's examination of modality, not least an ontology that helps to rethink uncertainty, anxiety, despair and related phenomena in a more rigorous and ultimately more hopeful light. I hope readers will find resources and insights in this volume to accompany them through times of spiritual sickness and in the face of problems that seem insurmountable. As Kierkegaard reminds us in *Sickness*:

> This is the struggle of faith, which struggles insanely, if you will, for possibility. For only possibility saves. When someone faints, people shout for water, eau-de-cologne, Hoffman's drops. But for someone who is on the point of despair it is: get me possibility, get me possibility, the only thing that can save me is possibility![55]

Notes

1 The German equivalent is *Möglichkeit*.
2 Aristotle, *Metaphysics*, VII:1 ZI, 1028a9ff.
3 This reading is influenced by Étienne Gilson, *Being and Some Philosophers*, 2nd ed. (Toronto: Pontifical Institute of Medieval Studies, 1952). The brief history presented here is adapted from the first chapter of Michael Wyschogrod's book *Kierkegaard and Heidegger: The Ontology of Existence* (London: Routledge & Kegan Paul Ltd., 1954). Wyschogrod names his first chapter 'Being and some problems', with a clear nod to Gilson.
4 G. W. F. Hegel, *Phenomenology of Spirit*, ed. and trans. Terry Pinkard (Cambridge: Cambridge University Press, 2018), 61–8: §95–110.
5 Søren Kierkegaard, *Philosophical Fragments* and *Johannes Climacus*, ed. and trans. Howard V. Hong and Edna H. Hong (Princeton, NJ: Princeton University Press, 1985), 210.
6 The exception, in Aquinas, is God.
7 Kierkegaard, *Philosophical Fragments,* 41: IV 209. The note here is worth quoting at length. Kierkegaard, speaking of Spinoza, claims that it makes sense to speak of levels of being and the perfection of being only when speaking of essence, what Kierkegaard calls 'ideal being'. 'With regard to factual being [existence], to speak of more or less being is meaningless, A fly, when it is, has just as much being as the

god [...] for the Hamlet dialectic, to be or not to be, applies to factual being. Factual being is indifferent to the differentiation of all essence-determinants, and everything that exists participates without petty jealousy in being, and participates just as much. It is quite true that ideally the situation is different. *But as soon as I speak ideally about being, I am speaking no longer about being* [existence] *but about essence*.

8 Kierkegaard, *Concluding Unscientific Postscript* to Philosophical Fragments, vol 1., ed. and trans. Howard V. Hong and Edna H. Hong (Princeton, NJ: Princeton University Press, 1992), 189–90.

9 See Gabriel Ferreira, 'Contingency', in *Kierkegaard's Concepts. Tome II: Classicism to Enthusiasm. Kierkegaard Research: Sources, Recourses, Reception*, vol. 15, ed. Steven M. Emmanuel, William McDonald, and Jon Stewart (London/New York: Routledge, 2014).

10 Kierkegaard, *Philosophical Fragments*, 80, IV 244.

11 Søren Kierkegaard, *The Concept of Anxiety*, ed. and trans. Reidar Thomte in collaboration with Albert B. Anderson (Princeton, NJ: Princeton University Press, 1997), 9–10.

12 See Immanuel Kant, *The Critique of Pure Reason* (Cambridge: Cambridge University Press, 1998), 567: A599 / B627.

13 This is a refutation specifically of Anselm's ontological argument, in which being is treated as a predicate that could be added to the essence of a thing (specifically to the concept 'that then which none greater can be conceived'). Kant claims, by contrast, that being (as existence) functions as a presupposition for any attribution of a predicate to a thing.

14 George Pattison, *God and Being: An Enquiry* (Oxford: Oxford University Press, 2011), 90.

15 Kierkegaard, *Philosophical Fragments*, 73–5.

16 See the discussion of the phrase *ab esse ad posse* in Chapter 2.

17 'All coming into existence occurs in freedom, not by way of necessity' (Kierkegaard, *Philosophical Fragments*, 75).

18 For a detailed account, see Furnal's introduction and Fabro's text on 'Actuality', both in *The Selected Works of Cornelio Fabro*, vol. 2. *The Selected Words of Cornelio Fabro vol 2: Selected Articles on Søren Kierkegaard*, ed. Nathaniel Dreyer (Chillum, MD: IVE Press, 2020). See also John Heywood Thomas, *The Legacy of Kierkegaard* (Eugene: Cascade Books, 2011), ch. 5. Kierkegaard's interest in Aristotle came in part through the work of F. A. Trendelenburg, for whom he had high praise. Furnal quotes one of Kierkegaard's journal entries from 1844 concerning his reading of Aristotle and Trendelenburg. 'But the Greeks remain my consolation. The damned mendacity which was ushered into philosophy with Hegel, the unending insinuation and betrayal and the marshalling and belaboring one or another Greek passage! Praised be Trendelenburg, one of the most sober-thinking philosophers I know' (SKS 18, 231 / Pap. V A 98 / KJN JJ:288 [1844–45]).

19 For more on Heidegger's relationship to Kierkegaard, see Noreen Khawaja, 'Heidegger's Kierkegaard: Philosophy and Religion in the Tracks of a Failed Interpretation', *The Journal of Religion* 95, no. 3 (2015): 295–317.
20 Pattison, *God and Being*, 12–45.
21 See Karl Jaspers, *Existenzphilosophie*, 4th ed. (Berlin: De Gruyter, 1974).
22 'Heidegger et Kierkegaard: Recherche des éléments originaux de la philosophie de Heidegger' was first published in *Recherches Philosophiques* 2 (1932–33): 349–70. It was republished with minor revisions in Jean Wahl, *Études kierkegaardiennes* (Paris: Fernand Aubier, 1938), 455–76, and republished again in Jean Wahl, *Kierkegaard: L'Un devant l'Autre*, ed. Vincent Delecroix and Frédéric Worms (Paris: Hachette Littératures, 1998).
23 Stewart, John, *Kierkegaard and Existentialism* (Farnham: Ashgate Publishing, 2007), 397.
24 Wyschogrod, *Kierkegaard and Heidegger*. See also the 1950 lectures of the Danish theologian K. E. Løgstrup on Kierkegaard and Heidegger, recently translated into English as 'Kierkegaard's and Heidegger's Analysis of Existence and its Relation to Proclamation', trans. Robert Stern (Oxford: Oxford University Press, 2020).
25 'A posited beginning is dialectically identical to its projected end: the beginning only really is once it shows itself as the beginning of a determinate, that is, concluded, process. Yet what attracts A's thinking is a beginning that never *departs toward* any end [. . .] Such would be an ab-solute or anarchic beginning' (David J. Kangas, *Kierkegaard's Instant: On Beginnings* (Bloomington, IN: Indiana University Press, 2007), 45–6).
26 Claire Carlisle, *Kierkegaard's Philosophy of Becoming: Movements and Positions* (Albany, NY: State University New York Press), 2005.
27 Søren Kierkegaard, *The Sickness Unto Death,* trans. Alistair Hannay (London: Penguin, 1989), 71. My emphasis.
28 Ibid., 64–5.
29 Ibid., 71.
30 Richard B. Purkarthofer, 'Origineity and Recognisability: On Kierkegaard's Ontology', *Rivista di Filosofia Neo-Scolastica* 105, no. 3–4 (2013): 805–21 (814).
31 Ibid., 808. Purkarthofer quotes from SKS 4, 448.
32 Kierkegaard, *The Sickness Unto Death*, 60.
33 See Jakub Marek's treatment of 'education through possibility' in Chapter 6.
34 Søren Kierkegaard, *Works of Love*, ed. and trans. Howard V. Hong and Edna H. Hong (Princeton, NJ: Princeton University Press, 1995), 251 / SKS 9, 250. This 'slime' emerges from 'cook[ing] over the slow or the merely earthly blazing fire of passions' a combination of attitudes that Kierkegaard associates with living without the eternal: 'habit, sagacity, aping, experience, custom and usage' (ibid.).

35 Kierkegaard, *Either/Or*, vol. 1, ed. and trans. Howard V. Hong and Edna H. Hong (Princeton, NJ: Princeton University Press, 1987), 294.
36 George Stack, 'Kierkegaard's Concept of Possibility', *Journal of Thought* 5, no. 2 (1970): 80–92.
37 Søren Kierkegaard, *The Concept of Irony*, ed. and trans. Howard V. Hong and Edna H. Hong (Princeton, NJ: Princeton University Press, 1989), 295.
38 Ibid., 295–6.
39 Lisette ironically ends her own life, that which ought to be the object of utmost interest, in a mode of aesthetic disinterestedness. She comes to view her death as artistically fitting and therefore necessary ('Lisette must die, must die now: that is the will of an iron fate!'). See Friedrich Schlegel, *Lucinde and the Fragments*, trans. Peter Firchow (Minneapolis: University of Minneapolis, 1971), 87.
40 Kierkegaard speaks in similar terms of the 'exhaustion resulting from reflection' in *The Present Age*. See also *The Sickness Unto Death*, 66, where the self 'exhausts itself floundering about in possibility'.
41 Ibid., 66.
42 Søren Kierkegaard, *Practice in Christianity*, ed. and trans. Howard V. Hong and Edna H. Hong (Princeton, NJ: Princeton University Press, 1991), 186.
43 Kierkegaard, *The Sickness Unto Death*, 61.
44 Ibid.
45 Stack, 'Kierkegaard's Concept of Possibility', 80.
46 *Either/Or*, vol. 1, 327. See also Kierkegaard's description of the occasion as understood in the aesthetic sphere (234–6).
47 Ibid., 291.
48 Kierkegaard, *Concept of Anxiety*, 38.
49 'Precisely by coming into existence, everything that comes into existence demonstrates that it is not necessary, the only thing that cannot come into existence is the necessary, because the necessary *is* . . . No coming into existence is necessary – not before it came into existence, for then it cannot come into existence, and not after it has come into existence, for then it has not come into existence. All coming into existence occurs in freedom, not by way of necessity' (Kierkegaard, *Philosophical Fragments*, 74–5).
50 'If the past has become necessary [. . .] it would follow that the future would also be necessary. If necessity could intervene at one single point, then we could no longer speak of the past and the future [. . .] The past has indeed come into existence; coming into existence is the change, in freedom, of becoming actuality' (Kierkegaard, *Philosophical Fragments*, 77 IV 241).
51 Kierkegaard, *The Sickness Unto Death*, 60.
52 For a discussion of these terms and their relationship, see Stephen Mulhall's *Inheritance and Originality: Wittgenstein, Heidegger, Kierkegaard* (Oxford: Oxford University Press, 2001). See also Purkarthofer, 'Origineity and Recognisability'.

53 See Chapter 1 of this volume. Hanson quotes from Kierkegaard, *Stages on Life's Way: Studies by Various Persons*, ed. and trans. Howard V. Hong and Edna H. Hong (Princeton, NJ: Princeton University Press, 1988), 442.
54 See Kierkegaard, *Stages on Life's Way*, 440.
55 Kierkegaard, *The Sickness Unto Death*, 69.

I

Possibility and the philosophical tradition

1

From possibility to actuality and back again

Kierkegaard's ontology of the possible and the actually ideal

Jeffrey Hanson

Søren Kierkegaard occasionally uses a pair of phrases drawn from classical logic: *ab posse ad esse*, which means 'from possibility to actuality', and *ab esse ad posse*, which of course means 'from actuality to possibility'. His use of these phrases, however, is anything but classical. Kierkegaard's deployment of *ab posse ad esse* and *ab esse ad posse* interjects him into the centre of an important philosophical discussion that has a long history in Western thought. These paired phrases are especially influential in the intellectual environment shaping Golden Age Denmark. Kierkegaard's interpretation of *ab posse ad esse* and *ab esse ad posse* represents a decisive and singular intervention into the history of metaphysics and logic in the wake of Hegel's transformative influence on the intellectual environment of Europe. Classical logic affirmed the validity of the *ab esse ad posse* principle while denying the validity of the *ab posse ad esse* principle. In their classical version, *ab esse ad posse* simply meant that from any given actuality it is valid to infer that the same actuality must ipso facto be possible. The converse naturally is not valid; from any given possibility one cannot infer that the same possibility is also actual.

I argue that Kierkegaard departs from this tradition and takes inspiration from Hegel by reading the principles as ultimately convertible. Hence, for Kierkegaard the movements 'from possibility to actuality' and 'from actuality to possibility' are co-implicated and reciprocally related. However, I further argue that Kierkegaard transposes these convertible principles from the realm of logic and applies them to the realm of freedom, choice and the attainment of ideal selfhood. Kierkegaard will therefore argue, contra the Danish Hegelians, that the two phrases cannot be united speculatively but only be united existentially:

by living out an ideal. He uses them to account for how he thinks human beings attain aimed-for ideals. This process of self-attainment proves to be a reciprocal means of allowing actual human situations to yield imaginatively yet further possibilities, which in turn present themselves for actualization.

In the first section of this chapter, I will exposit a very brief history of the *ab posse* and *ab esse* principles, including their deployment in the controversies surrounding Danish Hegelianism. This presentation helps us understand the intellectual context within which Kierkegaard operates and the novelty of his engagement of these principles in his writings. The second section of the chapter introduces important instances of Kierkegaard's engagement of the pair which are to be found in Climacus's *Concluding Unscientific Postscript* and Frater Taciturnus's 'Letter to the Reader' from *Stages on Life's Way*. It explains Kierkegaard's reasons for their use and demonstrates how Kierkegaard reconsiders the interplay of possibility and actuality that marks human existence. The third section presents Kierkegaard's essay on the Woman Who Was a Sinner as an exemplary text that illustrates how Kierkegaard's understanding of the reciprocal play of possibility and actuality might be put to work in a particular case meant by him to solicit our imagination and action.

Ab esse ad posse: A potted history

These phrases have a significant history. The full phrase *ab esse ad posse valet consequentia* 'from that a thing exists it follows that it is possible to be'– appears only once in Kierkegaard's journal. It is a Scholastic dictum, based on a reading of Aristotle, that was deployed to argue that if anything has happened or been thus actual, it must ipso facto have been possible.[1] A version of this formula appears in the writings of Duns Scotus. In his work on first principles he wrote, 'But I prefer to submit conclusions and premises about the possible, for if those about the actual are conceded, those about the possible are conceded, but not conversely.'[2] The fact that the principle was not convertible was recognized by the Scholastics. In the words of one commentator, this principle implied that 'what is true of the facts is true of their possibility, not vice versa.'[3] As late as Francisco Jacquier's 1787 *Institutiones philosophicae ad studia theologica* published contemporaneously with Immanuel Kant's *Lectures on Metaphysics*, Jacquier admits that one can conclude from actuality to possibility 'but not vice versa, because an artisan can conceive of the idea of a mechanism with his mind and clearly perceive it, such that the mechanism can exist, but for all that the same mechanism does not exist, from such it is plain that possibility is not a sufficient reason for existence'.[4]

Supporters of certain versions of the ontological argument would arguably wish to admit the converse of the *ab esse ad posse* principle in one instance: that of God, whose possible existence is meant to entail his necessary existence. Kant can be read as seeking to block the move from possibility to actuality in his influential criticisms of theoretical proofs for God's existence. One way of reading his attack on the ontological argument in the *Critique of Pure Reason* is as a claim that the converse of *ab esse ad posse* is never licit, not even in the singular case of the divinity. In his *Lectures on Metaphysics* Kant invoked the exact phrase *ab posse ad esse valet consequentia* in order to further complicate its use in the ontological argument. Kant uses this principle to argue that there can be no movement from the possibility of a thing's being to its actual being. This effectively blocks the ontological argument as classically conceived, because that chain of reasoning depends on drawing a conclusion about God's actual existence from the mere possibility of God's existence. In the *Lectures on Metaphysics*, Kant expressly argues that while it is true that one can, along with the Scholastics, argue from being to possibility, such that any actual existence is also thereby possible, the converse is not true, such that no possibility can be the basis of a sound inference to any actual existence. 'Possibility can be inferred from existence <*ab esse ad posse valet conseqentia*>, but not: existence can be inferred from possibility <*a posse ad esse valet consequentia*>. One can infer to possibility from existence, but not the reverse, to existence from possibility.'[5] Kant's innovation was to enforce this logic against the ontological argument as a specific and exceptional instance of concluding to actuality from possibility.[6]

While Kierkegaard of course largely accepts Kant's use of this principle, since he is sympathetic with Kant's criticisms of traditional proofs for God's existence,[7] I think he does not fully accept Hegel's variation on Kant's revised understanding of the logical principle. Kant deploys the *ab esse ad posse* theorem in order to refute a traditional form of rational argument about God, while the Danish Hegelians incorporated the principle into a revised logic inspired by Hegel himself, one that Kierkegaard sought to resist. Just as Hegel radically reinterpreted the fundamental Aristotelian logical principles of identity, non-contradiction and the excluded middle in his *Science of Logic*, so too the traditional assertion that if something actually is then it must also be already and also be possible must have seemed naïve, uncritical and unilluminating to Hegel.

A key moment in the reception of this Hegelian challenge to logic (and theology) occurred in 1839, when Johan Bornemann reviewed Hans Martensen's

1837 dissertation on the autonomy of human self-consciousness.[8] The review itself is largely forgotten, but for our purposes it is worth noting that the author uses the phrase *a posse ad esse*. This review can be read as a part of the significant debate in Golden Age Denmark over the legitimacy of Hegelian logic and especially its import for Christian theology. In the review, Bornemann characterizes Martensen as having followed Kant's *Religion within the Limits of Reason Alone* in proceeding from the autonomy of theoretical and practical reason in accord with the Cartesian principle that 'the beginning of all wisdom is to subject one's purported knowledge to a critique'.[9] The language here is unmistakable. The book of Proverbs declares that the fear of the Lord is the beginning of wisdom,[10] but Bornemann perceives that the modern imperative is to ground wisdom in doubt rather than the fear of the Lord. The critique that Bornemann proposes as a replacement for the fear of the Lord is of Cartesian inspiration: He here cites the maxim that becomes a satirical slogan in Kierkegaard's authorship: *de omnibus dubitandum*. If, Bornemann argues, we take seriously the Cartesian mandate *de omnibus dubitandum*, then the result would exclude all knowledge of God, 'for no inference from thinking to being is valid', and here he cites the Latin that we have been closely following: *a posse ad esse*.[11] The shorthand is obviously meant to assert that in the face of the modern philosophical project to begin with doubt, knowledge of God is cast into question because while one can think God one cannot know thereby whether God exists.[12] This line of argument is consistent with Bornemann's general dismissal of classical categories. As Jon Stewart has shown, Bornemann's seemingly cavalier manner of disposing of 'both rationalism and supernaturalism' 'in theology' as 'antiquated standpoints' caused quite a stir in Golden Age Denmark. In particular, the potential impact upon theology exerted by Hegel's revised logic was the issue that most exercised thinkers at the time.[13]

To appreciate this point of controversy it is important to see how the *ab posse* and *ad esse* principles were current in Danish speculative philosophy at the time Kierkegaard strategically revised them. One such prominent use of the *ab posse ad esse* principle is that of J. L. Heiberg. We find in his review of Valdemar Henrik Rothe's obscure treatise on the *Doctrine of the Trinity and Reconciliation* a deployment of the principles repeated by Kierkegaard in the course of Heiberg's thoroughgoingly Hegelian attack on the insufficiently speculative Rothe. The way Heiberg uses this principle and the association he makes between it and Kierkegaardian concerns make this treatise a plausible source of inspiration for Kierkegaard. Assuming he was familiar with the review, we could see it as a foil for Kierkegaard's own rejoinder to Heiberg's Hegelianism. That rejoinder can be read as of a piece with Kierkegaard's overall resistance to subscribing wholesale to Hegel's revision of classical logical principles. Just as Kierkegaard defends the binding force of contradiction when it comes to ethical freedom, choice and the attainment of selfhood, so too he seeks to preserve possibility's entailment by actuality. Arguably, Kierkegaard innovates further than his contemporaries by showing how the converse, actuality's entailment by possibility, is also a principle belonging to the realm of ethical choice and freedom, a converse that in fact is not part of classical logic as we have seen. So while Kierkegaard, like Hegel and his Danish followers, accepts the innovative interpretation that saw the two principles as co-implicated in a way that classical logic did not, he nevertheless insisted that they can only be substantively related in a concrete lived individuality, not as a function of speculative reasoning.

Heiberg's use of the principle occurs in the fourth of six sections in his review of Rothe, entitled, significantly for this study, 'Ideality and Idea'. Heiberg's overall complaint with Rothe is that he is insufficiently speculative, despite the fact that Rothe's treatise's subtitle proclaims it a work of speculative investigation. Heiberg's particular complaint in section four is that Rothe has confused the Ideal and the Idea rather than grasping them in their ultimate conceptual unity. The same problem bedevils Rothe's conflation of essence and phenomenon, substance and accident, and other such familiar speculative categories. Heiberg is stunned to discover Rothe plainly affirming a to him unbelievable truth in this sentence: 'When the spirit or essence of a thing is present, then the thing is also present – either it is thus present or it is not; or vice versa, when the essence is gone, the thing is gone.'[14] The problem here according to Heiberg is that Rothe is relying on 'a proposition that has been abandoned by formal logic: "*a posse ad esse valet consequentia*".'[15]

So the issue is that for Rothe when the essence of a thing is present, so also is the thing of which it is the essence; and vice versa, when the essence has eluded us so too has the thing. For this to be true, Heiberg argues, we would have to buy into the fallacious converse of the *ab esse ad posse* principle according to which being merely possible implies genuine actuality.

> But here the author [Rothe] seeks to oppose the general conviction of morality, art and religion that spirit is actual. For if every *posse* is an *esse* . . . then there can be no talk of spirit on the basis of the first determination. Another tacit presupposition is required because a spirit that does not realize its possibility, simply proves that it is not spirit. For spirit is more than a possibility, from which existence proceeds – as such it could hardly be called spirit. It proceeds from existence and has it as its presupposition.[16]

Heiberg's point here is that spirit is always actual. Rothe's mistake is that it is impossible to speak of spirit that has not yet realized its own possibility. To speak as Rothe does of a possibility merely implying its own actuality is to have failed to realize spirit in the first place. For Heiberg, spirit is always the speculatively grasped unity of possibility and actuality in their fundamental unity. Once again, Rothe has not gone far enough down the path of speculative reason, as his own example proves. Heiberg's indicts Rothe:

> For his proposition, '*a posse a esse valet consequentia*', says expressly that actuality (*esse*) is a necessary consequence (*consequentia*) of possibility (*posse*). Thus, the author [Rothe] requires that the determination of actuality be a necessary progress from possibility, while at the same time believing actuality need not be explicit but can remain in the bosom of possibility without hindering it or itself.[17]

Rothe illustrates his point that actuality necessarily progresses from a possibility while not needing to be explicitly actual by referring to a seed, which he claims 'contains the coming plant, far before it develops'.[18] Fair enough, Heiberg allows, but it must still be admitted that the seed is not the plant, such that if we are to speak of the spirit of the plant we must talk about the fully developed mature outgrowth of the seed, not the seed alone.[19] Or to use another example to which he turns at the close of this section, contra Rothe's claim that 'the bird's life is and remains the same, unchanged, whether it lies still in its egg or develops to become an inhabitant of the air', Heiberg points out that such a change is not at all inconsequential.[20]

Rothe's poorly chosen examples prove Heiberg's larger point that the Ideal is not the Idea, but rather its 'prophet', as he puts it. As in all things Hegelian, the positive and existing depend upon the negative and non-existing for their ground. Sounding very much like the master himself, Heiberg urges his readers to 'get beyond the common conception of these concepts' by grasping them in their covert unity.

> The common conception is exemplified in algebra textbooks whose standing example of positive and negative size is assets and debts, such that assets are always supposed to be the positive and debts the negative size . . . .. But assets are only positive for the person who does not have them. By contrast, for the debtor assets are negative and the debt positive.[21]

The true opposition is the one between categories that ultimately belong to one another: north and south are opposites, but it's the same distance travelled whether one is walking ten miles north or ten miles south.

The same revised logic goes for the Ideal and the Idea. Returning to Rothe's categories, Heiberg shows how essence is ideally present in its real phenomenon and substance is ideally present in its real accident. Essence and substance are negative, while phenomenon and accident are positive.[22] So it is with the Ideal and the Idea; in actuality the Ideal is always misunderstood and occulted, noticed only in what it produces. Only the Idea is its own ground and existence, a coincidence detectable in art and political life. The state has its ground in itself and has not its reality in the soil upon which its citizens dwell but in the invisible bond that unites those citizens. So also, fine art has its own ground and existence inasmuch as it is not meant to be put to any further use and exists not so much in its material composition as in the thought it expresses. To confuse the Ideal and the Idea then is a fatal mistake, one that drags the latter down to the realm of actuality where it does not belong.[23]

So what I am suggesting is that just as Hegel re-interprets the principles of identity, contradiction and the excluded middle, so too we might read Heiberg here in a Hegelian way trying to re-interpret the *ab esse ad posse* principle. For Hegelian logic, the classic principles are tautological at worst and uninformative at best. The same objection could be lodged against the *ab esse ad posse* principle: Of course, if something is actual then it is also possible. So what? Similarly, Heiberg treats the converse *ab posse ad esse* as not just invalid but vacuous in Rothe's handling of it. Of course, a seed grows up to be a plant and an egg hatches a bird that learns to fly. So what? The speculative truth, the interesting way to look at this principle, is to see that possibility and actuality are equally realized in the fully fledged existent.

Kierkegaard's appropriation of *ab esse ad posse*

Kierkegaard revises for his own purposes this speculative doctrine of the ultimate unity of actuality and possibility, in line with his broader existential dialectic. Kierkegaard adopts a form of the co-implicated structure that the Danish Hegelians, including Heiberg, promoted, while insisting on the relevance of this structure for understanding the formation of the self. For Kierkegaard, moving from possibility to actuality and back again is the fundamental means of grasping the ideal in its perfection, a perfection that for him, unlike in Hegel and the Danish Hegelians, can only be lived out, not grasped by speculation. What I want to argue is that what is true for Heiberg of the Idea, that here alone possibility and actuality are grasped in their true identity by speculative reason, can for Kierkegaard only be lived reality. A life lived by imagining possibilities and willing them into actuality is for Kierkegaard to live the true ideal and thus grasp it existentially, in the only sense that matters.

To see how Kierkegaard puts the *ab esse ad posse* and *ab posse ad esse* principles to work I begin with Johannes Climacus's approving citation of the paired phrases from Frater Taciturnus's 'Letter to the Reader'. In the *Postscript*, Climacus opens the section where he quotes Taciturnus with a remark on Aristotle's *Poetics*, which privileges poetry over history because history presents only what has occurred, while poetry presents what could and ought to have occurred, or, put another way, 'poetry has possibility at its disposal'.[24] Intriguingly, Taciturnus refers to the exact same Aristotelian point in the beginning of the section of his 'Letter to the Reader' where he uses the phrases *ab posse ad esse* and *ab esse ad posse*. There Taciturnus repeats 'the Aristotelian dictum that the poet is a greater philosopher than the historian because he shows how it ought to be, not how it is',[25] so obviously this eminent position of possibility with respect to poetry is on both author's minds. I will come back to this.

Climacus turns the observation about Aristotle to the point that while poetry has possibility at its disposal it is also thereby disinterested in his sense, that is, it is not invested in actual existence. As Climacus never tires of saying, 'there is only one interest, the interest in existing', and disinterestedness is indifferent to actuality.[26] Climacus is razor-sharp in his insistence on this point, which he presses aggressively against the confusion of categories he thinks characteristic of his age. Poetry tries to grasp possibility, speculation tries to arrive at actuality, while the ethical, which is interested in existing, is ignored, and 'what it means to exist is more and more forgotten'.[27]

While for aesthetics possibility is higher than actuality, it is just the opposite for ethics. For this reason, the ethical is militantly opposed to confusion and particularly insistent that observation is not what is at stake in ethics. It is strictly speaking impossible, Climacus argues, to observe ethically, because ethics demands that the individual meet its requirements. Or, to cite language that is even more apposite to the topic at hand, 'when the ethical inspects, it condemns every *posse* that is not an *esse*'.[28] The eye of the ethical so to speak is a judgemental one; any possibility not actualized is a demerit when it comes to ethical choice and action. Furthermore, ethics is not interested in others, only in the single individual and what the single individual must do. He writes:

> The ethical can be carried out only by the individual subject, who then is able to know what lives within him – the only actuality that does not become a

possibility by being known and cannot be known only by being thought, since it is his own actuality, which he knew as thought-actuality, that is, as possibility, before it became actuality; whereas with regard to another's actuality, he knew nothing about it before he, by coming to know it, thought it, that is, changed it into possibility.[29]

The crucial ethical point is to 'know what lives within' us; it is a form of self-knowledge that is involved here. To know what lives within us is to know an actuality that does not become transformed into a possibility by that very knowledge. Ordinarily, as this passage also intimates, to know an actuality is to change it into a possibility, because knowing makes of an actuality a possibility for me, which is not my actuality but that of another. Another's actuality only comes to be known by me as a possibility, because it was not my doing in the first place but that of another. As Climacus says on the same page, 'when I think something I want to do but as yet have not done, then what I have thought . . . is a possibility. Conversely, when I think something that someone else has done, therefore think an actuality, then I take this given actuality out of actuality and transpose it into possibility'.[30] The other's actuality stands to my knowledge of it as possibility in the same way that an act I am considering but have not done remains a possibility.

What I want to point out right away is that Kierkegaard then, writing as Climacus but consistent with a tack he has taken in other writings as well, resituates the import of the principles of *ab esse ad posse* and *ab posse ad esse*, which he is about to cite, into the terrain of the ethical. For Climacus too, as in Heiberg, these principles are about seizing upon the true ideal, but for Climacus that ideal can only be lived, and the principles are not interesting because of what they tell us about logic but because of what they imply about self-knowledge and living a life.

It is at this stage in the argument that Climacus refers to Taciturnus, so I will turn to him as well. The remarkable emphasis that Taciturnus places on his use of these phrases, underdeveloped in Climacus's account, is the role of a sort of regenerate aesthetics in moving back and forth from possibility to actuality in truly grasping the ideal. Taciturnus writes the following:

> In order to grasp the ideality, I must be able to dissolve the historical in the ideality or do (to use a pious expression) what God is said to do for one who is dying: shine upon it. Conversely, I do not enter into the ideality by repeating the historical jingle. Therefore, anyone who, with regard to the same thing, does not reach the conclusion just as well *ab posse ad esse* as *ab esse ad posse* does not grasp the ideality in this same thing.[31]

Again a dense passage, one that Climacus quotes exactly and in full. Taciturnus is here speaking on how to move into the religious ideality specifically, the ideality that Vigilius Haufniensis called the 'ideality of actuality'[32] (a phrase that Climacus uses as well).

I have explained this elsewhere at great length,[33] but I take the ideality of actuality, which Haufniensis equates with the religious ideal, to be for Kierkegaard the condition of having grasped a lived ideality. The lived ideal for him is one that is not as difficult to attain as the ethical ideal, which is impossible for sinful people, who always fail to fully live up to their ethical ideals. At the same time, the lived ideal is just as lovely as the aesthetic ideal, which is also impossible, inasmuch as again according to Haufniensis aesthetic ideals cannot cope with the gravity of sin without falsifying it.[34] Ethical ideals are unattainable because we always disappoint our own highest aspirations and betray our most cherished principles. Aesthetic ideals are remote from lived actuality because our actual lived existence never exhibits the poetic perfection that works of art exhibit when considering actuality in its ideal form, bound as they are to the necessarily limited power of poetics, which idealizes rather than seizes upon lived actualities. As Climacus argues, the ethical makes demands that we cannot satisfy and will not be dissuaded by temporalizing, while the poetic is concerned with possibility and therefore cannot attain true lived perfection.

The religious ideal or the ideal of actuality is the true perfection of lived experience in the light of an ideal that has aesthetic beauty and ethical force, recognizing that both of these ideals are imperfectly attained in actual life but that in that very same medium of actual life can be lived despite the unlovely aspects of our experience and our own ethical failings. To live the ideality of actuality is to live my own life as already ideal, not lacking by contrast to an imagined perfect ideal but sufficing already. For Taciturnus, to live the true ideal of actuality I must be able to move effortlessly from possibility to actuality in a kind of ceaseless oscillation between the two. This cannot be done on the basis of the historical when it comes to religious ideals. They do not rise and fall on historical truths, which are always uncertain and which Taciturnus says can only amount to 'raw material', a 'multiplicity of data' that the religious person knows how to dissolve into possibility and assimilate as actuality. 'There is nothing, therefore', he concludes, 'more foolish in the religious sphere than to hear the commonsensical question that asks when something is being taught: Now, did it actually happen this way for if it did one would believe it'.[35] History can only ever be inconclusive at best. I imagine Kierkegaard is thinking here of the infinite gulf that separates the believer from faith, one that cannot be traversed even by direct historical experience of a miracle, such that the disciple at second hand, to use the language of the *Philosophical Fragments*, is at no disadvantage, namely, to the disciple at first hand.

Implicit here is the claim that if history is not the foundation of the religious ideal, which again must be grasped in a continual re-imagining of that ideal as possible and then willed expression of that ideal in lived actuality, then aesthetics can play a role in this essential process. Recall that both Climacus and Taciturnus refer to Aristotle's prioritization of the possible over the actual in poetry. Both authors clearly place possibility, with which poetry is concerned, on an equal footing with actuality when the goal is grasping a lived religious ideal, an actual perfection expressed in life. Similarly, Taciturnus says that he has indirectly presented the religious paradigm by deliberately keeping it in the categories of immediacy and allowing it only to come to light indirectly. His method is aesthetic in a revised sense, and he claims that the aesthetic and religious have in common the necessity of issuing in a result. His own communication he says has no result because it is unfinished,[36] and it bears pointing out that he himself is not religious.[37]

Nevertheless, he argues that the dialectic of poetry and religion are the same. While the result of poetry is visible and external, the result of the religious is invisible and internal. The ethical is un-presentable for another reason, namely, that its demands are instantaneous, indeed so swift that there is no time to aestheticize them; as in Climacus, the ethical simply demands accountability. The goal is to combine the aesthetic and the ethical in the religious. The religious thus in Taciturnus's words 'plays the same role as the aesthetic, but as the superior'.[38] It slows down so to speak the ethical, so we can appreciate development and change, but it stages or gives expression to internal action, itself in principle invisible, in what Taciturnus does not hesitate to call the 'scene' of the external. 'This result', he maintains, 'is aesthetic-ethical and therefore can be shown in the external to a certain degree'.[39] This showing is a kind of staging or dramatization, by which we 'shine upon' the historical and thus grasp it as a possibility for ourselves, an act of imagination that makes a possibility precisely possible for me and affirms the actuality of who I am becoming as continuous with who I have always actually been.

The only questions that matter according to Taciturnus are 'Is what is being said possible?' and 'Am I able to do it?' It is evasiveness to ask, 'Did it actually happen?' and 'Has my neighbour Christophersen done it?' Faith, he concludes, 'is the ideality that resolves an *esse* in its *posse* and then conversely draws the conclusion in passion'.[40] I can only suppose that what he means by this is that to relate to the ideal in faith is to treat it as a real possibility for me to incorporate actually into my life and then passionately to will to do so. In this way faith is undeterred by the irresolvable question of whether history can provide the requisite degree of certainty to inspire my action and is undistracted by the irrelevant issue of whether my neighbour has actually lived in conformity with the ideal; faith rather wills to live the ideal myself with a passionate commitment in the face of uncertainty. It is perhaps no accident at all that these words from Taciturnus Climacus also approvingly quotes in his treatment of the same themes, which are of course perennial for him. The two authors agree that 'Ideality I know by myself, and if I do not know it by myself, then I do not know it at all, and all the historical knowledge does not help'.[41]

For both authors all that matters in relation to attaining the ideal is whether I can seize upon a possibility as relevant and compelling for myself and then make it actual by living it out. This is what it means to move from possibility to actuality and back again, in an endless interplay of becoming who I am. It is for this reason I suspect that in *Practice in Christianity* Anti-Climacus writes that the imagination is the 'first condition for what becomes of a person' while the will is 'the second and in the ultimate sense the decisive condition'.[42] It is by imagination that I can entertain a possibility, be enticed by it, and it is by the will that I actualize it. Notice also that possibility and actuality cannot be understood in the traditional fashion, as Kierkegaard has re-cast their meaning. Possibility in the crucial sense for him is tied to the call to ethical and religious transformation; it is not just an aesthetic object to be entertained – and actuality is not just brute facticity or a historical datum but a lived and accomplished reality that can inspire imitation.

My summary contention then is that in these short references Kierkegaard is taking up a familiar logical principle, one that has classical origins but was also a point of contention in the Danish reception of Hegelian logic. Departing from tradition, Kierkegaard depends on both possibility and actuality equally, and he re-configures both away from their traditional associations. Possibility is not a dim intimation of actuality but rather the essential precondition for change, a vital vision of what is genuinely real for me not as an abstraction but an available course of action and potential version of myself. Actuality is not simple facticity but what only I can be and do as myself in lived and willed affirmation. Together they result in the only true ideal, one that a renewed aesthetics can glimpse but that ultimately can only be lived out, from possibility to actuality and back again. Moving from possibility to actuality and back again is the very means by which we live an ideal existence.[43]

A case study: The Woman Who Was a Sinner

Taciturnus expressly says he does not want to linger with the aesthetic but 'go on to the religious', and for that, he must present the 'religious prototype' in a move that is strictly analogous to the poet's presentation of the tragic hero. Interestingly, Taciturnus says parenthetically that by a religious prototype here he means only 'devout individuals', a point that corroborates recent recognitions that while Kierkegaard of course upholds the quintessential case of Jesus Christ himself as the superlative prototype, he also refers to a number of other figures as possible prototypes. Wojciech Kaftanski has sensitized us to this wider use of the notion of prototype in Kierkegaard's writings, and here again we find a case where the prototype can be someone other than Christ.[44] Once more, however, it would be a mistake merely to relate to such a prototype historically, as if belief could follow smoothly upon the declaration by the speaker presenting the prototype that the prototype is historical and thus 'positively certain', such that the 'believing congregation believes everything, even that the speaker knows what he himself is saying'.[45]

So how can we get a better appreciation for how this process of knowing ideality by myself, by living it out, in this reciprocal pattern of moving between possibility and actuality, is meant to work? Is there a way to get a deeper appreciation for how a revised aesthetic can parallel and serve the religious by making it visible 'to a certain degree'? As I said, Taciturnus is primarily concerned with how to live out the ideality of a prototype, so to put a bit more meat on the bones of this argument, I would like to consider another figure that Kierkegaard explicitly calls a prototype who fits Taciturnus's reference to 'devout individuals' and is not Christ himself.

That prototype is the Woman Who Was a Sinner as she is celebrated by Kierkegaard in the third of his *Three Discourses at the Communion on Fridays*. Here Kierkegaard rhapsodizes on the love of the woman who in Luke chapter 7 anointed Christ's feet with costly oil in the house of a Pharisee. Her hatred of self and love of Christ makes of her nothing less than a 'prototype' for imitation, not a merely poetic ideal or possibility to be entertained with aesthetic light-mindedness.[46] Christ commends her for loving much, which results in the forgiveness of her sins, which it is implied are many. According to Kierkegaard's analysis, loving much is tantamount to having forgotten oneself entirely. To forget oneself is furthermore only to think of the other, in this case Christ himself, as the preeminent prototype.[47]

The Woman Who Was a Sinner does not speak; her power is not in words but in deeds, so again she communicates by her actual living, not by upholding a mere possibility for abstract consideration. She lives out the ideal of devotion to Christ in her very gestures. 'She says nothing', Kierkegaard writes, 'and therefore is not what she says, but she is what she does not say, or what she does not say is what she is. She *is* the symbol, like a picture'.[48] Beyond language, the Woman Who Was a Sinner communicates via her presence and actions. Kierkegaard repeats this phrase almost like a mantra, echoing again and again her likeness to a piece of visual art, or, more rarely, to a parable. Jesus, he argues, does not speak to her but speaks about her.

Significantly, he does 'look' at her, just as she looks at him, such that they are reciprocally related, one prototype to another, imaging one another with a surprising degree of mutual dependence, as we will soon see. Jesus comments on her action for pedagogical purposes. 'Presumably in order to make the application more impressive to those present', Kierkegaard says, 'he speaks not to her but about her. Although she is present, it is almost as if she were absent; it is almost as if he changed her into a picture, a parable'.[49] The parable of course is meant to communicate, and Kierkegaard here imagines that Christ communicates the meaning of self-forgetfulness, love and forgiveness of sins to Simon Peter by recounting the story of the Woman Who Was a Sinner to him. Yet the events that he would so narrate are in fact happening. Perhaps this is why Kierkegaard says 'it is almost like a story, a sacred story, a parable'. She cannot be entirely a story or parable because 'at the same moment the same thing was actually taking place on the spot'.[50]

By contrast, the companion Friday communion discourse on 'The Tax Collector' concerns a parable, one that is advertised as such. Luke recounts Jesus telling the parable of the humble and penitent tax collector who is despised by the self-important judgemental Pharisee in chapter 18. That episode actually is a parable, a sacred story, one that Jesus devises to instruct his disciples. But the Woman Who Was a Sinner is reported by Luke to be a real person, and so her story cannot be altogether a parable but as it were *becomes* a parable or a picture. Because the Woman's story is 'taking place on the spot' she is not a mere illustration but becomes a living prototype and exemplar. The Woman Who Was a Sinner by virtue of her self-forgetfulness and love receives the forgiveness of her sins. This transformation cannot 'be expressed more strongly, more truthfully than by this, that it is all forgotten, that she, the great sinner, is changed into a picture'.[51]

So she is not a contrived fictional parable but a sort of living, breathing parable. Though actual, she is idealized in a way that is not merely aesthetic but religious and edifying; rather than appeal only to her historicity, however, Kierkegaard imaginatively 'shines upon' her. Kierkegaard argues that the actual Woman Who Was a Sinner thus *becomes a work of art*. Numerous times he refers to her as if she were a 'picture' who had become an edifying spectacle, an artwork that is also simultaneously a real person. We can get further support from this reading from the same pages of *Stages in Life's Way* cited above. There Taciturnus says that 'the religious subjectivity has one more dialectical element than all actuality has, one that is not prior to actuality but after actuality'.[52] In the same vein, he says 'a religious ideality . . . comes after actuality'.[53]

Despite the parallels, there is thus a vital difference between aesthetics, which is capable of inventing its ideals from whole cloth, and a religious ideal, which depends on an actuality and comes 'after' it so to speak. The aesthetic ideal according to Taciturnus is 'higher than the actuality prior to the actuality, that is, in illusion'.[54] All aesthetics trades in idealization, and all poetry according to Kierkegaard idealizes an actuality. It takes an actuality, purges it of what is inessential to the ideal poetic vision, and so polished thus does the actual become idealized. Yet this aesthetic idealization is also necessarily falsifying. In this way it is prior to the actuality, since it has shorn, compressed and otherwise editorialized the actual. Again the difference cannot be simply that the one case is historical and the other not; yet it does seem to be the case that a constitutive relationship with an actuality is part of what makes the grasping of a religious ideal possible in its alternation between possibility and actuality. Possibility in the crucial sense is tied to the call to ethical and religious transformation, not just an aesthetic object, and actuality is not just brute facticity or a historical datum but a lived and accomplished reality that can inspire imitation.

We have noted that there is something provocative to be sure about Kierkegaard's claim that 'she became and is a prototype',[55] and Kierkegaard declares a blessing upon anyone 'who resembles her in loving much'[56] because of course the point of a prototype is to resemble it, and there can be no mistake about Kierkegaard's intent that his reader should resemble the Woman Who Was a Sinner in her self-forgetfulness and willingness to accept the forgiveness of her sins. This can be confirmed by a journal passage wherein he expressly says that 'the anonymous prototype constrains a person to think of himself insofar as this can be done'.[57]

This is perhaps why Kierkegaard is able to make the boldest suggestion advanced so far about the Woman Who Was a Sinner. Yes, he affirms, her sins are forgiven, but since she is a prototype she invites the imitation of all and each, and so the implication here is that each one must accuse himself as the

Tax Collector, forget herself as the Woman Who Was a Sinner, and love much and in so doing receive the forgiveness of sins for themselves. At this point in the text then Kierkegaard addresses the reader directly in the second person. 'It is true, in Christ your sins are forgiven you, but this truth, which therefore is said also to each one individually, is yet in another sense still not true; it must be made into truth by each one individually.'[58] The truth of the forgiveness of sins then is one that must be enacted; it remains abstract as a pronunciation until it is accepted and lived out, and in this instance specifically lived out by approaching the communion table and receiving the sacrament. It is this action surely above all others that makes the forgiveness of sins true for each person who performs it, for each one who plays her part in the drama of forgiveness and reconciliation. The true perfection is the one that is grasped as a possibility for myself and willed into actuality by myself.[59]

Finally, at the zenith of his discourse, Kierkegaard writes that 'This is how the woman is an eternal picture; by her great love she made herself, if I dare to speak this way, indispensable to the Savior'.[60] Now the Woman Who Was a Sinner is no mere picture but an eternal one, for her example can never dim. She is needed by the Saviour as much as she needs the Saviour because 'she made into truth'[61] the forgiveness of sins that he offers. She does so by her willingness to love another more than her own sin, and there is nothing people want to hang on to so much as their own sin, which they fear if they confess will leave them bereft of something essential to their identity. As we know from Kierkegaard's portraits of demonic defiance, there is no despair deeper than the despair of insisting on clinging to one's own sin, yet the Woman Who Was a Sinner truly earns the right to keep her title in the past tense, for she forever is the one who only was a sinner and now is no more.

As in Climacus, she does not become someone else, which is impossible but becomes herself in a new actuality, as one whose sins are forgiven. It is impossible that she become Christ; the task is to become *like* him. Climacus argues this at the very end of the *Concluding Unscientific Postscript*, when he shows that the biblical injunction to have the faith of a child means precisely not to become again a child, which again is impossible for grown people, but to become *like* a child.[62] Taciturnus again corroborates Climacus's point. He too writes that 'The difficulty with the forgiveness of sins ... is to become so transparent to oneself that ... one has become another person'.[63] This is what the Woman Who Was a Sinner has accomplished, and this is only possible when the religious ideal has been successfully grasped. In Kierkegaard's retelling of her story, she becomes an aesthetic object that is higher than actuality by being after it, and thus she makes the internal visible at least to a certain degree. No mere picture, she is also an incitement to action. Those who contemplate her example are not diverted from the essential questions but are rather confronted with them: Is this possible for me? Do I will it in actuality?[64]

Notes

1 See Jan Łukasiewicz, *Aristotle's Syllogistic from the Standpoint of Modern Formal Logic*, 2nd ed. (Oxford: Clarendon Press, 1957), 135–6.
2 'Sed malo de possibili proponere conclusiones et praemissas. Illis quippe de actu concessis, istae de possibili concedentur; non e converso'. Duns Scotus, *The De Primo Principio of John Duns Scotus: A Revised Text and Translation*, trans. Evan Roche (St. Bonaventure, NY: The Franciscan Institute, 1949), 41.
3 See Felix Alluntis, 'Demonstrability and Demonstration of the Existence of God', in *John Duns Scotus 1265–1965*, ed. John K. Ryan and Bernardine M. Bonansea, Studies in Philosophy and the History of Philosophy 3 (Washington, DC: The Catholic University of America Press, 1965), 133–70 (134).
4 '*Quod existit, id est possibile*: principium illud Scholasticorum verbis enuntiabimus: *ab esse ad posse valet consequentia*, seu quod perinde est: *ab existentia ad possibilitatem valet consequentia*: sed non viceversa, a posse ad esse valet consequentia.' See his *Institutiones Philosophicae ad Studia Theologica Potissimum Accommodotae*, Tomus II (Matriti: Ex Officina Ildephonsi a Lopez, 1787), 25–6. Translation my own.
5 Immanuel Kant, *Lectures on Metaphysics*, trans. and ed. Karl Ameriks and Steve Naragon (Cambridge: Cambridge University Press, 1997), 320.
6 'This is a warning against arguing directly from the logical possibility of concepts to the real possibility of things.' See Immanuel Kant, *The Critique of Pure Reason*, trans. Norman Kemp Smith (New York: St. Martin's Press, 1965), 503 n.[a].
7 See the classic discussion in Part III 'The Absolute Paradox (A Metaphysical Caprice)', in *Philosophical Fragments* and *Johannes Climacus*, ed. and trans. Howard V. Hong and Edna H. Hong (Princeton, NJ: Princeton University Press, 1985).
8 See Jon Stewart, *The Cultural Crisis of the Danish Golden Age: Heiberg, Martensen, and Kierkegaard* (Copenhagen: Museum Tusculanum Press, 2015), 247.
9 Johann Alfred Bornemann, 'Review of Martensen's *De autonomia conscientiae*', in *Mynster's "Rationalism, Supernaturalism" and the Debate about Mediation*, ed. and trans. Jon Stewart (Copenhagen: Museum Tusculanum Press, 2009): 57–92 (80).
10 Prov. 9.10.
11 Bornemann, 'Review of Martensen's *De autonomia conscientiae*', 80.

12 Descartes himself of course did advance his own version of the ontological argument, proving that for him at least the path of methodological doubt did not lead to scepticism about the divine. See Descartes's version of the ontological argument in part five of his *Meditations*.
13 Hans Lassen Martensen, 'Martensen's "Rationalism, Supernaturalism and the *principium exclusi medii*"', in *Kierkegaard Studies Yearbook,* trans. Jon Stewart (Berlin: DeGruyter, 2004): 583–94 (584).
14 Johan Ludvig Heiberg, 'Review of Dr. Rothe's *Doctrine of the Trinity and Reconciliation*', in *Heiberg's* Perseus *and Other Texts*, ed. and trans. Jon Stewart (Copenhagen: Museum Tusculanum Press, 2011), 85–149 (115).
15 Ibid.
16 Ibid., 115–16.
17 Ibid., 116.
18 Ibid.
19 Ibid.
20 Ibid., 124.
21 Ibid., 118.
22 Ibid., 119–20.
23 Ibid., 120.
24 Søren Kierkegaard, *Concluding Unscientific Postscript to* Philosophical Fragments, vol. 1, ed. and trans. Howard V. Hong and Edna H. Hong (Princeton, NJ: Princeton University Press, 1992), 318.
25 Søren Kierkegaard, *Stages on Life's Way: Studies by Various Persons*, ed. and trans. Howard V. Hong and Edna H. Hong (Princeton, NJ: Princeton University Press, 1988), 437.
26 Kierkegaard, *Concluding Unscientific Postscript*, 318.
27 Ibid., 319.
28 Ibid., 324.
29 Ibid., 320–1.
30 Ibid., 321.
31 Kierkegaard, *Stages on Life's Way*, 439.
32 Søren Kierkegaard, *The Concept of Anxiety*, ed. and trans. Reidar Thomte (Princeton, NJ: Princeton University Press, 1980), 17n.
33 See my *Kierkegaard and the Life of Faith: The Aesthetic, the Ethical, and the Religious in* Fear and Trembling (Bloomington, IN: Indiana University Press, 2017).
34 Kierkegaard, *The Concept of Anxiety*, 14–15.
35 Kierkegaard, *Stages on Life's Way*, 439.
36 Ibid., 441.
37 Ibid., 440.
38 Ibid., 442.

39 Ibid.
40 Ibid., 440.
41 Kierkegaard, *Concluding Unscientific Postscript*, 324; Kierkegaard, *Stages on Life's Way*, 438.
42 Søren Kierkegaard, *Practice in Christianity*, ed. and trans. Howard V. Hong and Edna H. Hong (Princeton, NJ: Princeton University Press, 1991), 186.
43 I have elaborated on these points further in 'After Actuality: Ideality and the Promise of a Purified Religious Vision in Frater Taciturnus', *History of European Ideas* 47, no. 3 (2021): 514–27.
44 See his *Kierkegaard, Mimesis, and Modernity: A Study of Imitation, Existence, and Affect* (London: Routledge, 2022), 133–9.
45 Kierkegaard, *Stages on Life's Way*, 439.
46 Søren Kierkegaard, *Without Authority*, ed. and trans. Howard V. Hong and Edna H. Hong (Princeton, NJ: Princeton University Press, 1997), 143.
47 Ibid., 140–1.
48 Ibid., 141.
49 Ibid.
50 Ibid., 142.
51 Ibid.
52 Kierkegaard, *Stages on Life's Way*, 428.
53 Ibid., 426.
54 Ibid., 423.
55 Kierkegaard, *Without Authority*, 142–3.
56 Ibid., 143.
57 Søren Kierkegaard, JP 1856 / SKS 22, 244, NB12:167.
58 Ibid.
59 I have explained more fully the sort of paradoxical perfection that Kierkegaard attributes to lived actuality by contrast to aesthetic ideality in my 'Imagination, Suffering, and Perfection: A Kierkegaardian Reflection on Meaning in Life', *History of Philosophy Quarterly* 38, no. 3 (forthcoming).
60 Ibid.
61 Ibid.
62 Kierkegaard, *Concluding Unscientific Postscript*, 595–8.
63 Kierkegaard, *Stages on Life's Way*, 483.
64 I would like to thank Erin Plunkett, Wojciech Kaftanski, Hjördis Becker-Lindenthal, George Pattison and Frances Maughan-Brown for their helpful and constructive feedback on the ideas presented in this chapter.

2

'What our age needs most'

Kierkegaard's metaphysics of *Virkelighed* and the crisis of identity of philosophy

Gabriel Ferreira

'What our age needs most'

In 1845, during the process of writing the *Concluding Unscientific Postscript*, published in February of 1846, Kierkegaard wrote a note in his drafts on what he considered to be one of the main problems of the philosophy of his time:

> Very likely what our age [*vor Tid*] needs most to illuminate [*belyse*] the relationship between logic and ontology is an examination of the concepts: possibility, actuality, and necessity. It is hoped, meanwhile, that the person who would do something along this line would be influenced by the Greeks. The Greek sobriety is seldom found in the philosophers of our day, and exceptional ingenuity is only a mediocre substitute. Good comments are to be found in Trendlenbur"s [sic] *Logische Untersuchungen*; but Trendlenburg [sic] was also shaped by the Greeks.[1]

The excerpt makes at least four interesting statements:

a. It is an evaluation of the philosophical *status quæstionis* concerning the relationship between logic and ontology.
b. This relationship must be clarified through an examination of the modal categories: Possibility (*Mulighed*), Actuality (*Virkelighed*) and Necessity (*Nødvendighed*).
c. That examination should be done by someone who is 'influenced by the Greeks'.
d. A good example of a person whose work is 'shaped' or educated (*dannet*) by the Greeks is Trendelenburg (misspelled here by Kierkegaard), and his

opus magnum, *Logical Investigations* (1st ed. 1840), is a good companion to such an enterprise.

Taken together, the four statements not only show how Kierkegaard had, despite the superficial appearances, a clear understanding of and interest in logical and ontological problems but also display how sensitive he was to the philosophical problems and debates of his time. Seen against the historical–philosophical background of the mid-nineteenth century, both the centrality of modal categories and the mention of Adolf Trendelenburg's work makes explicit Kierkegaard's awareness of the philosophical situation and of a way to overcome it. As we will see in the following section, the second half of the nineteenth century is generally recognized as a crisis point for philosophy, for several reasons. I suggest that this crisis is best understood as a crisis of metaphysics or, more precisely, a crisis concerning a particular understanding of metaphysics. After a historical reconstruction of that philosophical context, I will show how Kierkegaard's thought, mainly his metaphysics which orbits around the notion of *Virkelighed* (Actuality), fits in that background. Finally, I will explore how Kierkegaard's approach to metaphysics is a response to the crisis of philosophy as a crisis of metaphysics.

The crisis of metaphysics in nineteenth-century philosophy

In what way should we understand what Kierkegaard calls 'our age' or 'our time' [*vor Tid*]? I think we have mainly two possibilities. One of them is, as Stewart argues, to consider Kierkegaard's immediate intellectual context in nineteenth-century Denmark.[2] Following Stewart's main point, Kierkegaard's theoretical worries emerged primarily from published works and quarrels that originated from Copenhagen philosophical–theological circles. However, another way of reading Kierkegaard's preoccupation and proposals concerning his age is by widening the scope, confronting his analysis against the background of the complex set of problems, events and processes having place in the European intellectual world, beyond the limits of Denmark. What perspective should we assume?

There is no doubt that Jon Stewart's impressive work – both his major book on Kierkegaard's relationship to Hegel and translations of Kierkegaard's contemporaries' *opera*[3] – has changed the *status quæstionis* of the scholarship. By introducing new historical data, characters, works and quarrels, not only was the once commonplace acceptance of Kierkegaard's straightforward critique of Hegel profoundly revamped in the newest Kierkegaardian literature but also the landscape of theoretical references and connections in his works.[4] However, despite the obvious contributions made by Stewart's approach, such a perspective turned Kierkegaard into a 'parochial thinker'.[5] It is not a matter of the geographical aspect of making Kierkegaard an author who was more or less stuck inside the limits of the city of Copenhagen, but a philosopher whose theoretical framework was virtually insulated against the wider set of philosophical problems of the nineteenth-century philosophy. Those two ways of interpreting Kierkegaard's judgement of his age lead us to different results. Following one of those paths, we gain a deeper knowledge about Kierkegaard's immediate intellectual network, but we miss the perspective from which we could see his thought, philosophical and theological, as a relevant event in the intellectual history of the nineteenth century seen beyond the limits of Denmark. On the other hand, following the second path, we opt for seeing Kierkegaard within the wider philosophical scenario of the nineteenth century, but one could argue that, in so doing, we miss the focus of Kierkegaard's closest intellectual connections. What then?

Although both ways have their pros and cons, I think we can decide between those paths by looking to the very nature of the problem or topic. Considering the excerpt above, Kierkegaard is dealing with a problem – the relationship between logic and ontology – which is central not only to the whole history of philosophy but particularly to nineteenth-century philosophy. We can have a deeper understanding of the whole intellectual development of the period, and not only of philosophy, if we grasp the set of problems whose roots lie in the question of the nature, scope and object of metaphysics. Thus, the problem Kierkegaard is addressing cannot be fully understood and developed without the wider background of the period. 'Our age' here must be seen as the post-Hegelian age with all its features. Hence, I will attempt to briefly reconstruct it.

The standard view about nineteenth-century philosophy comes from a narrative that does not deviate very much from the story told by Löwith.[6] Following him, the main events in nineteenth-century philosophy can be found in reactions to Hegel, and the key moments are Kierkegaard's existential approach, Marx's historic–materialistic perspective and Nietzsche's nihilistic contributions, all of them shaping two major lines of twentieth-century philosophy: existentialism and Marxism. Though Löwith's work also mentions figures such as Ludwig Feuerbach, Max Stirner and Leo Strauss, their function is mainly to underscore those main narrative. Löwith's account, while significant, also omits major trends, figures and events that were crucial to shaping contemporary philosophy.[7] It is also noteworthy that, as Leo Freuler points out, the thought of Kierkegaard, Marx and Nietzsche was not widely discussed in the second half of the nineteenth century. In other words, the reception of those thinkers did not figure in the philosophical quarrels of the period, and their importance is much more a matter of a posteriori reconstruction of the intellectual scenario than a reliable example of a history of ideas of that period.[8]

Hence, in order to better understand the type of problems Kierkegaard had in mind when considering 'the relationship between logic and ontology', we must foreground what Schnädelbach first named as an 'identity crisis of philosophy' (*Identitätkrise der Philosophie*).[9] Whether 1831,[10] the year of Hegel's death, or 1840,[11] the year A. Trendelenburg first published his *Logische Untersuchungen*, the fact is that philosophy, at the end of the first half and the beginning of the second half of the nineteenth century, began to suffer a process from which it has not yet recovered, namely, a discredit that affected its roots as a field of knowledge.[12] Of the complex reasons for this turn, two of them, which are closely interconnected, are very important for my purposes here, namely, the dawn of absolute idealism and the success of the natural sciences.

We can see how those two major events are absolutely intertwined when paying attention to how the Hegelian view of both philosophy and natural sciences collided head-on with the main developments of the time. One of the distinctive marks of speculative idealism is its foundational perspective, or the view that the task of philosophy consists mainly in providing the bedrock for all other types of knowledge, especially the natural sciences. The basis of such a foundational view is precisely one of the central metaphysical theses of absolute idealism: the identity between being and thought and the consequent identity between logic and ontology.[13] Hence, the whole edifice of knowledge, including the natural sciences, rests upon the identity of being and thought, which is the very condition of possibility of any knowledge that aspires to be scientific, namely, universal and necessary knowledge. Particularly in Hegel's system, the identity between being and thought is the cornerstone for the solution of the problems bequeathed by Kant's remaining dualisms. That is why one of the principal aims of the beginning of Hegel's *Science of Logic* is to conquer such identity, which will make possible the overcoming of the *aporiai* of transcendental idealism.[14]

The view that philosophy must provide the metaphysical basis of epistemology, in other words, that philosophy serves a foundational role, gives birth to an approach to nature which sees it as an organic whole sustained by necessary and universal laws responsible both for its operations and its intelligibility. It makes the comprehension of nature and its phenomena necessarily dependent on metaphysical roots; the understanding of nature must be, therefore, a task of a *Naturphilosophie*.[15] However, it is precisely such a perspective that was progressively discredited. The success of the empirical, rather than an a priori, approach to nature, as well as the radical criticism of the very ground of a more radical speculative idealism in works like Adolf Trendelenburg's *Logische Untersuchungen* (1st ed. 1840) sealed the fate of a philosophy of nature, a *Naturphilosophie*, which, it was thought, should cede its place to natural sciences, or *Naturwissenschaften*. In fact, the title of an opuscule by Trendelenburg – *Die logische Frage*,[16] the logical question – began a movement that put into question the possibility of a pure dialectical identity between being and thought and, consequently, the validity of the Hegelian project of a foundational philosophy. As R. Vilkko presents it,

> After Hegel's death in 1831, there arose in the academic circles of Germany a lively discussion concerning the makings of logic both as a philosophical discipline and as a formal and fundamental theory of science which might clarify not only the logical but also the metaphysical foundations of science. In fact, this was perhaps the most popular theme in the philosophical exchange of thoughts in Germany during the mid-nineteenth century. The most characteristic slogans in the discussion were 'the logic question' and 'reform of logic'.[17]

Hence, the success of *Naturwissenschaften*, *qua* empirical sciences of nature, also had a metaphysical counterpart in the denial of a foundationalist perspective which, as Freuler points out, did not remain confined to a Hegelian or speculative idealist conception, but spread its doubts on the validity of philosophy in itself.[18] For the decades to come, such a dismissal led philosophers to re-think philosophical questions[19] under some new epistemological and methodological 'imperatives'.[20] Hence, it is possible to understand the whole development of late nineteenth-century philosophy through that perspective. However, as said above, the core of the story lies in metaphysics, insofar it is a certain view of metaphysics and its role upon which a great part of those debates rested. A significant number of late nineteenth-century philosophers rejected any sort of metaphysical project that suggested the return to a concept of philosophy that failed to take into account the evolution of natural sciences or that naively embraced speculative thought. Referring to the 'old days', Wilhelm Windelband, in 1894, summed up the 'spirit of the time' pointing to the 'metaphysical covetousness' (*metaphysische Begehrlichkeit*) of those speculative philosophers.[21] At first glance, this might appear to be, as Schnädelbach says, 'the end of philosophy as metaphysics',[22] giving rise to the myth of a metaphysical vacuum between Hegel and Heidegger.[23] But when we take a closer look at the philosophical projects in that period, we see that what was going on was not of a rejection of metaphysics or a metaphysical scepticism per se, but a dismissal of a sort of metaphysics, namely, the type bound by the presuppositions of speculative idealism, mainly the identity of being and thought. This opened a space for different types of ontologies with diverse candidates for the *relata* of thought: matter, meaning, value and so on. Within this frame, we see philosophers as varied as Trendelenburg, Fechner, Lotze, Brentano, Meinong, but also Wundt, Eduard von Hartmann, Lange, Frege and Husserl; these thinkers offered several distinct approaches that helped to design, or redesign, new metaphysical attitudes. That is why we can regard the crisis of philosophy in the late nineteenth century as a metaphysical crisis or, in other words, a crisis of a specific kind of metaphysical perspective.

Kierkegaard's metaphysics of *Virkelighed*

It is against the background presented above that we should see Kierkegaard's evaluation of the set of problems concerning the relationship between logic and ontology. This background also helps us to understand why Kierkegaard thought it necessary to examine modal categories of actuality, possibility and necessity, and to do it from a different standpoint. Despite his death in 1855, which did not allow him to see the further historical and philosophical developments, Kierkegaard was fully aware of his philosophical context, both the increasing role of the natural sciences as well as the philosophical dimension of the problems. Kierkegaard's suspicion of the natural sciences is very well known through the scholarship. Of course, Kierkegaard's criticism does not target the *Naturvidenskaben* in themselves. In fact, Kierkegaard acknowledges the epistemic value of laws of nature and the knowledge of them, as well as formal sciences such as mathematics and logic. The point is, precisely, the same which threatens some philosophers of that period, namely, the inclination of natural sciences to an absolute pervasiveness. In other words, Kierkegaard's criticism towards natural sciences was rooted in his sharp demarcation between a sphere which can be known and understood through the epistemic tools of sciences and a dimension that scientific knowledge cannot reach.[24] However, what distinguishes Kierkegaard from other philosophers who shared this concern is how he understands the aspect of reality that cannot be grasped by the scientific approach: the sphere of existence and its particular metaphysical structure.[25]

Despite a tendency in mainstream Kierkegaard scholarship to ignore areas like metaphysics and epistemology, theoretical concerns about logic and ontology were not foreign to his interests. In fact, Kierkegaard's papers are filled with expositions of such issues. Three of them are especially noteworthy for my purposes here. During 1844–45, Kierkegaard worked on what would be *Concluding Unscientific Postscript* (1846) under the title of 'Logical Problems' (*Logiske Problemer*),[26] with eight main problems, the first being 'What is a category. What does it mean to say that being is a category?' and the last 'What is existence? [*Existents*]?'[27] Though the book was never published under that name, these problems were central to *Postscript*. The problem of categories was a live philosophical issue after Hegel's death. Hermann Bonitz (1853), Eduard von Hartmann (1896), Franz Brentano (posthumously published in 1907) and F. A. Trendelenburg (1846) published works on the history and interpretation of the problem of categories due to its importance as one of the main *loci* of the metaphysical discussion concerning the relationship between being and thought.

Trendelenburg's *Geschichte der Kategorienlehre* had a singular impact on Kierkegaard. As he affirms in a *Papirer* entry from 1847,

> There is no modern philosopher from whom I have profited so much as from Trendelenburg. At the time I wrote Repetition I had not yet read anything of his – and now that I have read him, how much more lucid and clear everything is to me. My relationship to him is very special. Part of what has engrossed me for a long time is the whole doctrine of the categories (the problems pertaining to this are found in my older notes, on quarto pieces of paper). And now Trendelenburg has written two treatises on the doctrine of categories, which I am reading with the greatest [*yderste*] interest. The first time I was in Berlin, Trendelenburg was the only one I did not take the trouble to hear – to be sure, he was said to be a Kantian. And I practically ignored the young Swede travelling with me who intended to study only under Trendelenburg. O, foolish opinion to which I also was in bondage at the time.[28]

The 'older notes' to which Kierkegaard refers date from 1842 to 1843 and are a set of questions and claims[29] that, although they do not amount to a treatise on categories, identify fundamental points that were essential for Kierkegaard's ontology:

a) Can there be a transition from quantitative qualification to a qualitative one without a leap? And does not the whole of life rest in that?[30]

b) Every determination [*Bestemmelse*] for which being [*Væren*] is an essential qualification lies outside of immanental thought, consequently outside of logic.[31]

c) To what extent does imagination play a role in logical thought, to what extent the will, to what extent is the conclusion a resolution?[32]
d) What is the historical significance of the category? What is a category?[33]
e) Shall the category be derived from thought or from being?[34]
f) What is the relation between the speculating subject and historical existence [*Existents*]? What is continuity? What is primitivity?[35]
g) How is this [the relation between the speculating subject and historical existence] related to the world-historical development used so much now? In all ages man has had everything; the transaction takes place in cognition, feeling and will; they rank equally high. There are two goals: every man is *télos*, and the world-historical development is telos, but this telos we cannot penetrate.[36]
h) A pathos-filled transition – a dialectical transition.[37]
i) Every individual life is incommensurable for conceptualization; the highest therefore cannot be to live as a philosopher. In what is this incommensurability resolved? In action – that in which all men are one is passion. Therefore, everything religious is passion, hope, faith and love. Greatness is to have one's life in that which is essential for all and therein to have a difference of degree. To be a philosopher is a distinction just as much as to be a poet.[38]

Items 'b', 'e', 'f' and 'I' in particular relate to Kierkegaard's concern that any consideration of the problem of categories – the problem of the conceptual expression of the structure of reality, broadly understood – must consider the metaphysical aspect of reality that he makes explicit in another entry from *Papirer*:

On the Concepts ESSE and INTER-ESSE

A methodological attempt:

The different sciences ought to be ordered according to the different ways in which they accent being [*Væren*] and how the relationship to being provides reciprocal advantage.

Ontology ⎤
⎬ The certainty of these is absolute – here thought and being are
⎦ one, but on the other hand these sciences are hypotheses.

Mathematics

Existential-science [*Existentiel-Videnskab*].[39]

The importance of this entry cannot be overestimated. Kierkegaard lays out here both an epistemological/methodological and metaphysical perspective that is absolutely central to his thought. First, from a methodological point of view, Kierkegaard states that different 'sciences' must follow the ontological status of their objects, and, no less important, that the objects reciprocally determine the level of certainty of the respective sciences. Thus, Kierkegaard provides two different types or categories of science. The first, inside the bracket, includes 'Ontology' and 'Mathematics' as instances. It is noteworthy that by grouping ontology and mathematics together, Kierkegaard advances a concept of ontology as a formal science where the certainty is apodictic because in it being and thought are one; that is, the objects of that kind of ontology, as well as the objects of mathematics, are *entia rationis* or, in the best of cases, *abstracta*. Therefore, their unicity with thought is guaranteed by their very nature as beings *qua* in thought. By definition, there could not be any difference between such a being and thought. Connected with the title of the note, that sort of knowledge must be seen on the side of *Esse* (being).

Read without the broader context of the crisis of metaphysics that has as its cornerstone the identity between being and thought, this part of the entry could wrongly give place to a common misunderstanding regarding Kierkegaard's philosophical position, namely, that he is a fierce critic of metaphysics per se. However, as I have mentioned earlier, a number of philosophical projects of the period involved the rejection of both: (1) the identification between philosophy and natural sciences, and (2) of any return to an a priori metaphysical perspective. In this sense, an emblematic intellectual episode is the rise of an 'inductive metaphysics' in several late nineteenth-century philosophical projects, as a type of metaphysics without a priori grounding.[40] This seems close to what Kierkegaard had in mind with the second part of the entry. Besides the formal sciences and, especially, a particular kind of ontology, Kierkegaard recognizes in his scheme another type of science. It is not concerned with *Esse*, the pure being which, as he sees it, is identical to thought, but rather it has a different sort of object, namely, *Inter-Esse*. Falling outside of the bracket, its attributes must be different from those of ontology and mathematics. Hence, we can infer:

a. It does not have absolute certainty concerning its knowledge.
b. It is a science where there is no identity between being and thought.
c. It is not a science of 'hypotheses'.

The meaning of these features, as distinct from the features of mathematics and (a type of) ontology, are made clearer by the name that Kierkegaard gives to the science that would study them; it is an 'existential-science' (*Existentiel-Videnskab*). In other words, Kierkegaard is claiming that there is another 'science' which has existence as its proper object and that must conform to the methodological features listed above. It also means that ontology, at least understood as a knowledge whose object (being) is identical to thought, should not be responsible for dealing with existence, but should be reserved for another type of metaphysical thinking.

The methodological or epistemological differentiation between a traditional understanding of ontology, closer to a formal science, and an existential-science is not a trifling move by Kierkegaard, but reflects his deep view of the ontological structure of reality and, as a consequence, underlines his judgement about his age. This becomes clearer when we look at some excerpts from *Philosophical Fragments* and *Concluding Unscientific Postscript*.

In an extensive footnote in *Philosophical Fragments*, within the context of the discussion on the existence of God, Kierkegaard states:

> For example, Spinoza, who, by immersing himself in the concept of God, aims to bring being out of it by means of thought, but, please note, not as an accidental quality but as a qualification of essence. [. . .] But to go on, what is lacking here is a distinction between factual being and ideal being [*faktisk Væren og ideel Væren*]. The intrinsically unclear use of language – speaking of more or less being, consequently of degrees of being [*Grads-Forskjel i Væren*] – becomes even more confusing when that distinction is not made. [. . .] With regard to factual being, to speak of more or less being is meaningless. A fly, when it is, has just as much being as the god; with regard to factual being, the stupid comment I write here has just as much being as Spinoza's profundity, for the Hamlet dialectic, to be or not to be applies to factual being. Factual being is indifferent to the differentiation of all essence-determinants, and everything that exists participates without petty jealousy in being and participates just as much. It is quite true that ideally the situation is different. But as soon as I speak ideally about being, I am speaking no longer about being but about essence.

The distinction Kierkegaard stresses between two spheres or realms of being, factual and ideal, appears in a more sophisticated conceptual form in *Postscript*:

> This triumph of pure thinking (that in it thinking and being are one) is both laughable and lamentable, because in pure thinking there can really be no question at all of the difference. – Greek philosophy assumed as a matter of course that thinking has reality [*Realitet*]. In reflecting upon it, one must come to the same result, but why is thought-reality [*Tanke-Realitet*] confused with

actuality [*Virkelighed*]? Thought-reality is possibility, and thinking needs only to reject any further questioning about whether it is actual.[41]

Here we discover the insight that forms the ground of Kierkegaard's existential-science. While a speculative metaphysical approach sees the identity between being and thought as a necessary means to solve or dissolve all dichotomies – a move that Kierkegaard sees as 'laughable and lamentable' (*at lee og til at græde over*) – Kierkegaard, by contrast, draws attention to the absolute irreducibility of being *qua* actual to any sort of conceptual or thought movement. When grasped by thought, actual being is transmuted into being *qua* in thought, namely, a possible (*Mulig*) being. Such a mutation is not a perception or theoretical invention made by Kierkegaard. In fact, by distinguishing 'reality' (*Realitet*) and 'thought-reality' (*Tanke-Realitet*) from 'actuality' (*Virkelighed*), Kierkegaard is joining an eminent tradition,[42] which understands being possible – as thought entity (*de ratione*) – and being actual (its *actus essendi*) as radically distinct. The very terms used by Kierkegaard are, in truth, an inheritance of the medieval and early modern distinction between *Realitas* and *Actualitas*. *Realitas* was used to mean the definitory attributes (predicates) of a thing (*res*) and, as such, was understood as merely possible. Even if we look at Kant's table of categories, *Realität* falls under the category of quality, which is different from existence/actuality (*Dasein/Wirklichkeit*), a category of modality.[43] Heidegger explains:

> The concept of reality and the real in Kant does not have the meaning most often intended nowadays when we speak of the reality of the external world or of epistemological realism. Reality is not equivalent to actuality, existence, or extantness [. . .] When Kant talks about the *omnitudo realitatis*, the totality of all realities, he means not the whole of all beings actually extant but, just the reverse, the whole of all possible thing – determinations, the whole of all thing – contents or real – contents, essences, possible things. Accordingly, *realitas* is synonymous with Leibniz' term *possibilitas*, possibility.[44]

The impossibility of grasping being *qua* actual in thought is resumed once again in one of Kierkegaard's entries in his *Papirer*, dated 1850:

'Science' – The Existential.

'Actuality' [*Virkelighed*] cannot be conceptualized. Joh[annes] Climacus has already demonstrated this correctly and quite simply. To conceptualize is to dissolve actuality into possibility [*opløse Virkelighed i Mulighed*] – but then it is of course impossible to conceptualize it, for to conceptualize it is to transform [*forvandle*] it to possibility and is thus not to hold fast to it as actuality. As far as actuality is concerned, conceptualizing is a regression, a step backward, not a step forward. It is not as if 'actuality' were devoid of concepts – not at all, no, the concept that is found by conceptually dissolving it into possibility is also present in actuality, but of course there is something more: that it is actuality. From possibility to actuality is a step forward (except in connection with evil); from actuality to possibility is a step backward. But there is this ill-fated confusion in modern times, when people have incorporated 'actuality' into logic, and then in their distraction they forget that in logic 'actuality' is really only a 'thought actuality', [*tænkt Virkelighed*] i.e., a possibility [*Mulighed*].[45]

Kierkegaard's radical separation between *Virkelighed* and *Realitet* can be seen as the difference between actual and possible being. It distinguishes the proper domain of existence and its features, and it serves as the starting point to Kierkegaard's own ontological description of the structure of reality. First, because it prevents, once for all, the identity of being and thought and therefore also of logic and ontology. By insisting on the inapprehensibility of actual being, Kierkegaard also establishes an epistemological principle regarding actual being: 'all knowledge about actuality is possibility'.[46] Second, it serves as an ordering principle both for the proper understanding of existence and for its place in the general outlook of being.

Kierkegaard never wrote a metaphysical 'treatise' on *metaphysica generalis*. However, the emphasis on *Virkelighed* has theoretical consequences and developments in his ontological *Weltanschauung*, which can be assembled from some interesting statements from *Postscript*:

I. In the language of abstraction, that which is the difficulty of existence and of the existing person never actually appears; even less is the difficulty explained. Precisely because abstract thinking is *sub specie æterni*, it disregards the concrete, the temporal, the becoming of existence, and the difficult situation of the existing person because of his being composed of the eternal and the temporal situated in existence;[47]

II. God does not think, he creates; God does not exist [*existere*], he is eternal. A human being thinks and exists, and existence [*Existents*] separates thinking and being, holds them apart from each other in succession;[48]

III. But surely an existing individual human being is not an idea; surely his existence is something other than the thought-existence of the idea? Existing (in the sense of being this individual human being) is surely an imperfection compared with the eternal life of the idea, but a perfection in relation to not being at all. Existing is a somewhat intermediate state [*Mellemtilstand*] like that, something that is suitable for an intermediate being [*Mellemvæsen*] such as human being is;⁴⁹

IV. To exist as this individual human being is not as imperfect an existence as, for example, to be a rose. [. . .]. Philosophy explains: Thinking and being are one – but not in relation to that which is what it is only by existing [*at være til*], for example, a rose, which has no idea at all in itself, thus not in relation to that in which one most clearly sees what it means to exist [*existere*] in contrast to thinking; but thinking and being are one in relation to that whose existence is essentially a matter of indifference because it is so abstract that it has only thought-existence. But in this way one omits an answer to what was actually asked about: existing as an individual human being. In other words, this means not to be [*Være*] in the same sense as a potato is, but not in the same sense as the idea is, either. Human existence has an idea within itself but nevertheless is not an idea-existence [*Idee-Existents*];⁵⁰

V. The systematic idea is subject-object, is the unity of thinking and being; existence, on the other hand, is precisely the separation. From this it by no means follows that existence is thoughtless [*tankeløs*], but existence has spaced and does space subject from object, thought from being.⁵¹

From which we can draw the following hierarchy of modes of being:

a. not being at all (from III);
b. imperfect and finite actual being with no idea in itself (from IV);
c. imperfect, finite and intermediate being and composed by eternal and temporal in existence (*Existents/Tilværelse*) – *inter-esse* – capable of having/grasping ideas (from I, III, IV, and V);
d. eternal being (*Realitet*) of *sub specie æterni* ideas (from I, III and IV) and
e. eternal being (*Væren* and *Virkelighed*), but not *Existents/Tilværelse* of God (from I).

Now we can better understand the need for re-evaluation of the relationship between logic and ontology through the reassessment of modal categories proposed by Kierkegaard. From the Kierkegaardian standpoint, the speculative ontology of his age made the mistake of not separating, in a radical manner, the two regions or domains of being that could never be identified, namely, the actual and the possible. Even though in the being of *inter-esse*, the mode of being of human being, which enjoys the mode of being of existence, actuality and possibility are necessarily merged, they are not to be confused. To do so would risk deflating all ethical and religious questions. The irreducibility of actuality (*Virkelighed*) is the very condition of possibility of human existence in its ethical and religious fullness. And for Kierkegaard, in order for such re-evaluation to be undertaken, it must begin from a theoretical point of view distinct from that of his contemporaries. As Kierkegaard sees it, the major part of the history of modern philosophy is the history of the deflation of being *qua* actual. Now, it is noteworthy that Kierkegaard's evaluation regarding modern philosophy is virtually the same as that made by Hegel. Since the Cartesian *cogito*, 'thinking and being are thus inseparably bound together'.[52] Then, when we see Christian Wolff's systematization of metaphysics in the eighteenth century – his presentation of metaphysics as 'constituted by ontology, i.e. the doctrine of the abstract determinations of essence' – it is only the development of the progressive process of 'noetization' of being.[53] In fact, Wolff's account of existence as a mere *complementum possibilitatis* paves the way to the confusion Kierkegaard was denouncing, ironically, in Hegel himself and his contemporaries.[54] That is why Kierkegaard rightly claims that in his age 'the philosophical thesis of the identity of thinking and being is just the opposite of what it seems to be', namely, the unity of thinking and being is an identity insofar as it depletes (actual) being turning it into conceptual (possible) being.[55]

Hence, Kierkegaard's evaluation of the *status quæstionis* of the relationship between logic and ontology and his proposed metaphysics centred on *Virkelighed* has at least three important consequences: (1) it touches the bullseye of modern metaphysics in its progressive noetization of being, which deflates actuality; (2) it establishes ontological conditions for existential analysis insofar as it properly locates the mode of being of human existence within the whole structure of reality; and (3) from the broader point of view of the crisis of identity of philosophy as the crisis of a type of metaphysics, it offers an alternative centred on being *qua* actual which matches the exigence of a metaphysics open to a posteriori knowledge, whether in philosophy or the natural sciences.

Conclusion

From what I have intended to show above, I think we must draw at least three important conclusions.

First, concerning the intellectual landscape of the late nineteenth century, in contrast to what sometimes appears to be the standard view, the period cannot be seen as a time of a peremptory rejection of metaphysics *simpliciter*. On the contrary, the (partial) decay of speculative idealism, together with the rise of the *Naturwissenschaften*, occasioned new demands for metaphysics and, in consequence, for philosophy in itself. Those two boundaries – on the one hand, the renunciation of the thesis of the identity between being and thought, and, on the other, the threat of dissolution of philosophy into natural sciences – set new parameters for metaphysics that we still can see in action today.

When it comes to situating Kierkegaard within the broader context presented here, his metaphysical worries get other philosophical layers. If it is true that a considerable part of the standard reception interpreted Kierkegaard's criticism against 'Hegel' either as a straightforward argument with almost no contextualization (Thulstrup) or having almost nothing to do with the nineteenth-century intellectual problems beyond Denmark's borders (Stewart), it is also true that a more complex characterization of Kierkegaard's intellectual age is imperative. Therefore, when we read Kierkegaard's philosophical statements about modal categories, for instance, against the backdrop of the metaphysical crisis of nineteenth-century philosophy, we can have at least two payoffs, namely, a deeper understanding of Kierkegaard's own ideas and a clearer view of Kierkegaard's interaction with and impact on the history of philosophy. From that standpoint, Kierkegaard is not only fighting against his contemporary countrymen but is a major figure who is dealing with the greatest philosophical challenges of his time and can be seen as offering new and sophisticated analyses of and solutions for them.

Finally, another advantage that emerges from such a perspective is the awareness of Kierkegaard's possible contributions to contemporary philosophical debates. Kierkegaard's role as one of the main precursors of the philosophy of existence is well known and documented. However, the limited treatment of Kierkegaard's metaphysical positions obstructs our view concerning such a field of contemporary philosophical problems. Questions regarding the ontological status of existence or the existential predicate, as well as different ways of being, topics that are very central to Kierkegaard's thought, are among the most interesting topics in contemporary philosophy. If we pay attention to Kierkegaard's metaphysics of *Virkelighed*, as well as his general ontology that recognizes other kinds of beings along with human existence – like God, *abstracta*, and inanimate entities – we can see how Kierkegaardian thought can be related to current problems and positions such as ontological pluralism, and we can look to his works for arguments and insights regarding such questions.[56] Even in the landscape of nineteenth-century philosophy as a craving for new forms of metaphysics and, consequently, considering different sets of problems, we can establish connections between Kierkegaard and a motley group of nineteenth-century philosophers such as Meinong and his *Gegenstandtheorie*,[57] Lotze's *Mikrokosmus*,[58] among others. Along these lines, interpreting Kierkegaard's thought through the prism of the wider metaphysical problems of his age can open up new perspectives and deepen our understanding.

Notes

To my beloved *Doktorvater* and friend, Poul Otto Lübcke, *in memoriam*.

1. Søren Kierkegaard, *Søren Kierkegaard's Journals and Papers*, 7 vols., ed. and trans. Howard V. Hong and Edna H. Hong, assisted by Gregor Malantschuk (Bloomington, IN: Indiana University Press, 1967–1978), *Pap.* VI B 54:21 n.d., 1845.
2. Jon Stewart, *Kierkegaard's Relations to Hegel Reconsidered* (New York: Cambridge University Press, 2003b).
3. For instance, Jon Stewart, *Kierkegaard and his Contemporaries: The Culture of Golden Age Denmark* (Berlin: Walter de Gruyter, 2003a).
4. Compare to the former standard view from Niels Thulstrup, *Kierkegaard's Relation to Hegel* (Princeton, NJ: Princeton University Press, 1980).
5. See Merold Westphal, *Becoming a Self* (West Lafayette: Purdue University Press, 1996) and Daniel Watts, 'The Paradox of Beginning: Hegel, Kierkegaard and Philosophical Inquiry', *Inquiry* 50, no. 1 (2007): 5–33.
6. Karl Löwith, *From Hegel to Nietzsche: The Revolution in Nineteenth-Century Thought* (New York: Columbia University Press, 1964).
7. Beyond the main aspect of the 'philosophy crisis' I will deal with here, Löwith's reconstruction of the post-Hegel nineteenth century does not take into consideration, among other things, Frege and his developments, Neokantianism, *Psychologismusstreit*, the progress of *Naturwissenschaften*, and the rise of historicism and *Materialismusstreit*.
8. See Leo Freuler, *La crise de la philosophie au XIXe siècle* (Paris: Vrin, 1997), 7–9.
9. Herbert Schnädelbach, *Philosophie in Deutschland: 1831–1933* (Frankfurt am Main: Surkamp, 1983), 119.
10. See Ibid.
11. See F. Beiser, *After Hegel – German Philosophy 1840–1900* (Princeton, NJ: Princeton University Press, 2014).
12. There are at least two major questions that are legitimate heirs of the setting I am describing here. The current identity crisis of the whole edifice of the Humanities is one of them; the other is the radical 'parting of ways' of the two philosophical

trends, namely, analytic and hermeneutic-phenomenological philosophy. On the 'parting of ways', see Michael Friedman, *A Parting of Ways - Carnap, Cassirer, and Heidegger* (Chicago and La Salle: Open Court, 2000).

13 See, for instance, G. W. F. Hegel, *Encyclopaedia of the Philosophical Sciences in Basic Outline*, Part 1, Science of Logic (New York: Cambridge University Press, 2010), §24; §45.

14 On Hegel's reception of Kant's transcendental idealism problems, see Béatrice Longuenesse, *Hegel et la critique de la métaphysique. Étude sur la doctrine de l'essence* (Paris: Vrin, 1981).

15 Speculative idealism's *Naturephilosophie* is a consequence of a story that begins with seventeenth-century rationalism and its partial refusal of Aristotelian physics and the creation of mechanism. For an overview of Hegelian critique of mechanism, see James Kreines, 'Hegel's Critique of Pure Mechanism and the Philosophical Appeal of the Logic Project', *European Journal of Philosophy* 12, no. 1 (2004): 38–74.

16 Adolf Trendelenburg, *Die Logische Frage in Hegel's System. Zwei Streitschriften* (Leipzig: F. A. Brockhaus, 1843).

17 Risto Vilkko, 'The Logic Question During the First Half of the Nineteenth Century', in *The Development of Modern Logic*, ed. Leila Haaparanta (New York: Oxford University Press, 2009), 203–21 (204).

18 See Freuler, *La crise de la philosophie*, 42–3.

19 Schnädelbach's chapters are structured via the themes which had to be reconsidered (History, Science, Understanding, Value, Being and Man).

20 See Freuler, *La crise de la philosophie,* chapter 4.

21 Wilhelm Windelband, 'History and Natural Science', *Theory and Psychology* 8, no. 1 (1998): 5–22.

22 Schnädelbach, *Philosophie in Deutschland: 1831-1933*, 232.

23 See Ibid., 233.

24 Kierkegaard's *Papirer* have many entries that exemplify such a view. See, for instance, Søren Kierkegaard, JP 3, 240 / SKS 20, 60.

25 See also Kierkegaard's distinction between essential and non-essential knowledge (Søren Kierkegaard, *Concluding Unscientific Postscript to* Philosophical Fragments, vol. 1 (Princeton, NJ: Princeton University Press, 1992), 197–8 / SKS 7, 181). It is interesting to compare Kierkegaard's distinction to others like Windelband's differentiation between 'nomothetical' and 'idiographic', as well as to Dilthey's between 'explanation' and 'interpretation'.

26 See Gabriel Ferreira, '"O que nosso tempo mais precisa": Kierkegaard e o problema das categorias na filosofia do século XIX', *Kriterion: Revista de Filosofia* 58, no. 137 (2017): 333–50.

27 Kierkegaard, JP, VI B 13. See also VI B 89.

28 Kierkegaard, JP, VIII1 A 18 / SKS, 20, 93. On Kierkegaard and Trendelenburg, see A. Come, *Trendelenburg's Influence on Kierkegaard's Modal Categories*

(Montreal: Inter Editions, 1991); Dario González, 'Trendelenburg: An Ally Against Speculation', in *Kierkegaard and his German Contemporaries: Philosophy*, vol. 6, org. J. Stewart (Aldershot: Ashgate, 1997), 309–34; Richard Purkarthofer, 'Traces of a Profound and Sober Thinker in Kierkegaard's Postscript', *Kierkegaard Studies Yearbook* (2005): 192–207; Gabriel Ferreira, 'Kierkegaard Descends to the Underworld: Some Remarks on the Kierkegaardian Appropriation of an Argument by F. A. Trendelenburg', *Cognitio* 14, no. 2 (2014): 235–46.
29 *Pap.* IV C 87–IV C 96 / SKS 27, 269.
30 *Pap.* IV C 87 n.d., 1842–43.
31 *Pap.* IV C 88 n.d., 1842–43.
32 *Pap.* IV C 89 n.d., 1842–43.
33 *Pap.* IV C 90 n.d., 1842–43.
34 *Pap.* IV C 91 n.d., 1842–43.
35 *Pap.* IV C 92 n.d., 1842–43.
36 *Pap.* IV C 93 n.d., 1842–43.
37 *Pap.* IV C 94 n.d., 1842–43.
38 *Pap.* IV C 96 n.d., 1842–43.
39 *Pap.* IV C 100 n.d., 1842–43 / SKS 27, 271.
40 For a good overview of inductive metaphysics, see Kristina Engelhard, Christian. J. Feldbacher-Escamilla, Alexander Gebharter and Ansgar Seide, 'Inductive Metaphysics', *Grazer Philosophische Studien* 98, no. 1 (2021): 1–26. The term or analogous ideas can be found in the works of Gustav Fechner, Hermann Lotze, Wilhelm Wundt, Oswald Külpe and Franz Brentano.
41 Kierkegaard, *Concluding Unscientific Postscript to* Philosophical Fragments, 328 / SKS 7, 299.
42 The most famous ancestor to that position is Thomas Aquinas. See, for instance, Thomas Aquinas, *Summa Theologica* (New York: Benzinger Bros., 1948), I, 3, 4.
43 See Immanuel Kant, *Critique of Pure Reason,* trans. Paul Guyer and Allen Wood (Cambridge: Cambridge University Press, 1999), A 80 / B 106.
44 Martin Heidegger, *The Basic Problems of Phenomenology,* trans. Albert Hofstadter (Bloomington, IN: Indiana University Press, 1988), 34.
45 Kierkegaard, JP, Pap. X 2 A 439, 1850 / SKS 23, 72.
46 Kierkegaard, *Concluding Unscientific Postscript*, 316 / SKS, 7, 288.
47 Ibid., 301 / SKS 7, 274.
48 Ibid., 332 / SKS 7, 303.
49 Ibid., 329 / SKS 7, 301.
50 Ibid., 330–1 / SKS 7, 301.
51 Ibid., 123 / SKS 7, 118.
52 G. W. F. Hegel, *Lectures on the History of Philosophy vol. 3: Medieval and Modern Philosophy* (Berkeley, CA: University of California Press, 1990), 139.

53 Hegel, *Encyclopaedia of the Philosophical Sciences in Basic Outline*, § 33.
54 Christian Wolff, *Gesammelte werke,* vol. 3: *Philosophia prima sive ontologia* (Hildesheim: Georg Olms, 1962), §174.
55 Kierkegaard, *Concluding Unscientific Postscript*, 331 / SKS, 7, 302.
56 On Ontological Pluralism, see Kris McDaniel, *The Fragmentation of Being* (Oxford: Oxford University Press, 2017). On Kierkegaard as an ontological pluralist and how we can read him looking for such contributions, see Gabriel Ferreira, 'De Dicto and De Re: A Brandomian Experiment on Kierkegaard', *Revista de Filosofia Moderna e Contemporânea, [S. l.]* 7, no. 2 (2019): 221–38.
57 Despite Kierkegaard having some sort of 'prejudice in favour of actual', as denounced by Meinong, it would be interesting to see the connections between those two approaches.
58 Hermann Lotze, *Microcosmus* (Edinburgh: T&T Clark, 1885) builds a philosophical project mixing metaphysics and philosophical anthropology that resembles Kierkegaard's in many aspects.

II

Possibility and experience

3

Possibility, meaning and truth
Kierkegaardian themes in Proust

Rick Anthony Furtak

Readers of both Kierkegaard and Proust will notice involuntary echoes of *Either/Or* within *Remembrance of Things Past*. Witness what the aesthete 'A' writes in the penultimate of his 'Diapsalmata':

> Everything is quiet out on the street. It is Sunday afternoon. I distinctly hear a lark warbling outside a window in one of the neighboring courtyards, outside the window where the pretty girl lives. Far away in a distant street, I hear a man crying 'Shrimp for sale.' The air is so warm, and yet the whole city is as if deserted. – Then I call to mind my youth and my first love – when I was filled with longing; now I long only for my first longing.[1]

As in Copenhagen, so in Paris: within his apartment, Proust's narrator 'Marcel' can 'already tell what the weather [is] like' without having to look out the window, based on the 'sounds from the street'.[2] It is 'principally from [his] bedroom' that he experiences the 'outer world' at this time, whereas his 'captive' girlfriend Albertine is tellingly attracted by the sounds from outside, particularly the voices of food merchants: hearing the shellfish vendor, she exclaims, 'Oh, oysters! I've been simply longing for some', and wants to have 'all the shouts we're hearing transformed into a good dinner'.[3] She is alive to all the possibilities that the world offers, not only the edible ones – much to the chagrin of Marcel himself. He also knows what it is like to long for one's own longing, now that (as he claims) he does not love Albertine anymore.[4] To yearn for an earlier emotion is to yearn for what seemed possible then: so the aesthete asserts that 'If I were to wish for something, I would wish . . . for the passion of possibility, for the eye, eternally young, eternally ardent, that sees possibility everywhere. Pleasure disappoints; possibility does not. And what wine is so sparkling, so fragrant, so intoxicating!'[5] Beauty is appealing because it affords us 'a promise of happiness',[6] hinting at something valuable that remains to be unveiled. Despite the risks associated with pursuing the possible excessively or too exclusively, it is far from being a dangerous influence merely. Rather, the realm of the possible informs the meaningful features of our world, and we can therefore learn much from a literary figure such as Kierkegaard's 'A' or Proust's narrator Marcel.

I.

One of Marcel's characteristic attunements is towards what might be called *possibilities for romantic encounter*. Even when he is drawn towards an opportunity for superficial gratification, his attention is directed at the 'unknown quantity that another mind represents'.[7] When his eyes are oriented towards the beautiful Mademoiselle de Stermaria, the mysteries of her subjectivity evoke a more complex poetic account:

> From a certain look . . . in which one sensed that almost humble docility which the predominance of a taste for sensual pleasures gives to the proudest of women, who will soon come to recognize but one form of personal magic, that which any man will enjoy in her eyes who can make her feel those pleasures, an actor or a mountebank for whom, perhaps, she will one day leave her husband, and from a certain pink tinge, warm and sensual, which flushed her pallid cheeks, like the colour that stained the hearts of the white water-lilies in the Vivonne, I thought I could discern that she might readily have consented to my coming to seek in her the savour of that life of poetry and romance which she led in Brittany, a life [that] . . . she held enclosed in her body.[8]

Likewise with the girl he glimpses on the old bridge in Carqueville, who has 'a more serious and a more self-willed air' than other young women in the village, and who has been spending the day fishing:

> She had a tanned complexion, soft eyes but with a look of contempt for her surroundings, and a small nose, delicately and attractively modelled. My eyes alighted upon her skin; and my lips, at a pinch, might have believed that they had followed my eyes. But it was not only to her body that I should have liked to attain; it was also the person that lived inside it, and with which there is but one form of contact, namely to attract its attention, but one sort of penetration, to awaken an idea in it. And this inner being of the handsome fisher-girl seemed to be still closed to me. . . . I could have wished that the idea of me which entered this being and took hold in it should bring me not merely her attention but her

admiration . . . and should compel her to keep me in her memory until the day when I should be able to meet her again.⁹

We see here how the perception of another person can be charged with a potential for passionate contact; her skin (within which she 'lives') as *perhaps to be kissed by me*, and in each case the exotic (and hence intriguing) depths that she harbours of consciousness and personality, yet to be explored – as well as the capacity for scorn or admiration. One's affective comportment towards the world is thus an attunement, an emotional orientation, towards the possibilities that it holds. 'How boldly and saucily she looks around the world', as the author of *The Seducer's Diary* observes of one lovely young girl who appears 'more tempting, more seductive' when the 'puffing of the wind' reveals 'the beauty of her form'; it has the potential to blow her hat off into his hands, making him into the 'lucky fellow' who can return it to her.¹⁰ 'Good days are coming now', he adds, thinking of 'her hope, her future'.

As J. Hillis Miller points out, a 'recurrent motif' in Proust's novel is that, in our actual lives no less than in literary works of art, we are given a 'hint that there must be an immense proliferation of possible worlds'.¹¹ This includes the many universes to which human eyes open from their various perspectives, on which Marcel repeatedly comments,¹² as well as events that *might have been*, such as having met Albertine earlier than he actually did. In retrospect, declining the invitation to join his father at a dinner party where Albertine would be present takes on a significance unknowable to Marcel at the time. He reflects:

> So it is that the different periods of our life overlap with one another. We scornfully decline, because of one whom we love and who will some day be of so little account, to see another [whom] we might perhaps, had we consented to see her now, have loved a little sooner and who would thus have put a term to our present sufferings, bringing others, it is true, in their place.¹³

Sufferings related to Marcel's love (at the time) for Gilberte might have been replaced by a set of emotions different from what he in fact experiences in relation to Albertine after meeting her later. His love affair with Albertine would have been another story entirely, one that could possibly have had a less tragic – at least, a differently tragic – end.

The realm of possibility is so richly alluring to Kierkegaard's aesthete that he opts to retain the view, 'always ardent' or youthful, 'that sees possibility everywhere'. It would be a compromise to limit this realm by realizing certain possibilities and thereby eliminating others. Hence, his logic of possibility demands that 'when two people fall in love with each other and sense that they are destined for each other', they ought 'to break it off, for by continuing there is only everything to lose, nothing to gain'.[14] What is exhilarating about the things that *may* still come to pass is that 'the future is what exists as yet only in the mind',[15] as Marcel observes, and its strictly mental being makes it seem limitless. Alluding to the feeling of heightened existence that accompanies falling in love, Kierkegaard's 'A' muses that the 'most beautiful time is the first period of falling in love', when 'from every encounter, every glance, one fetches home something to rejoice over'.[16] Yet 'fetches home' is a loaded phrase.

> I swoop down into actuality and snatch my prey, but I do not stay down there. I bring my booty home, and this booty is a picture I weave into the tapestries at my castle. Then I live as one already dead. Everything I have experienced I immerse in a baptism of oblivion unto an eternity of recollection.[17]

He 'can describe hope so vividly that every hoping individual will recognize my description as his own; and yet it is forgery, for even as I am describing it I am thinking of recollection'.[18] He does not wish to actualize the ostensibly hoped-for possibilities that glimmer in the dawning of romantic love, but to weave them into his tapestry. This resonates with the theory of literary creation we find in Proust, whose narrator affirms that we may decide that an event through which our beloved 'has made us suffer' matters not nearly as much as 'the truths which it has revealed to us', a 'whole gamut of feelings' that have a profundity we can then inscribe into a work of art.[19] In the process, we switch from vulnerable exposure to the world of others to a position of self-sufficient control over our 'inner kingdom'.

One philosopher of the heart classifies hope as an 'epistemic' instead of a 'factive' emotion, in the sense that it is about what is uncertain, what *might* happen, rather than what is the case.[20] For all the talk we understandably hear about Marcel's jealousy, defined as an 'anxious need to be tyrannical' in 'matters of love',[21] he is arguably more often governed by *fear*, and worry, about Albertine, both of which are emotions having to do with uncertainties. He fears her infidelity and worries about whom she might be planning to meet for some secret tryst. He would 'sacrifice everything' in order 'to know at all costs what Albertine was thinking, whom she saw, whom she loved'.[22] And the issue of how to comport oneself regarding uncertainty is a prominent theme throughout Kierkegaard's writings.[23] What is most noteworthy in the present context is that our 'epistemic' emotions could not be felt if we did not feel aware of possibility – of what may be – in the same way that in a cloudy sky we can see the promise or threat of rain.

II.

Proust's narrator is by turns fascinated and tormented by the knowledge that his loves were shaped by contingent factors, and might have transpired in other ways than they did. 'Whoever it is who has determined the course of our life has, in so doing, excluded all the lives which we might have led instead'.[24] The abiding reality of these alternative worlds renders plausible a rather extravagant ontology:

> It is uncontroversially true that things might be otherwise than they are. I believe, and so do you, that things could have been different in countless ways. But what does this mean? Ordinary language permits the paraphrase: there are many ways things could have been besides the way they actually are. On the face of it, this sentence is an existential quantification. It says that there exist many entities of a certain description, to wit 'ways things could have been.' [. . .] I therefore believe in the existence of entities that might be called 'ways things could have been.' I prefer to call them 'possible worlds'.[25]

However, we may conceive of the metaphysical status of possibilities, we must agree that in our existence they have an experiential reality: indeed, without them many of the emotions we routinely feel could not arise. At one point Saint-Loup reminds Marcel of a philosophical book they read together, about 'the richness of the world of possibilities compared with the real world'.[26] This implies that all the alternative ways in which Marcel's relationship with Albertine might have unfolded vastly outnumber the one way it actually does. When he is tormented by a sense of how things may have been otherwise, there is an abundant supply of these ghosts for him to be haunted by.

And the present tense is not only filled to overflowing with the past. It is also 'big with the future', as Leibniz attests.[27] What a phenomenologist would designate as a 'horizon of possibilities' or 'a field of possibilities'[28] is present at each point in Proust's novel when his narrator first encounters any of the *jeunes filles* that spark his imagination. Marcel explains such an encounter in terms of 'that desire to live which is reborn in us whenever we become conscious anew of beauty', and of all the potential that it seems to hold.[29] It is because they are brimming with enticing possibilities that the young women have the power to renew his wish to be alive. Needless to say, the sense of possibility they awaken in him is passionately felt: it has a palpable emotional valence. As the enthralling Mademoiselle de Stermaria seems to embody a concealed life of poetry and romance, any new face that captivates Marcel represents a friend who may be made, an unknown subject with his or her own passions and aspirations, contingent history and individual outlook on the world. The beauty of a person, especially a potential beloved, indicates a good to be discovered, and in being moved by this beauty he wishes to have more of that good thing in his life.

In one memorable passage, Proust's narrator bursts out with an enthusiastic apostrophe to *jeunes filles*, in the following words: 'O girls, O successive rays in the swirling vortex wherein we throb with emotion on seeing you reappear while barely recognizing you, in the dizzy velocity of light. . . . O drops of gold, always dissimilar and always surpassing our expectation!'[30] Part of what intoxicates Marcel, in this little hymn of praise, is that the young women are (1) each singular and unlike any other, and (2) filled with possibilities that cannot all be anticipated in advance of being revealed. On his rides in the countryside with his grandmother and Madame de Villeparisis, he repeatedly catches sight of incarnate possibilities from every social class and of every description, girls about whom he says that, 'from the day on which I had first known that their cheeks could be kissed, I had become curious about their souls', and as a result 'the universe had appeared to me more interesting', since he now knows 'there is a reality which conforms' to his desire.[31] Here, Marcel's orientation to the world is typified above all by an alertness to a specific kind of possibility.[32] His condition is one in which, as he says, 'we desire, we seek, we see Beauty'.[33]

That is how he is disposed or attuned at the moment when he sees for the first time Albertine and her 'little band' of friends walking along the esplanade on the Balbec shore. As one critic has observed, literary works of art are especially adept at conveying 'atmospheres and moods', which 'belong to the substance and reality of the world'.[34] No abbreviated account can do justice to the eleven remarkable pages describing the narrator's initial impressions of the little band, and his heightened sense of all the enticing possibilities to be (perhaps) disclosed by them, yet this excerpt is representative of the whole:

> The girls whom I had noticed, with the control of gesture that comes from the perfect suppleness of one's own body and a sincere contempt for the rest of humanity, were advancing straight ahead, without hesitation or stiffness, performing exactly the movements that they wished to perform, each of their limbs completely independent of the others, the rest of the body preserving that immobility which is so noticeable in good waltzers. . . . They were known to me only by a pair of hard, obstinate and mocking eyes, for instance, or by cheeks whose pinkness had a coppery tint reminiscent of geraniums; and even these features I had not yet indissolubly attached to any one of these girls rather than another; and when (according to the order in which the group met the

eye, marvellous because the most different aspects were juxtaposed, because all the colour scales were combined in it, but confused as a piece of music in which I was unable to isolate and identify at the moment of their passage the successive phrases, no sooner distinguished than forgotten) I saw a pallid oval, black eyes, green eyes, emerge, I did not know if these were the same that had already charmed me a moment ago, [for] I could not relate them to any one girl whom I had set apart from the rest and identified.[35]

Soon he begins to differentiate the members of the group, even though there continues to be 'between their independent and separate bodies' an 'invisible but harmonious bond, like a single warm shadow, a single atmosphere, making of them a whole as homogeneous in its parts as it was different from the crowd through which their procession gradually wound'.[36] Although he compares their beauty to the beauty of flowers, reminding us of the younger Marcel's love for the hawthorn blossoms, what he finds most attractive about the girls is the unknown depths of subjectivity they harbour. 'If we thought that the eyes of such a girl were merely two glittering sequins of mica, we should not be athirst to know her.' However, 'we sense that what shines in those reflecting discs is not due solely to their material composition'.[37] Rather, it is their ideas, their plans, their desires, sympathies and aversions, as well as the entire sedimented biography of places they have been, friends they have made and homes to which they will return – all of this he thirsts for, as 'a parched land burns' for water, in yearning to know the group of young women.[38] Never before, he says, had he 'seen anything so beautiful', filled 'with so much that was unknown, so inestimably precious, so apparently inaccessible'.[39]

'A man sees only what concerns him', Thoreau writes, explaining how perception is shaped by the constitution of the perceiver.[40] And, doubtless, an indifferent observer nearby might fail to notice the group of young women walking along the esplanade. Marcel's emotional disposition renders him receptive to being impressed by them, allowing him to grasp and appreciate specific features of his world. Later on, he will view the roads in the area as 'simply the means of rejoining Albertine', since for him they do have this promise, just as a cube-shaped object holds the possibility of displaying other sides that are currently unseen.[41] In this manner, we see how a response to the world is filtered through the lens of one's subjectivity: deprived of that meaning, those roads would actually *look* different. Remarking on this phenomenon, Scheler notes that as our 'attitudes of interest and love' create in us 'a readiness for being affected', our felt sense of what is significant is 'peculiar to each' of us.[42] When Proust's narrator loses interest in communicating with a person, it is because she no longer seems to contain, 'like a nest of boxes, all the possibilities' for encounter,[43] and for becoming an important part of his life, that she once did. What he describes as the death of a self that loved another particular human being could equally well be termed the loss of a world in which this other subject teems with possibilities that seem relevant to him.

III.

A lamentable kind of self-doubt troubles Marcel at such moments as when he composes a letter to Gilberte, no longer loved by him, and is astonished that he can now write her name with utter calm, 'without emotion, and as though finishing off a boring school essay', when he had earlier passionately written her name all over page after page of his notebooks.[44] Sceptical once again of his affective vision, he reflects that perhaps at the time he loved her she had simply been illuminated by a glow that emanated from within *him*. It is similar to when a person is in a disenchanted mood and, unable to step outside of it, questions how the world had ever seemed to contain anything worth hoping for, pursuing, or even avoiding. Everything now appears weary, stale, flat and worthless.[45] In the words of Kierkegaard's 'young man' in *Repetition*, life seems nauseating, 'without salt or meaning'.[46] In *Either/Or*, 'A' concurs: 'how empty and meaningless life is'; and, 'my life is utterly meaningless'.[47] Longing only for his old longing, the aesthete may believe that the significance with which things *once* seemed to be animated was merely illusory. Proust's narrator tends to be tempted by this line of thought, to wonder if – as a common cliché suggests – a person's moods lend a false colouring to the (factually colourless) world.

As relatively trivial a modification of subjectivity as fatigue, dizziness or nausea can be lived through as a pervasive atmosphere,[48] enhancing the sense that our disposition is highly variable. Marcel notices how much his emotional comportment has altered after he has drunk himself into a state of generalized 'euphoria' (supposedly for medical reasons) on the train to Balbec:

> When at the first stop I clambered back into our compartment I told my grandmother how pleased I was to be going to Balbec, that I felt that everything would go off splendidly, that ... the train was most comfortable, the barman and the attendants so friendly that I should like to make the journey often so as to have the opportunity of seeing them again.[49]

Finding him in this amiable, outgoing mood, Marcel's grandmother just looks at him with concern and suggests that he take a rest. Instead, he promptly finds himself staring in wonder at the blue window-blind:

> The contemplation of this blind appeared to me an admirable thing.
>
> ... The blue of this blind seemed to me, not perhaps by its beauty but by its intense vividness, to efface so completely all the colors that had passed before my eyes from the day of my birth up to the moment when I had gulped down the last of my drink and it had begun to take effect, that compared with this blue they were as drab, as null, as the darkness in which he has lived must be in retrospect to a man born blind whom a subsequent operation has at length enabled to see and to distinguish colours.[50]

Such a passage might lead us to think: there is *something* to be said for objectivity, after all. Yet is our hero oblivious to the world at this moment, or is he making contact with it in an unusual manner? It seems that the latter is what we must conclude, if we are adopting as our principle of interpretation that, as Heidegger affirms, for any mood there is some 'peculiar truth or manifestness that lies in this attunement as in every attunement'.[51] When we imagine that moods are a comprehensively distorting influence, we are conceiving of them as an epistemic embarrassment – as if *any* human vantage point is devoid of any determinate characteristic whatsoever. Yet, at the same time, we would regard it as a pity if Marcel were to place greater importance on his enraptured view of the window-blind than, for example, the colourful sunrise that he subsequently watches *through* the window, after having slept, and whose beauty he ornately depicts.[52]

It makes sense to keep in mind that all our perception, including our affective perception, is a way of seeing from somewhere – and in some way. To speculate about what things are like *entirely* apart from 'interpretation and subjectivity' is, as Nietzsche says, to entertain 'a quite idle hypothesis'.[53] And if we were to aspire towards the ideal of the universe's own impersonal perspective, 'from which all is seen but nothing is cared for',[54] we would be dead to the meaning of things, lacking the focus and orientation that are required for the conduct of life and the pursuit of knowledge. The reason why it is a pity to be 'stuck' in a depressive mood, or one of irascibility or of sentimental nostalgia, or of being awestruck by the brilliant colour of the window-blind, is that the way the world seems to us when we are depressed, or irascible, or in one of these other states, is not the *only* way it is. The window-blind contemplator is out of touch with much that is worthy of his attention, as is the nostalgic sentimentalist. What is needed by any of us is the ability to inhabit a diversity of moods, affective standpoints and perspectives,⁵⁵ and not to close our minds to what an atypical mood, maybe even a morbid or impaired state, might be able to reveal. When our affective vision is functioning somewhat oddly for subjective reasons, we do not find ourselves in a self-enclosed realm, but rather with an angle of interpretation on the world.

Hence, the manner in which we are *tuned in* to our environment, the mood that we embody at a given time, opens us towards what is not ourselves and conditions how it seems. To be affectively disposed in some way is to sense how things are going in our world of concern, and to have an idea of what is real and significant. That is what a mood can disclose, which is why it is far from being objectless or lacking intentional world-directedness altogether. Possibilities are by their very nature uncertain: nevertheless, they are not for this reason to be dismissed as somehow artificial. Our somatic, affective experience testifies to the meaning of our encounters with what is other than us – and to how, in the words of one phenomenologist, 'we bear witness to that which has moved us'.⁵⁶ Each person's attunement is both outwardly and inwardly truth-revealing, since it brings to light aspects of the environment (what we love) while also showing who we are at heart (in *how* we love, our way of loving). Proust's narrator is on a search for truth, with the emphatic aim of understanding the varieties of truth that are at stake in our lover's quarrel with the so-called 'external' world.⁵⁷ To learn from it we must avoid throwing out the baby with the bath water, so to speak. For if we reject the potential truthfulness of all moods due to the silliness of Marcel's enraptured state of mind as he apprehends the window-blind, we will be unable to appreciate the profundity of how he 'finds himself' as he uses hundreds of pages in *The Fugitive* to explain how it feels to recognize too late one's love for a person whom one has irretrievably lost.

IV.

A prominent doctrine in Kierkegaard's Christianity is that the life of the finite person has an eternal significance; another is that we are nothing but dust, to which we shall return in the end. For we cannot follow every 'hint from God', not as finite beings who can only actualize *some* of what is possible. He views it as feasible, if rare, to feel 'at one and the same time how great and how insignificant' one is;⁵⁸ more characteristically, these standpoints would be occupied in succession, within different changing moods. Such a person just *might* achieve integration across the polarities, uniting the self over time throughout the fluctuations of having possibility either exceedingly present or else apparently absent. Since these categories or factors are always at issue in human existence, they bring into sharp relief an opportunity or challenge that each of us faces. Due to the very structure of the human psyche, we are burdened with the task of being both limitless and mundane simultaneously. Kierkegaard's God for whom all things are possible, and by virtue of whom enticing possibilities dawn in the midst of 'contingent finitude', pervades our experiential world such that, ideally, 'the divine inhabits the finite and finds its way in it',[59] and an eternal power is thereby expressed. Putting this in Proust's more secular terms, we might note that Marcel writes, 'I have always been more open to the world of potentiality than to the world of contingent reality. This helps one to understand the human heart, but one is apt to be taken in by individuals.'[60] Our emotional awareness of what is possible can draw us into intimate relations with what surrounds us – as long as it does not become so dizzying that it launches us beyond the finite world and leaves us floating in mid-air, volatilized and intoxicated in a bad way. But this, far from being an actual romance, is only a flirtation. Like love itself, our feeling of enticing possibilities ought to enhance our participation, rather than allowing us to stagnate in a self-contained, vertiginous state. The power of possibility, like any other sacred inspiration, has its dangers and needs to be handled with care. After all, we live in only *one* of all possible worlds. Yet that world is enhanced by our sense of possibility, and when we glimpse the riches of possibility we feel convinced that life is worth living.

Notes

1 Søren Kierkegaard, *Either/Or*, vol. 1, trans. Howard V. Hong and Edna H. Hong (Princeton, NJ: Princeton University Press, 1987), 42.

2 Marcel Proust, *Remembrance of Things Past*, 3 vols, trans. C. K. Scott Moncrieff and Terence Kilmartin (New York: Vintage Books, 1982), III: 1.

3 Ibid., 122–3.

4 See, e.g., Ibid., 4, 13–14. Marcel is protesting too much, as time will tell.

5 Kierkegaard, *Either/Or*, vol. 1, 41.

6 Proust, *Remembrance of Things Past*, III: 136. On various 'radiating emanations of womanly beauty', see Kierkegaard, *Either/Or, Part I*, 428–9, from 'The Seducer's Diary'.

7 See Proust, *Remembrance of Things Past*, II: 779–81.

8 Ibid., I: 740–1.

9 Ibid., 769–70. On experiencing the possible, see Jean-Paul Sartre, *Being and Nothingness*, trans. Hazel E. Barnes (New York: Washington Square Press, 1992), 147–55. See also page 478: 'if Love were in fact a pure desire for physical possession, it could in many cases be easily satisfied . . . [yet] Albertine escapes Marcel even when he is at her side'.
10 Kierkegaard, *Either/Or*, vol. I, 354–9. The girl herself looks 'so exuberant, so full of longing and anticipation', containing her own wealth of possibility.
11 J. Hillis Miller, *On Literature* (London: Routledge, 2002), 64.
12 See, e.g., Proust, *Remembrance of Things Past*, III: 189–90. 'It is not one universe, but . . . almost as many as the number of human eyes and brains in existence, that awake every morning'.
13 Ibid., I: 674. See also Joshua Landy, *Philosophy as Fiction: Self, Deception, and Knowledge in Proust* (Oxford: Oxford University Press, 2004), 121: the 'non-event has *become* something worth talking about'.
14 Kierkegaard, *Either/Or*, vol. I, 298. This is from the 'Rotation of Crops' essay.
15 Proust, *Remembrance of Things Past*, III: 426.
16 Kierkegaard, *Either/Or*, vol. I, 24. Cf. E. F. N. Jephcott, *Proust and Rilke: The Literature of Expanded Consciousness* (London: Chatto & Windus, 1972), 36.
17 Kierkegaard, *Either/Or*, vol. I, 42. Clare Carlisle notes that in 'repetition', as contrasted with recollection, 'a possibility is actualized, brought into existence'. See her 'How to Be a Human Being in the World: Kierkegaard's Question of Existence', in *Kierkegaard's Existential Approach*, ed. Arne Grøn, René Rosfort, and K. Brian Söderquist (Berlin: Walter de Gruyter, 2017), 113–30 (113). Recollection, by contrast, does *not* actualize possibilities, but preserves them as if in a state of unchanging stasis.
18 Kierkegaard, *Either/Or*, vol. I, 36.
19 Proust, *Remembrance of Things Past*, III: 944–5. Cf. Martha C. Nussbaum, *Love's Knowledge* (Oxford: Oxford University Press, 1990), 273–4. See Kierkegaard, *Either/Or*, vol. I, 32: 'As soon as I have recollected a life relationship', it 'has ceased to exist'. See also Sharon Krishek, *Kierkegaard on Faith and Love* (Cambridge: Cambridge University Press, 2009), 23: 'Recollection is indeed protected from the passage of time; it constitutes the little inner kingdom of the one who recollects'.
20 Robert Gordon, *The Structure of Emotions* (Cambridge: Cambridge University Press, 1987), 26–7, 45–85. Factive emotion-types outnumber epistemic ones.
21 Proust, *Remembrance of Things Past*, III: 86.
22 Ibid., 91–2.
23 As I have spoken about elsewhere: see Furtak, 'Varieties of Existential Uncertainty', in *The Kierkegaardian Mind*, ed. Adam Buben et al. (London: Routledge, 2019), 376–85. Regarding how our sense of possibility underlies modes of doubt and belief, see Edmund Husserl, *Analyses Concerning Passive and Active Synthesis*, trans. Anthony J. Steinbock (Boston, MA: Kluwer Academic Publishers, 2001), § 13.

24 Proust, *Remembrance of Things Past*, III: 955.
25 David K. Lewis, *Counterfactuals* (Cambridge, MA: Harvard University Press, 1973), 84.
26 Proust, *Remembrance of Things Past*, II: 115.
27 Gottfried Wilhelm Leibniz, *Theodicy*, trans. E. M. Huggard (New Haven, CT: Yale University Press, 1952), 341. This caught Kierkegaard's attention around the time he was writing the first page of *Repetition*.
28 See, e.g., Maurice Merleau-Ponty, *Phenomenology of Perception*, trans. Donald A. Landes (London: Routledge, 2012), 156n and 188. See also Edmund Husserl, *Ideas II*, trans. Richard Rojcewicz and André Schuwer (Dordrecht: Kluwer Academic Publishers, 1989), 38–42, 72.
29 *Remembrance of Things Past*, I: 705. Cf. Alexander Nehamas, *Only a Promise of Happiness* (Princeton, NJ: Princeton University Press, 2007), 129–30: 'Even the narrowest judgment of beauty has far-reaching consequences', since 'you can't know in advance the sort of person it will make you'. Therefore, to 'think of beauty as only a promise of happiness' requires being 'willing to live with ineradicable uncertainty'.
30 Proust, *Remembrance of Things Past*, III: 58–9.
31 Ibid., 764–6. See also, e.g., III: 145.
32 That it takes no more than a momentary glance for his curiosity to awaken, as in the case of the girl who emerges from the train station at a stop on the way to Balbec, shows this attunement in Marcel: *Within a Budding Grove*, I: 705–7. On how possibilities exist not as merely private thoughts, but also not apart from subjects, see Sartre, *Being and Nothingness*, 150–1.
33 Proust, *Remembrance of Things Past*, I: 845. He adds later, alluding to Stendhal, 'It has been said that beauty is a promise of happiness'. See III: 136.
34 Hans Ulrich Gumbrecht, *Atmosphere, Mood, Stimmung*, trans. Erik Butler (Stanford, CA: Stanford University Press, 2012), 12, 20. Italics removed.
35 Proust, *Remembrance of Things Past*, I: 847. The passage is marked throughout by what one commentator calls 'the affect of possibility', namely 'amazement'. Rok Bencin, '"*Sans Cause*": Affect and Truth in Marcel Proust', *Filozofski Vestnik* 38, no. 3 (2017): 53–66 (59).
36 Proust, *Remembrance of Things Past*, I: 850–1.
37 Ibid., I: 851–2.
38 Ibid., I: 852–3. He finds extremely appealing and yet unlikely 'the supposition that I might some day be the friend of one or other of these girls, that these eyes, whose incomprehensible gaze struck me from time to time and played unwittingly upon me like an effect of sunlight on a wall, might ever, by some miraculous alchemy, allow the idea of my existence' to 'interpenetrate their ineffable particles'. Kierkegaard also talks about longing for meaning as a parched land thirsts for moisture: Kierkegaard's *Journals and Notebooks*, vol. 1, ed. Niels Jørgen Cappelørn, Alistair Hannay, David Kangas, Bruce H. Kirmmse, George Pattison, Vanessa

Rumble, and K. Brian Söderquist (Princeton, NJ: Princeton University Press, 2007–2020), 19–20. Journal AA: 12.

39 Proust, *Remembrance of Things Past*, I: 855.

40 Henry David Thoreau, 'Autumnal Tints', in *Collected Essays and Poems*, ed. Elizabeth H. Witherell (New York: Library of America, 2001), 367–95 (394).

41 Proust, *Remembrance of Things Past*, II: 1044–5; on the cube, see, e.g., Merleau-Ponty, *Phenomenology of Perception*, 308. Regarding our perception of things as tinged with a sense for the possibilities they do or do not harbor, see Matthew Ratcliffe, *Experiences of Depression* (Oxford: Oxford University Press, 2015), 211–12.

42 Max Scheler, 'Ordo Amoris', in *Selected Philosophical Essays*, trans. David Lachterman (Evanston, IL: Northwestern University Press, 1973), 101, 107.

43 Proust, *Remembrance of Things Past*, II: 378–9. On his eventual loss of interest in Gilberte and, hence, the death of the self that loved her see, e.g., II: 739 & III: 92.

44 Ibid., 765–6.

45 Echoing Hamlet, Simon Blackburn notes that for those in certain affective states the world at present simply *is* 'weary, stale, flat, and unprofitable'. See *Ruling Passions* (Oxford: Clarendon Press, 1998), 8–9,131. On how one form of sceptical doubt about axiological matters 'is the view that there is really nothing worth caring about', see Harry G. Frankfurt, *The Importance of What We Care About: Philosophical Essays* (Cambridge: Cambridge University Press, 1988), 91n.

46 Søren Kierkegaard, *Repetition/Philosophical Crumbs*, trans. M. G. Piety (Oxford: Oxford University Press, 2009), 60. Letter of 11 October from the young man to Constantin Constantius.

47 Kierkegaard, *Either/Or*, vol. I, 29, 36.

48 Dan Zahavi, *Self-Awareness and Alterity: A Phenomenological Investigation* (Evanston, IL: Northwestern University Press, 1999), 125. See also Heidegger on *soma* and *psuchē*: *Zollikon Seminars*, 76–80. Cf. Matthew Ratcliffe, *Feelings of Being: Phenomenology, Psychiatry, and the Sense of Reality* (Oxford: Oxford University Press, 2008), 106–29 and *Experiences of Depression*, 75–91.

49 Proust, *Remembrance of Things Past*, I: 700–1. See Gernot Böhme, *The Aesthetics of Atmospheres*, ed. Jean-Paul Thibaud (London: Routledge, 2017).

50 Proust, *Remembrance of Things Past*, I: 702.

51 Martin Heidegger, *The Fundamental Concepts of Metaphysics: World, Finitude, Solitude*, trans. William McNeill and Nicholas Walker (Bloomington, IN: Indiana University Press, 1995), 139.

52 'There gathered behind it reserves of light. It brightened; the sky turned to a glowing pink which I strove, gluing my eyes to the window, to see more clearly, for I felt that it was related somehow to the most intimate life of Nature, but, the course of the line altering, the train turned, the morning scene gave place in the frame of the window to a nocturnal village, its roofs still blue with moonlight, its pond encrusted with the opalescent sheen of night, . . . and I was lamenting the loss of my

strip of pink sky when I caught sight of it anew, but red this time, in the opposite window which it left at a second bend in the line; so that I spent my time running from one window to the other' (Proust, *Remembrance of Things Past*, I: 704).

53 Friedrich Nietzsche, *The Will to Power*, ed. Walter Kaufmann (New York: Vintage Books, 1968), § 560.

54 Margaret Olivia Little, 'Seeing and Caring: The Role of Affect in Feminist Epistemology', *Hypatia* 10, no. 3 (1995): 117–37 (125).

55 For examples of how both Thoreau and Nietzsche describe this capacity and its importance, see Rick Anthony Furtak, *Knowing Emotions: Truthfulness and Recognition in Affective Experience* (Oxford: Oxford University Press, 2018), 172–3. On the topic in more general terms see Giovanna Colombetti, *The Feeling Body: Affective Science Meets the Enactive Mind* (Cambridge, MA: MIT Press, 2014), 77–80. With regard to the physiological basis of a particular mood, see Paul Redding, *The Logic of Affect* (Ithaca, NY: Cornell University Press, 1999), 158: 'Reason must navigate on a sea of biological and other natural forces that do not belong to it, but without which it could go nowhere. Affect is our most immediate awareness of the fact that we sail on such a sea'.

56 David Michael Levin, *The Body's Recollection of Being: Phenomenological Psychology and the Deconstruction of Nihilism* (London: Routledge and Kegan Paul, 1985), 103. See also page 95, on why authentically becoming oneself is 'an *individual* realization of the universal relatedness-to-Being which defines every one of us in a primordial way'.

57 I trust that I need no more cite 'external world' than I do the notion of having a 'lover's quarrel' with it. Yet I do bear in mind what Merleau-Ponty says about love, that 'as the thing, as the other, the true dawns through an emotional and almost carnal experience', it is not so much 'understood' as it is 'welcomed or spurned'. *The Visible and the Invisible*, trans. Alphonso Lingis (Evanston, IL: Northwestern University Press, 1968), 12. On the way that Marcel enacts 'in his own body the general human quest for knowledge', see Malcolm Bowie, *Freud, Proust and Lacan: Theory as Fiction* (Cambridge: Cambridge University Press, 1987), 50–1.

58 *Kierkegaard's Journals and Notebooks*, vol. 1, 10. Journal AA: 6.

59 Søren Kierkegaard, *Works of Love*, Ed. and trans. Howard V. Hong and Edna H. Hong (Princeton, NJ: Princeton University Press, 1995), KW 16: 3; then, *Kierkegaard's Journals and Notebooks, vole. 11, Part 1*, 236. Paper 264: 1. With regard to fulfilling one's 'eternal validity' amidst finitude and contingency, see also Clare Carlisle, *Kierkegaard's Philosophy of Becoming: Movements and Positions* (Albany, NY: State University New York Press, 2005), 25.

60 Proust, *Remembrance of Things Past*, III: 16. The despair of too much possibility is diagnosed in Kierkegaard's pseudonymous *The Sickness Unto Death: A Christian Psychological Exposition for Upbuilding and Awakening*, ed. and trans. Howard V. Hong and Edna H. Hong (Princeton, NJ: Princeton University Press, 1980), 30–1, 35–6.

4

The secrecy of possibility in Kierkegaard's 'pattern'

Frances Maughan-Brown

Pattern surrounds us

Pattern surrounds us. Out of the window, on the left, the river's rippling against the flow of its current; on the right, the forest leaves repeated in hundreds in trickles of light and shadow. What indicates pattern? The repetition: many of the same leaves, or similar leaves, make the pattern of leaves; otherwise, I must admit it is just a tree I am looking at, or a segment of the forest. The many tiny folds on the surface of the water, and if the water weren't disturbed in this way, it would show me a picture, and if I didn't look at the ripples as they move across its surface I might imagine the river's deeper movement 'towards the sea'. These patterns play with my eyes, interrupt my reading of the visible world, interest me in its visibleness – in surfaces as surface. And they do it by likeness, reproduction of likeness, likeness followed by likeness – and thereby make likeness the subject and put it into question. The similarity between one ripple and another, one leaf and another, should be straightforward. For Kierkegaard, it is not; he challenges what we take for granted in our perceptions of nature – he reminds us that even this basic example of resemblance is uncertain.[1] But if it *were* straightforward, it would be a good foil to pattern in a more serious sense – a sense which presumably holds a stronger or more rigorous possibility. This stronger pattern, I will argue, referring to *Fear and Trembling* and to *Philosophical Fragments* as well as to Kant's *Critique of Judgment*, opens up an unexpected way of thinking about Kierkegaard's idea of faith.[2]

The simplest way of drawing the distinction between pattern and pattern is by moving from nature to craft. In dressmaking, for example, if a dress is patterned, if, rather than depicting the image of a tree, if it is instead covered in a pattern of little leaves, this is only a matter of the print of the fabric. In a more fundamental way, the 'pattern' of the dress is the paper model which dictates how it is to be cut – or rather the drawing which can be printed over and over onto many papers, and used to cut numberless new dresses. The real pattern of the dress is its origin, that which has the power to generate the dress, which holds its possibility.[3]

In this sense of pattern, the likeness that operates is sequential rather than simultaneous, temporal rather than spatial: the issue is not so much that several dresses cut to the same pattern resemble each other, but that the resemblance between all of them is the result of each dress resembling the pattern. Pattern in this sense is a way of thinking of image or copy in its potential. The pattern itself is never yet a complete dress; it is always only the potentiality of the dress, the dress-that-could-be, the invitation or call to dressmaking. The copy of a pattern makes the pattern actual and in such a way that it exhausts the possibility of the pattern. Not because subsequent versions might not be made but because in this particular instance possibility is annulled, or consummated; to use the language from *The Sickness Unto Death*, it is now actual.[4] But then, what was essential about the pattern – its potentiality – seems to be lost in making the copy. Would there be a way of copying the pattern such that its possibility remained to invite again? To investigate such a question about the possibility of possibility requires turning from an account of craft or equipment (such as dressmaking) to one of art or work (such as Kierkegaard's own essay writing), which is the move that the first section of this chapter attempts.[5]

To start over (to begin from nature again): Kierkegaard (like Nietzsche) says there is *no* resemblance between one leaf and another. 'In all that is visible there is nothing, not even a leaf, that resembles another or is its image. If that were the case, then the image would be the object itself.'[6] Kierkegaard writes this subversive rejection of resemblance into the first of his Lily Discourses, the 1846 'What We Learn from the Lily in the Field and the Birds of the Air'. No leaf resembles another leaf! This is not the only place where Kierkegaard tries our common sense; but his argument is sound. If a leaf really resembled another leaf, or were its image, it would *be* that other leaf; in other words, nothing in nature gives us the means for understanding resemblance. Resemblance is not something we simply *see*, and if I insist that I *do* see resemblance, then that tells me that my sight is not a simple phenomenon. However, insofar as there is a resemblance between leaves, or if we want to talk about a perceived resemblance, the question would be how, or according to what principle, the leaves all turn out 'the same'. For instance, oak leaves, with their distinctive indentations, tell me this tree is an oak – its leaves look like other oak leaves.

Perhaps more urgently, I need to be able to recognize a poison ivy leaf in shade or in sunlight, big or small, up the trunk of a tree or just sprouting, if I want to avoid a nasty surprise. Each 'vision' of each leaf, each sensory image, will be different; but if I can recognize it, I will find each leaf also conforms to a specific pattern. How this happens is neither simple nor uninteresting: the second half of Kant's *Critique of Judgment* investigates the back-and-forth between our pre-scientific assumption of the 'whole', which is to say the organism as teleological, and our ability to even identify the leaf as part of the tree, let alone as similar to its sister leaves. Assuming we can take natural teleology for granted (an assumption Kant throws into some uncertainty), we would attribute the pattern of the leaves to the generating principle of the plant, to its genes. This kind of natural pattern-making will not be sufficient as a 'model' for what Kierkegaard means by pattern (*Mønster*): a true pattern will not be merely natural.

Thus, at the start of *Fear and Trembling*, in the 'Eulogy on Abraham', Johannes de Silentio describes several patterns in nature: 'forest foliage', 'the singing of birds in the forest', the passing of a 'ship through the sea, as wind through the desert'.[7] What these leaves, songbirds and winds have in common is that – like the ship – they come and go without leaving a trace. De Silentio says that this can't be all there is to human life. 'If', de Silentio says, '[i]f such were the situation, if there were no sacred bond that knit humankind together, if one generation [*Slaegt*] emerged after another like forest foliage, if one generation succeeded another like the singing birds of the forest, if – [he goes on . . .] how empty and devoid of consolation life would be. But precisely for that reason it is not so.'[8] There is more to human life than the so-called patterns of nature, de Silentio promises, because the patterns of nature – as this list demonstrates – cannot retain resemblance on their own, and even the passage of a vessel (which could as easily be one of nefarious trade as of scientific discovery) is not enough to anchor and hold the likenesses of these patterns such that they might amount to anything, might last or endure. The ship on the sea joins the wind and birds and leaves in leaving no mark behind. In all of nature we find merely this 'unthinking and unproductive performance', and in much of our navigation of nature too. Johannes de Silentio seems sure though: there *must* be a kind of generation available to us as human beings which goes beyond the pattern of the foliage. What I am arguing is that, for Kierkegaard, this is not, after all, something to be sure about. Any pattern that is stronger than nature's, that is not available immediately for sense or cognition (and as we've seen *even* natural patterns are not really available in this way) will have to remain utterly uncertain.

As something that might leave a mark in the way nature cannot, Johannes de Silentio's 'generations' are ultimately not a sound candidate. Do human generations not succeed one another like forest foliage? In *Philosophical Fragments*, Johannes Climacus argues very convincingly that one generation succeeds another generation without changing anything. That is to say, each generation has just as much chance of learning the truth as the preceding generation had; each generation has to start all over again.[9]

There are two ways of understanding this: the Greek way and a distinctly Christian way. The first is that each generation has equal chance, because there is no truth that can be learned except for the truth of one's own ignorance – of the difference of each person from the other; and the second is that each generation has equal chance, because the truth that can be learned, can be learned only by each person, singularly, by means of the grace of a pattern which grants the learning. According to the first model, the model of Socrates, who says that we each have nothing to learn except who we are, one person's learning can never provide a shortcut for another's. According to Climacus's hypothesis, the hypothesis of Christianity, there *is* something more to be learned; there *is* some trace, something which exceeds the proliferation of leaves and the blowing of sand; there is a teacher, a pattern – but it would be no more easily accessible to this generation than to the generation which could see and touch 'it', which is to say to see and touch Christ as the *Forbillede*: Kierkegaard's Danish word that is translated by Lowrie as 'Pattern', or as 'Prototype' by the Hongs.[10]

Which generation one belongs to will make no difference when it comes to perceiving this pattern: that is, when it comes to perceiving it *as pattern*. In other words, when it comes to discovering its possibilities. To following it, being transformed by it and acting according to it, when it comes to receiving or preserving or making something that could defy the oblivion of bird song. And, thus, the ground beneath the distinction Silentio was obliged to set up in order to begin *Fear and Trembling*, between the way generations of people progress and the way nature continues, threatens to shudder and collapse.

This collapsing difficulty that distinctions keep facing as we try to separate a flatter or simpler sense of pattern from a stronger or more rigorous one could be called their 'uncertainty' – the uncertainty of patterns. It has to do with the fact that the distinction cannot be made fast by any rule. For instance, as laid out above, we cannot definitively distinguish between patterns of leaves, which are all similar, and patterns of people, who are all different, because leaves are not all similar; and on the other hand, we cannot simply distinguish between patterns of leaves and generations of people, because the generations are actually all the same. That is not to reduce everything to a dichotomy (nature and human beings), but rather to point out that this particular distinction is unstable, uncertain, at *both* ends.

There are other discourses in which Kierkegaard writes more directly about the uncertainty of pattern, but it is in *Philosophical Fragments* that the myth of generations is dispelled so ruthlessly.[11] If the teacher once walked and talked and fished and kissed, it seems as if (or so the myth would have it) it should have been easier during that time to learn the truth from him – at any rate there was a generation of people who walked alongside him, and then a second generation who could talk to the first, and another generation who learnt from the second, and so on until Kierkegaard's generation or our own. All of which might lead one to say, well, if it wasn't easier for the very first followers, perhaps it was harder, and is easier for us! There must be some difference! Climacus's point is that it cannot be easier for any of us – those in the past or those to come, those who were traded as slaves or those who did the trading – those who bore the children or those who fathered them. There is no simple rule or shortcut. *If* there is this rupture in the manifold of forest leaves and song, *if* there is a clearing, such that 'all is not despair', such that something new can be learnt, this can only happen in a way which would be absolutely singular for each individual.[12]

To return to Johannes de Silentio's generations: in the textual succession of the fragments which make up *Fear and Trembling*, the account in the Eulogy comes after a pattern of stories about generations – the four stories of God, Abraham and Isaac – and a counter-pattern, a supporting pattern (as woof supports warp) of stories about weaning.[13] Usually, when we talk of the pattern of generations, it is not to describe the way one succeeds another, as if from afar, but the ways in which one repeats inside the other: yes, I was weaned just as my mother before me was, but more to the point, I too will wean my baby, as my mother before weaned me. And will I do it in the same way, bound by the same pattern, will I feel such guilt, will I tell my daughter the story of my guilt for years and years until she too has to wean her daughter and confront that – would it be the same – guilt? If one generation does not emerge from another like the waves on the sea, if humankind is different, it is because each generation has to be weaned. This weaning implies being ripped out of continuity – condemned to freedom – to knit a bond with one another. *And yet*, that is not enough to prevent the generations from simply succeeding each other as part of nature: not because weaning is 'natural' – which it isn't, as it requires the kind of passion and faith with which one marries – but because such passion doesn't last – it must be repeated.

Repeated: by each generation to come – in the mother's relationship to her baby over and over again in acknowledgement of her separateness – by her baby who becomes an adult and affirms her freedom; in every act of faith, which is the only thing that lasts, that leaves a trace and yet must be continually taken up again and in writing, again and again, four times at least, into a pattern that can decorate a treatise, as if at its four corners, as a kind of frame.

Another way of saying that something must be repeated is to note that it is, as yet, just a fragment. A pattern is made up of nothing but fragments – much more so than a 'whole' is; for a whole may or may not be fragmented, at least in theory, while a pattern must be. The question is: What kind of pattern can philosophical fragments make? Can they make the type of pattern that leaves a trace – that generates something different – despite the uncertainty of the generations?

Can the fragment present itself as such – as part of a pattern – as the pattern that generates a pattern different from all of nature – in such a way that it does indeed generate? Can we go 'beyond' the Socratic, in other words, beyond the image of the midwife?

Socrates's paradox of learning can be put in terms of the Sorites paradox: How many fragments must I look at to be able to recognize the pattern? For Socrates, I will never be able to recognize the fragment if I do not already possess the pattern; and so I do not learn anything new, there is no authentic teaching (except that which reminds me of my difference, my ignorance). And therefore, no matter what tricks his students played on him, Socrates would not be seduced into seducing. He made fun of the idea that some touch might transfer knowledge from one person to another, that a teacher might touch her student and thereby confer wisdom. Teaching is not seduction. But for Socrates there is no means *other* than touch either, for transferring knowledge from teacher to student. And thus, there is *no* transfer of knowledge. There is either seduction – or nothing; either seduction – or Socratic irony.

Climacus's project is to suggest that there might be something else – some teaching that is not seduction, some touch, some intimacy, some transformation that does not stop at midwifery, but grants a rebirth, a regeneration, new life, possibility. The teacher who might generate this response would be called the archi-image, the prototype – the pattern. And the teacher would look just like Socrates: to eyes, which see the visible (to vision, which sees light and shadow, ripples and leaves); and to the understanding, which decodes the trends and recognizes what it already fundamentally knew. The visible pattern of the thing, the principled reliable pattern of the tool – be it a jacket or a textbook – does not give an indication of the difference that Climacus is after: it does not issue a call, and it does not originate a new response. It repeats, but not *forwards*.[14] Climacus persists, however, and suggests that there might be one more possibility, one invisible, improbable, impossible possibility (a repetition forwards, an archi-image, prototype).

This possibility – invisible, untouchable, uncertain – Climacus puts in terms of *belief*; de Silentio, of *faith*. But instead of following what might be considered the established trajectory and moving from the 'aesthetic' surface to the depths of religion, I am contending that there is reason to think about what Kierkegaard means by faith in relation to aesthetics – to the work of art. This thinking would of course entail not only a rethinking of what Kierkegaard means by faith but also a rethinking of what it might be possible to mean by the philosophical category of the aesthetic.

The precedent for such a move, however, had already been written down by one of Kierkegaard's most significant predecessors; perhaps we could go as far as to say one of his teachers. Kant, in the *Critique of Judgment*, describes a judgement of taste as one which holds true universally, and yet is absolutely singular. What this means is that it must follow the pattern set by a prototype. And yet, this 'following' (*Nachfolge*), Kant says, cannot be a simple 'imitating' (*Nachahmung*).[15] In Danish, the word '*Efterfolgelse*' (following) is used to mean the imitation of Christ, and this is the term Kierkegaard uses when he describes our response to the prototype as one of *following*.

My daughter says, 'look at the wrinkles in the water', and when I say, 'these ripples, in this light, are beautiful', I am making a claim which I expect you will agree with – I require you to agree with the claim, it is a universal truth claim, Kant says, the claim is made 'to *everyone's* assent'.[16] However, I will not be able to show the concept that makes it true, since there is not a concept that makes it true – each person has to recognize the beauty of the patterned water herself. According to Kant, 'To say, "This flower is beautiful", is tantamount to a mere repetition of the flower's own claim to everyone's liking'.[17] My claim repeats the water's claim, the flower's claim and it does so without recourse to a concept.

Kant does not spend many pages worrying about a situation in which a child or a student is trying to learn what is true about the beautiful, about which setting or flower or painting or poem or set of fragments is beautiful. But in a marvellously succinct two-page section at the beginning of the Deduction, titled, 'The First Peculiarity of the Judgment of Taste', Kant lingers on the problem of learning for just a few paragraphs. It is a matter, Kant says, of the pattern, the model, the prototype – and of how to *follow*.

Kant says that in relation to a judgement of taste 'we demand that [a person] judge for himself: he should not have to grope about among other people's judgments by means of experience, to gain instruction'.[18] Judge for yourself! Fine. But does that mean there are no teachers, that all instruction would be no more than groping? How can a teacher teach me, if I am to judge for myself? Yes, there are teachers, Kant says,

> if each subject had always to start from nothing but the crude predisposition given him by nature, many of his attempts would fail, if other people before him had not failed in theirs; they did not make these attempts in order to turn their successors (*die Nachfolgenden*) into mere imitators (*zu blossen Nachahmern*), but so that, by their procedure, they might put others on a track (*auf die Spur zu bringen*) whereby they could search for their own principles within themselves and so adopt their own and often better course.[19]

The generations do not succeed one another like forest foliage, then for Kant, too, not just de Silentio, there is this assurance that some mark (*Spur*) can be left, some learning happen. As Climacus will do, Kant arranges generations of teachers into roughly two groups: 'the works of the ancients as models (*die Werke der Alten zu Mustern*)', on the one hand, and a different group, religious teachers, who might offer 'an example of virtue and holiness (*ein Beispiel der Tugend oder Heiligkeit*)', on the other. Kant does not dwell on the difference between these groups as Climacus does: in both cases there is no 'concept' which will make learning possible, and a simple 'imitation' will not replace learning. In both cases the prototype demands a *follower*:

> Following (*Nachfolge*) by reference to a precedent, rather than imitating (*Nachahmung*), is the right term for any influence that products of an exemplary author (*exemplarischen Urheber*) may have on others; and this means no more than drawing on the same sources from which his predecessor himself drew, and learning from him only how to go about doing so.[20]

All the learner has to do is to learn from her teacher how *she* learnt from *her* teachers. And with that we will all be able to pronounce the right flower truly beautiful.

It is almost as if Kierkegaard took up this passage, specifically, to respond to – it is not simply in relation to the Lutheran tradition but in relation to Kantian aesthetics that he makes his intervention, that he introduces the archi-image. In *Philosophical Fragments* one can read a repetition of Kant – but not without a difference. That which is able to speak, to call, to originate, is not merely imitation. No: if Kierkegaard repeats Kant he also splits apart those two generations, the two great generations of teachers, the philosophers and the believers, so that their difference becomes or appears to become absolute.

And yet we are now obliged to return to the work of philosophy, or of art. And just as we have had to ask about faith (Is such a thing possible, a communication of truth via the pattern?) now we have to ask, Would it be possible for a work of art, for a text, to be an origin? Would it be possible for a dialectical lyric or a set of philosophical crumbs to present the kind of pattern that generates something lasting, something new, to teach? That has to remain uncertain, but with the uncertainty that is faith's uncertainty, with unsureness, Climacus says,

> Immediate sense perception and cognition do not have any intimation of the unsureness (*Usikkerhed*) with which belief approaches its object, but neither do they have certitude (*Visheden*) that extricates itself from the incertitude (*Uvisheden*).[21]

As there is pattern and pattern, there is uncertainty and uncertainty! With regard to the possibility of a radical teaching, a strong pattern, there is the deepest uncertainty: de Silentio, repeating Philippians 2:12, called it 'fear and trembling'. This 'unsureness', this fear and trembling, is not merely an 'incertitude' which might vacillate in doubt, unable to act. Belief stops doubt: belief acts. But in stopping doubt, in 'extricating itself from incertitude', belief doesn't thereby conquer uncertainty, or unsureness. The pattern to which belief testifies is not available either for 'immediate sense perception' or for 'cognition': it is secret in this sense – I can't see it or, nothing in what I can see is certainly *it*.

Then, the pattern that I recognize in a work such as *Philosophical Fragments*, if it is the kind which interrupts the hungry oblivion of nature, is something that will always be uncertain – not just because I can't see it with my eyes but because to see it is to copy it, and in such a way that I preserve the originating, invite a new copy to be brought forth. What is imperative about the pattern must be *repeated* in the copy: it cannot be lost, as happens in the manufacture of equipment. It always remains to generate, and it is all that the pattern was to begin with, since there is, after all, no prototype for a work except in this sense – that it teach, and not seduce.

Pattern summons us

Pattern summons us: asks us to enter into it, with works in response to it, by making a mark as part of it. Were one to make such a mark, it would not just interrupt, complicate, trouble, supplement, affirm, repeat, what went before it: it would also, itself, call for another, a different, response, in turn. A response, not made by rule, retains, renews the pattern's call.

Pattern summons us – from out of the pages of a book, say – and it isn't just scholars either, those of us who make our living pattern-seeking with the child's enthusiasm for circling the matches and crossing the odd ones out. To circle a pattern is not quite the same as responding to it, to notice it is not quite the same as being summoned by it in the full sense, falling in love: and yet, neither is it very helpful to cross out 'scholarship' or 'criticism' ahead of time. Kierkegaard himself, so virulently opposed to 'paragraph gobbling', adored the genre of criticism.[22] This distinction between 'circling', on the one hand, and 'responding', on the other, in which 'circling' marks the close of possibility and 'responding' invigorates possibility in the pattern, is the very one that will keep eluding definition and *refuse* to be governed by a rule.

Not just passively available for circling, the pattern *invites* one to sign, in turn, some part of its sequence. For instance, the way Kierkegaard writes his discourses on the gospel, responding to it by adding: *take* 'Christ as *Forbillede*', that is, 'Christ as Archi-image', or 'Pattern'. He does so, as we have seen, in such a way that he emphasizes the non-imitative following – *Efterfolgelse* – which is the way both to recognize a pattern and to respond to it. That is, to circle the pattern in its strongest sense as summons, and to repeat it, follow it, in such a way that the pattern is extended in a renewed call. What I have suggested is that Kierkegaard's texts which trace this pattern themselves can be read as a response, not just to the gospel but also to Kant's *Third Critique*. Here, looking more closely at the way Kierkegaard uses the term 'pattern' itself – *Mønster* – particularly in some of the early 'aesthetic' texts in *Either/Or*, I extend and develop that argument. Kierkegaard's concept of the archi-image is as much a repetition of Kant's *Urbild* as of the biblical idea of Christ-to-be-followed.

Reading Kierkegaard in the pattern of the gospel, and reading Kierkegaard in the pattern of Kant, need not be considered incompatible interpretations: unless one is determined to imagine that for Kierkegaard the 'religious' is something entirely removed (two stages away) from the 'aesthetic'. To argue (as I will do here) that we are best able to understand the concept of summons – in the religious sense – in terms of pattern is to argue that the aesthetic and the religious are incorrigibly intertwined in Kierkegaard.

What makes Kierkegaard's work part of the pattern that includes both the gospel and Kant is the way in which it maintains the summons that it reads in those texts: maintains and repeats that summons in such a way that it continues to call to us.²³ To be summoned, and to respond in such a way that the summons is not ignored, to answer in such a way that the summons is re-traced, that the summons marks itself into the response, to say 'Here I am' when one is called in such a way that the call will be remembered: that is, to testify to, to repeat, the pattern.

What I am proposing is a reading of Kierkegaard's figuring of the call and response (between God and Abraham, we might say, or between the teacher and her student; between the artist and the artist-to-come; between Oedipus the father and Antigone the daughter; between Sophocles, or Kant, or *Matthew* and Kierkegaard) that takes the call and response as *patterned*. The consequences of such an approach would include an emphasis not just on the uncertain, but on the fragmentary, interrupted, responsive, inviting, nature of such a relation. The repetition of pattern in this sense requires an account of creativity or productivity that not only is not simply 'from nothing' but is also not ever 'finished', because it 'opens' to the future, which is also to say, allows itself to be *interrupted* by it. And this is the sense in which Kierkegaard means 'repetition' when he distinguishes it from 'recollection' – it is forwards, it is for that which is to come, it maintains the summons.

In its simplest, most casual sense, a pattern is just a repetition of marks. In its strong sense, it is a call, a model, but one which is never entirely complete, never a 'rounded-off whole', always referring back to what went before it as well as reaching towards what might still come.²⁴ The repetition in the simple pattern, the mechanical imitating of what went before, is what has to be distinguished from Kierkegaard's sense of 'repetition' – the repeating *forwards*, that is, repeating non-mechanically, in such a way that the future is opened towards and not closed off.

The Danish word for 'pattern' is *Mønster*; Kierkegaard uses it a few times, here and there, and generally in the sense of 'model', gesturing towards, playing with, the stronger sense of pattern. The full sense of 'summons' is checked, however, by appearing within contexts of the most conventional bourgeois social–familial notions (which reminds us that the 'strong' sense of pattern is always threatening to fall back into the weaker sense). So, in *The Concept of Irony*, for instance, Kierkegaard admits Socrates was not a 'model' husband, and in *The Concept of Anxiety*, Vigilius Haufniensis suggests that it is harder to live with the idea of God's existence than it is to be a 'model' husband.²⁵ In *Either/Or*, A writes that Antigone was a 'model' daughter – but *how*, that was her secret: the secret of how one could be a model, a pattern, in this strong sense, is what Kierkegaard was after throughout his work – and we'll return to the example of Antigone.²⁶

In 'The Seducer's Diary' in *Either/Or*, Kierkegaard has Johannes the seducer play with the alternative meanings of the word 'pattern'. Johannes first uses it to describe an almost-image, a not-quite-yet image, a won't-hold-still image, which is too light, too much in motion, without adequate frame, to be an image proper and thus tormenting to the seducer, who is desperate for the image (the image is of the girl he has fallen for). Johannes is referring to pattern in the weaker sense, the repetitive decorative design sense, but in such a way that it gets put in relation to the image: the image that might, just possibly, be an archi-image, a summons or pattern in the stronger sense. The relation is that the weaker pattern forms a frame for the stronger one. *Before* seeing, or in order to see, the image *as an image*, it must be clothed and situated properly (the aesthetic is not the natural; the flower we find beautiful is already severed from its place in the garden by our aesthetic judgement of it). The pattern that, as we'll see, frustrates the impatient Johannes so terribly is a stage in that setting. Johannes has just seen Cordelia for the first time, and become so excited, that he can't remember what she looked like (only later will he see her again and be able to remember and hold her image as beautiful):

> Then, when I have chafed in impatience and have calmed down, it is as if presentiment and recollection were weaving an image that still does not take definite shape for me, because I cannot make it stand still in context; it is like a pattern [*Mønster*] in a fine weaving – the pattern is lighter than the background, and by itself it cannot be seen because it is too light.[27]

Patterns are of course native to weaving, they belong properly to textiles, which repeat fragments of an image decoratively, in order to adorn and warm the one wrapped in them.[28] But this 'lighter' pattern, this decorative 'space' carved out of the dark background, this hesitating, scintillating, tantalizing, *becoming* sense of pattern, bears Kierkegaard's own signature. He develops it a little further in the text. In one of the many 'interruptions' of the main narrative, Johannes takes a break from describing his pursuit of Cordelia and includes this fragment as an aside. Johannes is 'out in Frederiksberg' watching the 'servant girls' on a Sunday afternoon:

> First come the peasant girls holding hands with their sweethearts, or in another pattern [*Mønster*], all the girls in front holding hands and the fellows behind, or in another pattern, two girls and one fellow. This flock forms the frame.[29]

So, as if in a kind of kaleidoscope, the girls come in patterns – none of these girls is interesting in herself, she is just a pretty peasant in brightly coloured clothing changing places with the others, taking up different positions, patterning the square. Each girl repeats the others in the backwards sense of repetition. This pattern of skirts forms a swirling frame for a central figure, who is, according to Johannes, a 'pattern' in the *other* sense. The 'prettiest girl in Copenhagen', Marie, takes the stage before these interchangeable others. She is 'an ornament and a pattern [*Mønster*] for all servant girls'.[30] She is (for a moment in the text) a model, someone to be emulated (and for this moment she is therefore like her namesakes, Mary Magdalene, the archi-image, the pattern and the Virgin Mary, the knight of faith[31]). This passage demonstrates Kierkegaard's deliberate use of the two senses of pattern, which play off one another. Out of the decorative, framing pattern, emerges a pattern, a model.

Marie-the-pattern, however, in the seducer's narrative, soon becomes no more than another girl, another plain Marie, in the background, twirling with all the others, framing the story of Cordelia, part of a merely decorative pattern. That, again, is the trouble, the uncertainty, when it comes to pattern: the model and the ornament can be conflated, and are never finally distinguished by rule. The one who stood out might turn out to be just the same as the others after all.[32]

But if repetition (in the backwards sense) is the great risk, Kierkegaard's repetition is perhaps the best way of understanding what he means by the 'following' that recognizes and responds to the archi-image, in such a way that the pattern continues: as in, continues to call. To the extent that this following cannot be executed by rule or concept, it will have to rely on a kind of secret: and here we have to turn to Kierkegaard's Antigone, the 'mother' as much as the 'daughter' – the pattern – of secrecy.

Earlier in *Either/Or*, in an essay called 'The Tragic in Ancient Drama Reflected in the Tragic in Modern Drama: A Venture in Fragmentary Endeavor', Kierkegaard has author 'A' re-write Sophocles's character Antigone – revivify her, renew her, repeat her for modernity.[33] Antigone is the daughter of Oedipus, the man who slept with his mother, who was blind to his own origin. The 'reflected' version in Kierkegaard's text describes the whole community as blindfolded, so no one knows the secret of the origination – except Antigone herself. This Antigone, A says, 'is extolled in the land as a pattern [*Mønster*] of a loving daughter, and yet this enthusiasm is the only way in which she can give vent to her sorrow. Her father is always in her thoughts, but how – that is her painful secret.'[34] Antigone is the image of a loving daughter, she looks for all the world as if she loves her father, Oedipus, enthusiastically, and it is impossible for anyone to guess that she has discovered his secret. She doesn't give any clues, not even to her father, and so she doesn't know whether *he* knows the painful secrecy in which she is kept by keeping his secret. The way in which she loves her father, then, is hidden from the world, and this hiddenness, which Sophocles's Antigone already quietly carried, and the author A discovered and responded to – 'reflected' in his modern sketch – is what makes her the pattern. A says, 'Purely aesthetically, [Antigone] is *virgo mater* [virgin mother]; she carries her secret under her heart, concealed and hidden.'[35] Not only Oedipus's child then, but the Virgin Mary's in another sense, Antigone is the 'mother' of secrecy, not only its daughter. If A talks about Antigone as his 'creation', and about himself as her 'father', he also admits that she seems always to be 'ahead' of him, 'before' him, allowing him to witness and repeat her movements, though only according to a mechanism he doesn't entirely understand and cannot ultimately control. The secret of her generation – as origin and originator of this text by A – is not only about the past but also about what is to come. That is, it works as a kind of a call: one that cannot be determined by rule. [36]

To say that the call retained in pattern defies determination by rule is also to say, as the first section does, that it bears an uncertainty. This uncertainty, as we have seen, is also the uncertainty that Kant's judgement of taste carries. The aesthetic judgement, for Kant, is not rule-based. It is now possible to articulate that uncertainty in terms of a secrecy – of Antigone's secrecy. To interrupt, in this way, the philosophical reception of Kant by introducing into it the aesthetic figure of Antigone as *virgo mater* is exactly the kind of wildly unanticipated future the *Third Critique* opens itself to and calls for, provided only that we take the motif of pattern sketched out there seriously, as a work of art in its own right. Were it possible to define all beautiful objects conceptually, there would be no need for aesthetic judgement, for taste – looking at artworks (including Kant's text) would not require anything significantly different from learning lists of dates, names, concepts or styles. But the work of art *is* different from anything that can be learned exclusively by rote, its beauty – considered 'purely aesthetically', the way A considers 'his' Antigone, as the silent bearer of Kant's legacy – is *not* defined by rules – and that is to say, in author A's terms, there is something secret about it, both in its origin and unpredictable future.

The work of art isn't *merely* individual or 'subjective' as one says; for Kant, the claim that something is beautiful is a peculiar kind of truth claim, it applies universally, we *require* others to agree with us, and yet no rule can be produced to adequately explain it, or to guarantee that our claim is justified. The only way we can learn what is beautiful, then, is by *following* a teacher – and, as we saw in the first section of this chapter, in explaining this idea Kant distinguishes between '*Nachfolge*' and '*Nachahmung*' – to follow without aping – the very distinction Kierkegaard will later 'repeat' when describing how we relate to the archi-image as '*Efterfølgelse*' that is not '*Efterablelse*' – to *follow* without *aping*.[37] Repeat, in other words, but not backwards, not mechanically, but rather, freely, forwards. Repeat, but not in such a way that possibility is curtailed, but rather so that possibility is opened up. Kant not only provides the terms for a following that does not ape, he also uses the term *Urbild*, which in Kierkegaard's Danish would be *Forbillede*, for the model that must be followed. Kant says, in *the Ideal of Beauty*:

> We regard some products of taste as *exemplary*. This does not mean that taste can be acquired by imitating someone else's (*indem er anderen nachahmt*). For taste must be an ability one has oneself; and although someone who imitates a model (wer *aber ein Muster* nachahmt) may manifest skill insofar as he succeeds in this, he manifests taste only insofar as he can judge that model (*Muster*) himself. From this, however, it follows (*Hieraus* folgt aber) that the highest model, the archetype (*das Urbild*) of taste, is a mere idea, an idea which everyone must generate (*hervorbringen muss*) within himself and by which he must judge any object of taste.[38]

Judge for yourself, Kant says – but this judgement is not simple: it requires *both* a careful consideration of the model, the pattern, and, in order to respond without merely repeating backwards or imitating, *also* a reflection of this model in relation to the future: it requires a call for, a generation of, an archi-image or archetype.

Kierkegaard's fourth *Lily Discourse* is found in his posthumously published *Judge for Yourself* and is titled 'Christ as *Forbillede*'. The translation I propose is 'Christ as Archi-image' (while, as we have seen, the Hongs have 'Christ as Prototype', and Lowrie has 'Christ as Pattern'). Since in *Either/Or* and other places Kierkegaard uses *Mønster* to mean decorative pattern, the terms must be kept separate. It is also the case that *Forbillede* is specifically the word used in the Danish Lutheran Church for Christ-to-be-followed (*imitatio Christi*), Christ as a very special *image* which calls for (summons, generates, originates, makes possible) a response. Nevertheless, what I am arguing is that Lowrie's rendering of *Forbillede* as pattern is not without merit (that, therefore, the terms cannot be kept absolutely separate), because the concept of pattern – in the strong sense lent to it by Kierkegaard – does precisely mean this summons that is the archi-image;[39] and also because the play with pattern in the weaker sense is helpful for understanding more clearly how the archi-image works. Kant uses *Urbild* – in the passage above translated as 'archetype' – for both the image of

Christ-to-be-followed, and the *aesthetic* model.⁴⁰ Kierkegaard clearly takes up this pattern again.

The Kantian concept of the *Urbild* has precisely the qualities of pattern that Kierkegaard emphasizes. On the one hand, it is never 'the highest' without there being a 'still higher standard'; in other words, there is always some more originary image that can be referred back to, that is repeated or reflected in this standard or model. On the other hand, no matter how high the standard, it means nothing unless it is approached freely by a reader, by a student; for without this freedom, *'there can be no fine art'*, Kant says. In other words, the pattern has to be thought in terms of possibility, has to call to a future, to one who can recognize and receive it, which is to say, repeat it, respond in such a way that, as part of the pattern, one's response continues to call, again and again. Kant says, in section 60, the Appendix and last section of the first part of the *Critique of Judgement*:

> The master must stimulate the student's imagination (*die Aufweckung der Einbildungskraft des Schülers*) until it becomes commensurate with a given concept; he must inform the student if the latter has not adequately expressed the idea, the idea that even the concept cannot reach because it is aesthetic; and he must provide the student with sharp criticism. For only in this way can the master keep the student from immediately treating the examples offered him as if they were archetypes (*Urbilder*), models that he should imitate as if they were not subject to a still higher standard and to his own judgment, [an attitude] which would stifle his genius, and along with it would stifle also the freedom that his imagination has even in its lawfulness (*mit ihm aber auch die Freiheit der Einbildungskraft selbst in ihrer Gesetzmässigkeit erstickt werde*), the freedom without which there can be no fine art (*keine schöne Kunst*), indeed not even a taste of one's own by which to judge such art.⁴¹

Without rules, Kant points out, the teacher and student have only examples to work with: but the risk is that the student repeats the examples in the shallow sense, imitating them. What she needs to see is that the archetypes, the archi-images, are always 'subject to a still higher standard', in other words, they themselves are just responses to other works, but responses that call out to the student; and the archetypes, or archi-images, cannot call except to the 'freedom' of the student's imagination – they cannot prescribe beforehand who it is who will respond, their call is open – it is a call to 'freedom'.

Instead of following rules, Kant says in the next paragraph, becoming an artist or a critic requires that we 'expose ourselves' to the humanities, in order to develop two qualities – one of 'the universal *feeling of sympathy*', and the other of 'the ability to engage universally in the most intimate *communication*'.[42] The pattern from which we learn has to be both 'universal' – open to anyone, opening, calling, inviting, who knows who, 'my reader', and all the others – and also 'most intimate' – secret, hidden, available only and exclusively to one single individual, for as long as she is faithful. If Antigone is the model, that 'most intimate' communication is not even revealed as communication between the father and the daughter – Antigone doesn't tell her father she knows his secret, and so doesn't know for sure whether he even really knew it himself. Did Kant *know* what he was writing, when he wrote the *Urbild* that Kierkegaard found and took up again?

When this paradox of the pattern is expressed as a communication that is both 'universal' and 'intimate', it is the 'universal' part that serves to remind us of the interrupted and open aspect. If the call and response could be between two discreet totalities, two 'rounded-off wholes', if the communication – the teaching, the art, the ethical practices – between them could be contained, there would be no need for the 'response' to retain a 'call'. Rules could be ditched without further ado in light of the utter singularity of the relation. The response could refer solely to the initial call, end of story. But this communication, as intimate as it is, is *also* universal – it can be overseen, overheard, interrupted by a third party: by the laughing Isaac, as Kierkegaard reminds us in *Fear and Trembling*. There is Kant interrupting the straightforward religious inheritance Matthew leaves Kierkegaard, and here we are listening at the door, interfering in what they have left us to read. To say that the response contains a call is also to say that it can't be completed once and for all, that it is a mere fragment, a moment in a pattern without end, or telos.

Interrupting himself in the middle of his Antigone essay, in a way which he will call 'anacoluthic' (in a manner which does not follow the path, or follows without following), Kierkegaard's author 'A' states:

> [it is] characteristic of all human endeavour in its truth that it is fragmentary, that it is precisely this which distinguishes it from nature's infinite coherence, that an individual's wealth consists specifically in his capacity for fragmentary prodigality and what is the producing individual's enjoyment is the receiving individual's also, not the laborious and careful accomplishment or the tedious interpretation of this accomplishment but the production and the pleasure of the glinting transiency, which for the producer holds much more than the consummated accomplishment, since it is a glimpse of the idea and holds a bonus for the recipient, since its fulguration stimulates his own productivity [for den *Reciperende indeholder et Mere, da dens Fulguration vækker hans egen Productivitet*] –[43]

To think the call and response, the summons, in terms of pattern is to think it as fragmentary – is to acknowledge the way each moment repeated – even when it is repeated forwards in Kierkegaard's sense – is only a fragment, not a whole, and a fragment not *of* a whole, but of something which could never be whole, which constantly interrupts itself, repeating itself, anacoluthic, exposing itself to the laughter which makes it live again. In a pattern, 'the master must stimulate the student's imagination', says Kant, and the author A says, the *fulgurating* – the shining, scintillating, dancing – idea, stimulates the recipient's – the student's, the daughter's, the follower's – productivity. That 'productivity' cannot but respond to what has 'stimulated' it, but if it really responds, it will contain its own 'stimulation', its own arousal of something still to come, by virtue of which it will be forever unfinished, which is to say, anticipatory, a 'glinting transiency'. Merely, that is, part of a pattern.

Notes

1. See 'What We Learn from the Lily in the Field and the Bird of the Air', particularly the second discourse: 'How Glorious it is to be a Human Being' in Søren Kierkegaard, *Upbuilding Discourse in Various Spirits*, ed. and trans. Howard V. Hong and Edna H. Hong (Princeton, NJ: Princeton University Press, 2009).
2. Søren Kierkegaard, *Fear and Trembling*, ed. and trans. Howard V. Hong and Edna H. Hong (Princeton, NJ: Princeton University Press, 1983) and *Philosophical Fragments* and *Johannes Climacus*, ed. and trans. Howard V. Hong and Edna H. Hong (Princeton, NJ: Princeton University Press, 1985). Immanuel Kant, *Critique of Judgment*, trans. Werner S. Pluhar (Cambridge: Hackett Publishing Company, 1987).
3. The Danish word for 'pattern', or 'model', is *Mønster*: in the section 'Pattern Summons Us' I return to consider Kierkegaard's use of this word in more detail.
4. Søren Kierkegaard, *The Sickness Unto Death: A Christian Psychological Exposition for Upbuilding and Awakening*, ed. and trans. Howard V. Hong and Edna H. Hong (Princeton, NJ: Princeton University Press, 1980), 3.
5. 'Equipment' and 'work' are, of course, Heidegger's terms, as he writes them into 'The Origin of the Work of Art', in *Basic Writings*, ed. David Krell (San Francisco: Harper, 1993), 139–213.
6. Søren Kierkegaard, *Upbuilding Discourses in Various Spirits*, Ed. and trans. Howard V. Hong and Edna H. Hong (Princeton, NJ: Princeton University Press, 2009), 192. For Nietzsche's version of leaves that do not resemble one another, see 'On Truth and Lies in a Nonmoral Sense', in *Philosophy and Truth: Selections from Nietzsche's*

Notebooks of the Early 1870s, ed. and trans. Daniel Breazeale (Atlantic Highlands, NJ: Humanities Press, 1979), 79–97.
7 Kierkegaard, *Fear and Trembling,* 15 / *SKS* 4, 112.
8 Ibid.
9 Johannes Climacus sometimes uses the same word as Johannes de Silentio, '*Slægt*' (for instance *SKS* 4, 267, 300 / *Philosophical Fragments,* 66, 104), although he also uses the word '*Generation*' (for instance *SKS* 4, 271 / *Philosophical Fragments,* 71).
10 For the Hongs' version see for instance the discourse 'Christ as the Prototype', in *For Self-Examination* and *Judge for Yourself,* ed. and trans. Howard V. Hong and Edna H. Hong (Princeton, NJ: Princeton University Press, 1990), 145–215. For Lowrie's see *For Self-Examination* and *Judge for Yourself* and *Three Discourses,* trans. Walter Lowrie (London: Oxford University Press, 1944).
11 See for instance 'The Cares of the Pagans' in Kierkegaard's *Christian Discourses Christian Discourses* and *the Crisis and a Crisis in the Life of an Actress,* ed. and trans. Howard V. Hong and Edna H. Hong (Princeton, NJ: Princeton University Press, 1997), 3–91. In *The Lily's Tongue* (Albany: State University of New York Press, 2019), I argue that this text should be read as *patterned* and as being about pattern; see 'Paper Flowers' 41–80.
12 The motif of the forest clearing, the interruption in the natural patterning of the foliage, the shift from pattern in the simple sense to that of a call or origination, is developed in Heidegger's 'Origin of the Work of Art'.
13 Kierkegaard, *Fear and Trembling,* 10–14.
14 Here is another way of putting the difference between surface-pattern and the stronger type: it is the difference between ordinary or vulgar repetition, and repetition forwards, repetition in the sense developed by Kierkegaard in the text called *Repetition.* The 'Pattern Summons Us' section of this chapter explores the pattern in terms of repetition in more detail.
15 Kant, *The Critique of Judgment,* 146 / *KU,* 212. German citations are taken from: *Kritik der Urteilskraft,* vol. 10 of *Werkausgabe,* ed. Wilhelm Weischedel (Frankfurt am Main: Suhrkamp, 1978).
16 Kant, *The Critique of Judgment,* 145.
17 Ibid.
18 Ibid.
19 Ibid., 146; Kant, *Kritik der Urteilskraft,* 212.
20 Ibid., 146–7; Kant, *Kritik der Urteilskraft,* 212.
21 Kierkegaard, *Philosophical Fragments,* 82 / *SKS* 4, 281.
22 Including, for example, his very first book, *From the Papers of One Still Living;* the 'occasion' that *The First Love* is for author A in *Either/Or;* and the later and more overtly political *A Literary Review* ('From the Papers of One Still Living', in *Early Polemical Writings,* ed. and trans. Julia Watkin (Princeton, NJ: Princeton University Press, 1990); 'The First Love', in *Either/Or: Part I,* ed. and trans. Howard V. Hong

and Edna H. Hong (Princeton, NJ: Princeton University Press, 1987), 231–81; *Two Ages: The Age of Revolution and the Present Age: A Literary Review*, ed. and trans. Howard V. Hong and Edna H. Hong (Princeton, NJ: Princeton University Press, 1978).

23 To take a concrete example: the pattern was able to call again from Kierkegaard's texts to Heidegger, whose *Origin of the Work of Art* responds in its turn to the question of call, of origination, *Ursprung* of 'a work' as something that waits for a 'preserver' to read and respond to it.

24 Søren Kierkegaard, *Either/Or*, vol. 1, ed. trans. Howard V. Hong and Edna H. Hong (Princeton, NJ: Princeton University Press, 1987), 236.

25 Søren Kierkegaard, *The Concept of Irony*, ed. and trans. Howard V. Hong and Edna H. Hong (Princeton, NJ: Princeton University Press, 1989), 192 and *The Concept of Anxiety*, ed. and trans. Reidar Thomte in collaboration with Albert B. Anderson (Princeton, NJ: Princeton University Press, 1997), 141. One has to be suspicious here of Kierkegaard's regard for 'model husbands' – that this would be a type in the simplest kind of mechanically reproduced pattern seems almost inevitable: this an example of how the 'strong' sense of pattern slides back into the weakest sense.

26 Kierkegaard, *Either/Or*, vol. 1, 161.

27 *Either/Or*, vol. 1, 324.

28 As explored in the dressmaking example from the first section of this chapter.

29 Ibid., 413 / SKS 2, 401.

30 Ibid., 414 / SKS 2, 401, translation modified.

31 For Kierkegaard's account of Mary Magdalene as archi-image, see 'The Woman Who Was a Sinner', in *Without Authority*, ed. and trans. Howard V. Hong and Edna H. Hong (Princeton, NJ: Princeton University Press, 1997), 135–44; for the Virgin Mary as Knight of Faith see *Fear and Trembling*.

32 Is there an image, in The *Seducer's Diary*, that calls out in such a way that the pattern to which it is responding is left forever disrupted? I argue in 'Kissing the Image: An Allegory of Imagination in "The Seducer's Diary"', *History of European Ideas*, Routledge 47, no. 3 (2021): 528–42 that Cordelia is just such an image, in that 'she' intervenes in the philosophical attempt to understand the role of the aesthetic in mediating our access to actuality.

33 A, incidentally, Kierkegaard's fictitious editor of *Either/Or* suggests, is also responsible for having created the character of Johannes the seducer.

34 Ibid., 161, translation modified.

35 Ibid., 158.

36 To identify Antigone as the pattern (as A does in relation to Sophocles's Antigone) is itself to respond to that call (so that A 'the author' or 'the father', is also one of the children of Antigone). There is a lot more to be said about the peculiar way in which Antigone can be read as A's 'mother'. Here see Kevin Newmark's 'Modernity Interrupted: Kierkegaard's Antigone', in *Irony on Occasion: From Schlegel and*

Kierkegaard to Derrida and de Man (New York: Fordham University Press, 2012), 66–96. A similar reversibility also occurs in 'The Seducer's Diary'.

37 Martin Gammon's article, 'Exemplary Originality: Kant on Genius and Imitation', *Journal of the History of Philosophy* 35, no. 4 (1997): 563–92, is an illuminating look at the difference between imitation and following in Kant, 'in light of the forcefield of concepts Kant has employed to characterize [this difference]: *Nachfolge, Nachahmung, Nachmachung,* and *Nachaffung*', *Journal of the History of Philosophy* 35, no. 4 (1997): 563–92 (564).

38 Kant, *The Critique of Judgment,* 79; Kant, *Kritik der Urteilskraft,* 149–50.

39 'A *Forbillede* is certainly a summons [*Opfordring*]', Kierkegaard says in 'Christian Discourses', in 'The Care of Lowliness' (*Christian Discourses,* 42 / SKS 10, 52).

40 For the *Urbild* as a religious concept in Kant, see especially *Religion Within the Bounds of Bare Reason,* trans. Werner Pluhar (Cambridge: Hackett, 2009). For an investigation on the difference between *Urbild* and *Vorbild* in Kant's use of the terms ('archetype' and 'prototype') see Paolo Diego Bubbio's 'Christ as Symbol in Kant's Religion', in *God and Self in Hegel* (New York: State University of New York Press, 2018).

41 *The Critique of Judgment,* 231 / KU, 299–300.

42 Ibid., 231, translation modified. 'By exposing ourselves beforehand to what we call the *humaniora*; they are called that presumably because *humanity* [*Humanität*] *means both the universal* feeling of sympathy, *and the ability to engage universally in the most intimate* communication' (Ibid., 231). The paradoxical juxtaposition of the 'universal' and 'the most intimate' at first seems to refer back to the Christian command to love one's neighbour, which Kant formalizes in terms of duty, and Kierkegaard thematizes in terms of 'neighbour-love'. But in the context of Kant's closing remarks in his work on aesthetics, we should perhaps not jump so quickly to the ethical or religious viewpoint – it is also a very original way of understanding what is going on with the pattern.

43 *Either/Or,* vol. 1, 151–2 / SKS 2, 151.

5

Kierkegaard and Deleuze

Anxiety, possibility and a world without others

Henry Somers-Hall

Introduction

In his appendix to the *Logic of Sense* on Tournier's novel, *Friday*, Deleuze conjoins two quotations concerning possibility: one from William James, and one from Kierkegaard. For William James, 'in the universe of Hegel – the absolute block whose parts have no loose play, the pure plethora of necessary being with the oxygen of possibility all suffocated out of its lungs – there can be neither good nor bad, but one dead level of mere fate'.[1] In relating to Kierkegaard, Deleuze tells the story of 'the bourgeois who takes his breakfast and reads his newspaper with his family and suddenly rushes to the window shouting, "I must have the possible, or else I will suffocate".[2] While the latter anecdote and quotation do not appear to be found in Kierkegaard's work itself, we can nonetheless find a number of similar expressions of this sentiment in Kierkegaard's writings.[3] Why does Deleuze focus on the notion of possibility here? We can begin by noting that both quotations can be read in light of the dominance of Hegel's metaphysics. James and Kierkegaard develop kindred criticisms of Hegel. For James, the difficulty with Hegel's thought is that Hegel's assumption that the essence of an object is defined relationally implies that the determination of any part of the universe implies the whole:

> The proof lies in the *hegelian* principle of totality, which demands that if any one part be posited alone all the others shall forthwith *emanate* from it and infallibly reproduce the whole. In the *modus operandi* of the emanation comes in, as I said, that partnership of the principle of totality with that of the identity of contradictories which so recommends the latter to beginners in Hegel's philosophy. To posit one item alone is to deny the rest; to deny them is to refer

to them; to refer to them is to begin, at least, to bring them on the scene; and to begin is in the fulness of time to end.[4]

As James notes, there is nothing inherently problematic with the principle that to understand an object or event fully we must understand the whole, but Hegel combines this principle with the idea that such a whole is in fact given with the individual. He fails to consider that the effect may not be latent within the cause, and thus the possibility of genuine novelty emerging within the causal nexus. The world thus becomes, as Merleau-Ponty would say, 'a crystal cube, where all possible presentations can be conceived by its law of construction'.[5] James's criticisms of Hegel here arise from two claims: that Hegel has an illegitimate conception of the transition between categories, and that Hegel has transposed the representation of logical thinking onto the physical world. In doing so, Hegel has removed any possibility of explaining the contingency and novelty we experience in the world.

Kierkegaard's criticisms of Hegel follow a similar line, arguing that Hegel's logic illegitimately takes for granted a concept of transition in order to allow itself to develop. As he puts it, 'the system is supposed to have such marvellous transparency and inner vision that in the manner of the *omphalopsychoi* it would gaze immovably at the central nothing until at last everything would explain itself and its whole content would come into being by itself'.[6] For Kierkegaard's Hegel, much as for James's, Hegelian logic operates through a process whereby a fragment generates the whole, and it does so by understanding transition in immanent terms, bringing in an illegitimate understanding of transition as necessity. In fact, Kierkegaard notes that transition itself is not a logical category at all, but nonetheless plays a fundamental role in allowing the dialectic to relate categories together.[7] It can only do so by misconceiving transition in what Kierkegaard calls 'quantitative' terms. That is, it is only if transition takes a determinate route that we can understand the necessary development of the Hegelian logic. Kierkegaard's claim is that this representation of transition in logic is a falsification of transition as it is found in actuality, which is a qualitative determination. We will return in detail to Kierkegaard's account of transition when we turn to anxiety in the final sections of this chapter. Much as with James's analysis, therefore, for Kierkegaard, the effect is not latent within the cause but requires the addition of a qualitative leap that transcends any quantitative determinations.

I do not want to explore the legitimacy of these criticisms in detail here. We could note that there is a notion of contingency in Hegel that emerges in the

Philosophy of Nature, where the logic externalizes itself, and in the process opens the way to deviations from the strict path of the logic. Contingency here seems to operate in a negative manner, however, merely as a deviation from the Idea generated by the 'impotence of nature'.[8] We do not have here the Jamesian or Kierkegaardian analysis of the possibility of genuine novelty, but rather simply the deficient adherence of nature to a logical category. What interests me, instead, is the reason Deleuze introduces these quotations. Deleuze's opposition to Hegel is well known, and *Difference and Repetition*, written at the same time as the *Logic of Sense*, defines its own context as one of a 'generalised anti-Hegelianism'.[9] In that work, Kierkegaard appears as an ally in the attempt to break free from Hegel's influence, even if this allegiance involves a degree of ambivalence. In the essay on Tournier, however, Deleuze distinguishes his position from Kierkegaard's on the basis of the concept of possibility. Rather than Kierkegaard's claims about Hegel positioning him as a fellow traveller for Deleuze here, then, Kierkegaard's claims about possibility are seen as highlighting a fundamental problem with Kierkegaard's worldview. In the rest of this chapter, I want to explore why Deleuze feels that possibility is such a misstep by looking at Deleuze's reading of Tournier's *Friday*, which is itself a reworking of Defoe's *Robinson Crusoe*, before considering whether Deleuze is right in his assessment.

A world without others

In citing the notion of possibility in Kierkegaard and James, Deleuze argues that in both cases, 'they are only evoking the a priori other',[10] an evocation here that Deleuze understands in a negative manner. To prefigure Deleuze's argument, his claim will be that if possibility rests on the other, and if in turn, the other acts as a principle of ordering that overwrites the natural order of experience, then a move to possibility leaves us little better off than the Hegelian dialectic. Rather than move from representation to actuality, we have moved from one form of representation (a representation of immanence) to another (a representation of possibility). We can see why Tournier's novel is therefore of interest to Deleuze. If Deleuze can show that the structure of experience differs in the absence of the other from both the dialectic and from possibility, then he opens a new path away from the representation of the world we find in Hegel. Tournier's examination of Robinson's experience free from others offers a glimpse of this path.

Tournier describes his novel as having a tripartite structure that mirrors Spinoza's three kinds of knowledge, though we can understand the novel in terms of a number of different frameworks, with Bergsonian elements visible throughout. Each moment therefore represents a different way of relating to the world. The first two parts of the novel loosely follow Defoe's *Robinson Crusoe*, with the arrival of Friday leading to a radical divergence from its original form. Robinson, shipwrecked on a desert island, at first attempts to escape what he names the 'Island of Desolation'. When the ship he fashions proves too heavy to launch, he 'gives up', retreating to a primitive state in what he calls the 'mire',[11] where he wallows in his own faeces, eating 'unmentionable foods' and falls into a state of dissolution. 'He moved less and less, and his brief excursions always ended in his return to the mire. Here, in his warm coverlet of slime, his body lost all weight, while the toxic emanations of the stagnant water drugged his mind. Only his eyes, nose, and mouth were active, alert for edible weed and toad spawn drifting on the surface'.[12] Recovering from this initial period of apathy, Robinson attempts to reassert the structures of the European society from which he has been separated. Robinson begins to call himself governor, and to institute a legal code, developing an economy for the environment, draining the mire and so on. He maps the island, and invents a water clock to measure time. When Friday arrives, Robinson contrives to pay Friday for his labour in coin taken from the ship, with Friday allowed to use his wages to buy time off from work, and various trinkets taken from the ship. While much of these first two parts follows the structure of a traditional robinsonade, even before the arrival of Friday, there is a divergence. As well as the quantified and ordered Speranza that Robinson institutes, he also experiences several encounters with 'another Friday'[13] and 'another island'[14] that point not to the abandonment of order of the mire, but to another form of understanding. Here, the world is not understood according to Robinson's own practical concerns, but rather the island shows itself according to its own purposes. After stopping the water clock, Robinson is drawn into this aspect of the island, covering himself in milk before slipping into a womb-like cavern in the heart of the island, and also copulates with the earth, giving rise to mandrake plants that Robinson takes to be his daughters. Friday's arrival exacerbates this ambivalence, with Robinson attempting to civilize Friday, with some apparent success, while at the same time it becomes apparent that Friday has a mind of his own, which subverts this process.

The third moment of the novel begins with Friday's accidental destruction of all of the civilized structures of the island by igniting Robinson's stores of powder carefully stored from his ship, the *Virginia*. Robinson's response to this development is one of relief rather than exasperation, and he recognizes a pre-existing drive towards the kind of nomadism represented by Friday. With the destruction of the civilization, and the water clock, Robinson enters into a kind of eternity on the island, with each day having its own splendour, and the island no longer understood in terms of 'possible points of view'. Rather, Robinson lives on the island in a 'state of innocence'. The transformation is so radical that when a ship, the *Whitebird*, finally does arrive at the island, it is Friday, rather than Robinson, who departs. Robinson is instead left with the cabin boy of the ship, who takes Friday's canoe and returns to the island, Robinson now taking on a position to the cabin boy similar to Friday's in relation to himself. Tournier originally planned a more 'rigorous' ending to the novel, with Robinson alone on the island, like a 'stylite, standing immobile on a column in the sun'.[15] We will return to this third stage when we discuss Deleuze's account of the transcendental field, but for now, let us turn to Deleuze's analysis of the structure of the novel.

While there are a number of incidental deviations from Defoe's original (in Tournier's novel, for instance, Robinson attempts to kill Friday, but misses through the intervention of his dog, rather than attempting to save him), Deleuze sets out three claims which he holds to be the essential divergences of Tournier's work. He sets these out as follows:

> [Tournier's Robinson] is related to ends and goals rather than to origins; he is sexual; and these ends represent a fantastic deviation from our world, under the influence of a transformed sexuality, rather than an economic reproduction of our world, under the impact of a continuous effort.[16]

The first here is perhaps the most important. Deleuze points out that unlike Defoe's Robinson, Tournier's Robinson does not relate to the past, but to a future horizon that differs from the world from which he has been shipwrecked. Deleuze's characterization of Robinson in terms of goals and ends does not adequately characterize the ambivalence and creative evolution of Robinson here, but we can note that at least it does capture the way in which Tournier's Robinson does not reassert the values that he has left behind. These deviations in both the sexuality of Robinson, and his understanding of the world, emerge for Deleuze from the relation to the other for Deleuze. At the heart of Deleuze's reading here is a distinction between two different kinds of other: the structure-other (or a priori other) and the concrete other. The a priori other structures our perception, while the concrete other is a specific instantiation of the other.[17] I will turn to how these structure experience in a moment, but for now, we can provide a schematic reading of how these fit in the text. In the first moment of despair, the structure-other is still present, but has no particular concrete instantiation. This leads to enervation, since the lack of any concrete other can only be understood negatively as a privation of what gives meaning to the world. Deleuze sees the second moment as occurring once the concrete other is replaced with an attempt to preserve the a priori other by other means. The incessant accumulation, the water clock and the reinstatement of the economy all play this role, as does Robinson's attempt at 'superhuman filiation'[18] with the island. In the final moment of the narrative, the a priori other disappears in its entirety, such that Friday is ultimately unable to be incorporated into Robinson's world as a concrete other at all:

> What is essential, however, is that Friday does not function at all like a rediscovered Other. It is too late for that, the structure has disappeared. Sometimes he functions as a bizarre object, sometimes as a strange accomplice. Robinson treats him sometimes as a slave and tries to integrate him into the economic order of the island – that is, as a poor simulacrum – and sometimes as the keeper of a new secret which threatens that order – that is, as a mysterious phantasm. Sometimes he treats him almost like an object or an animal, sometimes as if Friday were a 'beyond' with respect to himself, a 'beyond' Friday, his own double or image. Sometimes he treats him as if he were falling short of the Other, sometimes as if he were transcending the Other.[19]

Perception and the other

How does such an account of the other lead to a critique of possibility? To understand this, we need to introduce a more precise specification of the other. Deleuze gives two aspects of the other: first, the other determines the nature of the perceptual field. Second, the other presents a possible world to us. I want to focus here on the first aspect, which ultimately relates the other to the phenomenological account of perception.

The two accounts Deleuze seems to be engaging with are those of Sartre and Merleau-Ponty.[20] Sartre's account of the other seems to influence Tournier's reading of the changes to the psychology of Robinson Crusoe's character, and *Vendredi* can be seen as working through the implications of Sartre's assertion in *Huis Clos* that hell is other people by considering what consciousness is in the absence of others. Ventura in his analysis rightly sees Tournier as here borrowing heavily from Sartre.[21] As Petit[22] has also noted, Tournier's account of Robinson's gaze at Friday which does not objectify seems to suggest that Tournier is critical of Sartre, providing a deliberate counterpoint to Sartre's account of the look. Deleuze suggests that 'Sartre is here the precursor of structuralism, for he is the first to have considered the Other as a real structure or a specificity irreducible to the object and the subject'.[23] Ultimately, Sartre does not develop the concept of an a priori other, since Sartre 'was satisfied with the union of the two determinations [of subject and object], making of the other an object of my gaze, even if he in turn gazes at me and transforms me into an object'.[24] Of course, Sartre would see the absence of an a priori other as a strength of his theory, since for Sartre, all relations with others are ultimately contingent and between particular individuals, and, as it were, necessarily so, since it is the absence of a category of the other that makes possible real relations with other people.[25] As such, it is not clear how successful Deleuze's criticism of Sartre is here.

While Deleuze refers to Sartre in passing, I would suggest that Merleau-Ponty is the main target of his account. Deleuze refers to several of the central mechanisms of Merleau-Ponty's account in his description of the influence of the other on the perceptual field, namely the figure-ground structure,[26] the law of transition between perspectives[27] and depth as the horizon of perception.[28] Each of these is a central aspect of Merleau-Ponty's account of the organization of the perceptual field, and each for Deleuze is determined by the other. For Merleau-Ponty, perceiving involves attending to a figure which presents itself against an indeterminate background. Rather than seeing space as a homogeneous field within which we find a range of determinate objects, space is instead understood perspectivally, as a field of depth from which objects become determinate by pressing themselves forward against a background of indeterminacy. It is this structure of determinacy and indeterminacy that allows us to explain what it is to attend to an object. As Deleuze puts it, 'around each object that I perceive or each idea that I think there is the organization of a marginal world, a mantle or background, where other objects and other ideas may come forth in accordance with laws of transition which regulate the passage from one to another'.[29] Now, Deleuze's claim is that what allows us to shift our attention from one figure to another is the possibility of another perspective, given by another individual: 'And what is *depth*, for me, in accordance with which objects encroach upon one another and hide behind one another, I also live through as being possible width for Others, a width upon which they are aligned and pacified (from the point of view of another depth). In short, the Other assures the margins and transitions in the world.'[30] Our perceptual field, therefore, is full of distractions that point us to the point of view of others.[31] Deleuze's analysis here is curious, and we will return to it in due course, since in effect it elides the distinction between Merleau-Ponty's analysis of the perceptual field and his analysis of what he calls objective thought, a term that Merleau-Ponty himself traces back to Kierkegaard.³²

Here, then, is the source of possibility for Deleuze, in the fact that the perceptual field contains within itself a reference to the other. Insofar as it does so, it includes the perspectives of others, and it is the presence of these perspectives that allows the transition between our own present perspective and future perspectives. Tournier expresses this as follows:

> Each of these men was a possible world, having its own coherence, its values, its sources of attraction and repulsion, its centre of gravity. And with all the differences between them, each of these possible worlds at that moment shared a vision, casual and superficial, of the island of Speranza, which caused them to act in common, and which incidentally contained a shipwrecked man called Robinson and his half-caste servant. For the present this picture occupied their minds, but for each of them it was purely temporary, destined very soon to be returned to the limbo from which it had been briefly plucked by the accident of the *Whitebird's* getting off course. And each of these possible worlds naively proclaimed itself the reality. That was what other people were: the possible obstinately passing for the real.³³

Deleuze's thesis here, therefore, is that the synthesis of the perceptual field is not to be understood as involving intuition and an ego but rather the perceptual field is synthesized by the presence of the structure of an other. It is this other that introduces possibility into the world by generating the background against which the figure emerges. The other therefore represents another possible world, which serves the purpose of constituting both possibility and the individuated perspective of the self.

So what is Deleuze's response to this analysis? Here we get to the heart of Deleuze's project:

> In defining the Other, together with Tournier, as the expression of a possible world, we make of it, on the contrary, the a priori principle of the organization of every perceptual field in accordance with the categories; we make of it the structure which allows this functioning as the 'categorization' of this field. Real dualism then appears with the absence of the Other. But what is happening, in this case, to the perceptual field? Is it structured according to other categories? Or does it, on the contrary, open onto a very special subject matter, allowing us to penetrate into a particular informal realm? This is Robinson's adventure.³⁴

In effect, we have something like the Kantian relation between intuition and the understanding, but here, instead of the understanding schematizing intuition, it is the other that performs this role. Just as for Kant, the subject is implied once the understanding has schematized intuition to allow us to make a distinction between our representations and objects themselves, the other brings in the notion of the subject. Here, however, is Deleuze's question. If it is the other that is responsible for the schematization of the phenomenal field, what happens when the other is no longer present? Deleuze suggests the possibility that the transcendental field could either be schematized in another manner, or it could be the case that with the absence of the other, we could encounter a field that is structured, but not through the imposition of a form. Here, finally, we see the opposition to Kierkegaard in this early work. Kierkegaard rightly opposes the dialectic of Hegel for being merely a representation of motion, but since he opposes it to possibility, which still relies on the categorization of the phenomenal field by the other, we still find ourselves caught within a realm of representation:

> The perverse world is a world in which the category of the necessary has completely replaced that of the possible. This is a strange Spinozism from which 'oxygen' is lacking, to the benefit of a more elementary energy and a more rarefied air (Sky-Necessity). All perversion is an 'Other-cide', and an 'altrucide', and therefore a murder of the possible.[35]

The transcendental field

So what is the structure of the transcendental field prior to the structure of the other, and hence prior to the possible? Here, I want to introduce three aspects of the transcendental field. First, the transcendental field differs from the representations it gives rise to. Second, the transcendental field does not contain the structure of the other or of the self. Finally, the absence of the other leads to a different conception of temporality.

The first aspect is that experience is presented as something that differs in kind from our representations, but which provides a ground for them. Deleuze sets this out clearly by noting the two different forms of organization at play in Tournier's text.[36] First, there is the transcendental field, which is governed by process and operates prior to the other, and second, there is the field of representation, which is the transcendental field schematized by the other. For Deleuze, thinking itself operates through the movement between this transcendental field and our representations of it, even in the case of a thinker of representation such as Descartes.[37] What gives movement to thought is the intensive ground of representations, and so rather than thought involving synthesis on the plane of representation, it involves an oscillation between representation and its intensive grounds. This is one of the reasons Deleuze is critical of the notion of possibility, since rather than operating through a movement between two planes that differ from each other structurally (the transcendental field and representation), possibility does not involve any transposition, since the only difference between the possible and the actual is that the actual exists.[38] As such, it provides a poor basis for an account of the genesis of the new. As Kant puts it, 'the real contains no more than the merely possible. A hundred real thalers do not contain the least coin more than a hundred possible thalers'.[39] The transcendental field itself for Deleuze is empty of possibility, as well as its relation to representation not being structured in terms of it. In *Immanence: A Life*, Deleuze defines this impersonal field as being that which is expressed in the individual, but is itself pre-individual. The 'a' of 'a life' here does not signify generality, but rather the sense that life falls outside of the numerical distinctions that we normally take to individuate our mental lives:

> A life is everywhere, in all the moments that a given living subject goes through and that are measured by given lived objects: an immanent life carrying with it the events or singularities that are merely actualised in subjects and objects.[40]

This brings us to the second aspect: this difference in structure is played out in that the transcendental field contains neither the elements of the subject nor the other. We can see Robinson as being moved back from the economic world of time understood in spatial terms, emphasized by his invention of the water clock, with its focus on calculation and representation, to the pure becoming of the island itself. Robinson on this reading would undergo a process of returning upstream from the individuated representational thought to a field of pure duration. Within such a field of pure duration, the notions of subject and object no longer operate. Robinson would here be moving between an understanding of the world in terms of subjects, objects and others, to a world of impersonal processes. Here, consciousness becomes a mere 'phosphorescence'[41] pervading the field, a description Sartre also gives of Bergson's account of consciousness, though Sartre gives it in a critical spirit.[42] Elsewhere, Deleuze takes up this description as that of the central concept that underlies while giving rise to our representations, the transcendental field:

> What is a transcendental field? It can be distinguished from experience in that it doesn't refer to an object or belong to a subject (empirical representation). It appears therefore as a stream of pure a-subjective consciousness, a pre-

reflexive impersonal consciousness, a qualitative duration of consciousness without a self.[43]

Finally, these Bergsonian references to duration suggest that the transcendental field involves a different relation to time. Rather than the time of the subject, we have for Robinson something radically different. Tournier's account of Robinson, in his move away from selfhood, falls away from the temporal world:

> What has most changed in my life is the passing of time, its speed, and even its direction. Formerly every day, hour and minute leaned in a sense toward the day, hour, and minute that was to follow, and all were drawn into the pattern of the moment, whose transience created a kind of a vacuum.[44]

As Bogue notes, Tournier's account here is very close to the intensive time of Deleuze's reading of the eternal return.[45] Without the measured structures of linear time, Tournier describes time as involving a strange combination of repetition and singularity that accords with Deleuze's sense of the intensive as giving rise to representation while not being reducible to it.

Here we come to the conclusion of Deleuze's account. While Kierkegaard has the same aim as Deleuze in escaping from representation, because he does so in terms of possibility, he is ultimately unable to escape from the structures of representation to arrive at a proper understanding of the transcendental field. We can see something of this relation between possibility and the other in Kierkegaard's analysis of the police agent who is able to infer the concrete other on the basis of the a priori other:

> One who has properly occupied himself with psychology and psychological observation acquires a general human flexibility that enables him at once to construct his example which even though it lacks factual authority nevertheless has an authority of a different kind. The psychological observer ought to be more nimble than a tightrope dancer in order to incline and bend himself to other people and imitate their attitudes, and his silence in the moment of confidence should be seductive and voluptuous, so that what is hidden may find satisfaction in slipping out to chat with itself in the artificially constructed non-observance and silence. Hence he ought also to have a poetic originality in his soul so as to be able at once to create both the totality and the invariable from what in the individual is always partially and variably present. . . . His observation will have the quality of freshness and the interest of actuality if he is prudent enough to control his observations. To that end he imitates in himself every mood, every psychic state that he discovers in another.[46]

We can note that Kierkegaard's entire analysis of moods points to the importance of perspective in analysing a philosophical problem, with the account of pseudonyms likewise pointing to the importance of one's perspective in providing a point of escape from the movement of the dialectic. *The Concept of Anxiety* concludes with a discussion of the different ways in which the eternal and the temporal may be synthesized together that provides a taxonomy of different perspectives, in effect, a potential mapping of the structure of the a priori other.

The phenomenological response

How are we to respond to this account? For the rest of this chapter, I want to pursue two lines of response to Deleuze's account. First, I want to look in more detail at the structuring role of the other to see how coherent Deleuze's account is here. In this respect, I want to look at it in relation to the phenomenological tradition, which seems to be the natural target of Deleuze's detailed account. Second, I want to turn to Kierkegaard directly, and look at what appears to be Kierkegaard's own model of the transcendental field, the pre-dialectical structure of innocence which Kierkegaard sets out in *The Concept of Anxiety*.

Beginning with Merleau-Ponty, we in fact do find that for him the presence of the other leads to a schematization of the world that establishes the subject and the object. The other leads to the idea of the objective world in much the way that Deleuze suggests, where we find ourselves confronted with a crystalline world of objects. This occurs when we recognize that the object that we are considering can be seen from a number of different perspectives simultaneously:

> Each object, then, is the mirror of all the others. When I see the lamp on my table, I attribute to it not merely the qualities that are visible from my location, but also those that the fireplace, the walls, and the table can 'see.' The back of my lamp is merely the face that it 'shows' to the fireplace. Thus, I can see one object insofar as objects form a system or a world, and insofar as each of them arranges the others around itself like spectators of its hidden aspects and as the guarantee of their permanence.[47]

Here, already, we can immediately see a difference from Deleuze's account, however, in that the other that schematizes the object is not an a priori other that has its roots in the human, but merely the possibility of another perspective. Deleuze here illicitly humanizes the notion of perspective in

Merleau-Ponty's ontology.[48] The structure of the perceptual field for Merleau-Ponty is a figure against a background, and so operates in terms of a movement between determinacy and indeterminacy. If we were to move to the position of the fireplace, in Merleau-Ponty's example, then while another aspect of the lamp would become determinate, this would only happen at the expense of our original perspective falling back into indeterminacy. Each perspective, therefore, gives a part of the object, but only on condition of the rest of the object falling into indeterminacy. In this sense, perception is a play of immanence and transcendence. For Merleau-Ponty, it is not the other that schematizes this account of perception, but memory. With memory, we can remove from consideration the fact that each of these perspectives on the object is revealed in time, and see them all as existing simultaneously. In doing so, we leave to one side the idea that a determinate perception can only present itself against an indeterminate background. While perspectives cannot be aggregated since each necessarily operates in terms of determinacy and indeterminacy, when we *represent* perspectives outside of time, we *can* see them as co-existing. This lets us assume a fully determinate object underlying our perspectives, and as soon as one object is considered this way, then, following from Kant's third analogy, all objects become understood as objects in this sense. Once thought has travelled down this path, we have a characterization of the world as objective that indeed involves the other, since it presents a world abstracted from any individual perspective. We should note that what makes this possible, however, is that we have already moved to a position of seeing each perspective on the object as being a representation, such that they can be taken together as aggregates, and the indeterminacies of perception can be ignored. For Merleau-Ponty, therefore, representation gives rise to a problematic conception of the other, but the other does not have to be understood in terms of representation.

Deleuze recognizes that beneath our representations of the world, there may be another mode of organization that escapes the categorization of representation. Deleuze fails to recognize that what is at the heart of our representations for the phenomenologist is the removal of time, which constitutes a space free from perspective, and hence open to an equalization of all others. Here, therefore, perspectivism is the organization that occurs prior to the schematization of objective thought, and with it, and in this prior moment we also find possibility, which occurs not through a *comparison* of perspectives, but through the intention of every perspective towards others. 'My gaze can only be compared with previous acts of seeing or with the acts of seeing accomplished by others through the intermediary of time and language.'[49] The subject here is secondary, not to the other, but to perception itself. By seeing representation as independent of our relationship with the other, rather than the other determining us to see the world in terms of representation, Merleau-Ponty opens up the possibility of a distinction between authentic relations with others, and inauthentic relations with others mediated by objective thought. 'In the experience of dialogue, a common ground is constituted between me and another; my thought and his form a single fabric, my words and those of my interlocutor are called forth by the state of the discussion and are inserted into a shared operation of which neither of us is the creator.'[50] Dialogue sets out clearly the problem with Deleuze's account here. The analysis of transition in terms of the other assumes that all perspectives are given all at once, effectively reducing them to representations. Here, for Merleau-Ponty, the dialogue operates neither in terms of subject nor other, and is generative rather than simply aggregative. Such an account is not possible for Deleuze, for whom 'discussion has no place in the work of philosophy. The phrase "let's discuss it" is an act of terror.'[51] The failure of Deleuze's analysis of the other as a site of representation in this regard should give us pause in relation to Kierkegaard. When Merleau-Ponty sets out his distinction between objective thought and perspectival perception, he cites Kierkegaard, seeing in Kierkegaard's search for a relation to the world prior to dialectic a precursor of his own efforts to understand the world prior to representation. Similarly, just as perspectives for Merleau-Ponty lack the commensurability that they would require for Deleuze's account of the structuring role of the other to be coherent, so the different perspectives for Kierkegaard are of necessity incommensurable. It is this incommensurability that disrupts the unifying role of the other, and forces Kierkegaard's use of indirect communication.[52]

The Kierkegaardian response

In this final section, I want to turn to Kierkegaard's work directly, and to the notions of innocence and anxiety in his thought. The eponymous Robinson Crusoe understands his exile on the island in terms of his original sin of disregarding the will of his father,[53] while Tournier's Robinson can be seen as reversing this direction, with Robinson experiencing something like a return to innocence in the island. I want to conclude this chapter by exploring this notion of innocence, and the place it occupies in Kierkegaard's thought.

Tournier himself describes Robinson's state on the island as a 'moment of innocence'.[54] What characteristics does this innocence hold? To begin with, for

Deleuze, a world of innocence does not contain the structure of the other. This does not mean that there cannot be others in such a world (such as Friday), but rather, that such others do not conform to the structure of the a priori other. As we have seen, this in turn means that there is no structure of the possible in such a world. In turn, without the structure of the possible, I am unable to imagine a world which differs from the one I occupy, and hence to distinguish my self from the world. 'Before the appearance of the Other, there was, for example, a reassuring world from which my consciousness could not be distinguished. The Other then makes its appearance, expressing the possibility of a frightening world which cannot be developed without the one preceding it passing away.'[55] The key claim here is that without the organization of the other, we do not merely have an empty immediacy, but rather a new mode of structure opened up by the removal of the other. Here, we have something like pure intuition. For Tournier, therefore, what Deleuze calls the transcendental field is a state of innocence that Robinson returns to once freed from the influence of the other. Here we can turn to Kierkegaard, who also provides a complex discussion of the notion of innocence in relation to Adam and sin, and it is here that his 'concept' of anxiety is introduced. In this section, I want to turn to Kierkegaard's concept of innocence, since there are substantial affinities between Kierkegaard's account and Deleuze's of the transcendental field.

Kierkegaard's own account of innocence emerges in his analysis of original sin. Kierkegaard is keen to explore the ambiguous situation of Adam prior to the fall, who is in a state of innocence, yet is still responsible for the sin he commits. Since the concepts of good and evil do not come into existence until Adam eats the fruit of the tree of knowledge, he cannot understand the act as evil. Kierkegaard begins by claiming that we cannot understand sinfulness as 'an epidemic that spreads like cowpox',[56] and so Adam's move from innocence to sin needs to be understood in terms of a transition that is neither arbitrary nor fully determined. Kierkegaard describes Adam as in a state of anxiety, which he characterizes as 'entangled freedom, where freedom is not free in itself but entangled, not by necessity, but in itself'.[57] Kierkegaard's claim will be that the movement from innocence to sin through anxiety is a movement in each individual's life, and that anxiety is in fact ever present in the processes of both sin and redemption. Now, it would be tempting to see the movement from innocence to sin as the actualization of a possibility, but in fact, Kierkegaard is clear that anxiety is not possibility but 'the possibility of possibility'.[58] What is important here is that the movement from innocence to sin is not a movement within one plane of organization, but the constitution of another way of organizing the world (the form of knowledge).

While possibility presupposes the actual object as a model, as Bergson argues, anxiety has no object, and so fits badly with the kind of account of possibility Deleuze criticizes, and in his early lectures on grounding, Deleuze himself seems to recognize this movement in Kierkegaard.[59] Rather, just as Deleuze sees thinking as moving between representation and the transcendental field, anxiety operates between the planes of innocence and knowledge. Let us return now to the three characteristics of the transcendental field that we outlined above.

First, as with Deleuze, we have a genetic account here. The innocence of Adam is one that has a structure different in kind from that of one's represented world. For Hegel, innocence is equated with immediacy, but as we know from the *Science of Logic*, immediacy for Hegel dialectically transitions into mediacy, since without mediation, we cannot attribute any determinations to the object of our enquiry, and so it remains indistinguishable from its opposite. As Kierkegaard notes, Hegel's error is to represent innocence within logic according to the category of the immediate. While the immediate turns into the mediate through its own immanent development, as Kierkegaard argues, we cannot understand the loss of innocence of Adam as involving sin if guilt were immanent to his innocence. Innocence cannot be equated with immediacy, and more than this, innocence escapes any dialectical qualification. In fact, more deeply, Kierkegaard notes that innocence, qualified as ignorance, can only be understood in categorial terms by relating it to knowledge. Innocence therefore has a double nature, as a category within the dialectic, but also as a wild state that is prior to its sedimentation into the oppositional categories of Hegel's logic.[60] In its wild state, innocence is not a simple immediacy, and 'only a prosaic stupidity maintains that [innocence] is a disorganization'.[61] As such, the structure of innocence differs in kind and is generative of, the structure of knowledge, in a manner which foreshadows Deleuze's account of the transcendental field.

Second, just as for Deleuze, in Adam's innocence, he exists prior to the formation of the self, and prior to the object. Prior to the fall Adam is outside of all dialectical categories, and, as with Robinson, is unable to use such categories themselves: 'here there is language, though in an imperfect way similar to that of children who learn by identifying animals on an ABC board'.[62] Moreover, there is no subject or object in the state of innocence, just as they are absent from the transcendental field. Within the stage of innocence, neither of these categories have yet to have emerged. Spirit is 'dreaming':

> the real 'self' is posited only by the qualitative leap. In the prior state there can be no question about it. Therefore, when sin is explained by selfishness, one

becomes entangled in indistinctness, because, on the contrary, it is by sin and in sin that selfishness comes into being. If selfishness is supposed to have been the occasion for Adam's sin, the, explanation becomes a game in which the interpreter finds what he himself first has hidden.[63]

Finally, we can note that in innocence, there is no temporality for Adam, but purely a stream of duration. It is only with the introduction of the moment that we can clearly divide time into past, present and future. Prior to this, time is purely infinite succession, but such a succession that, as with Bergson's duration, cannot be reduced to a discrete multiplicity of moments:

> If in the infinite succession of time a foothold could be found, i.e., a present, which was the dividing point, the division would be quite correct. However, precisely because every moment, as well as the sum of the moments, is a process (a passing by), no moment is a present, and accordingly there is in time neither present, nor past, nor future. If it is claimed that this division can be maintained, it is because the moment is spatialized, but thereby the infinite succession comes to a halt, it is because representation is introduced that allows time to be represented instead of being thought.[64]

As such, we find in Kierkegaard not the structure of possibility that we find in Deleuze's critique of the other but something radically different that operates across different planes of structure, rather than simply within the field of representation. Perhaps we could say here that Deleuze is simply too quick to assimilate all forms of possibility to those engaged with by Bergson. In the conclusion, I want to draw out some of the implications of these limitations to Deleuze's account.

Conclusion

So we find in Kierkegaard's account of innocence something like the 'moment of innocence' that is present in Tournier, and which mirrors Deleuze's own transcendental field. In this sense, we could view Deleuze's own philosophy as an account of the fall, with the movement from pure difference to difference as diversity, where, just as for Kierkegaard, Adam's fall is characterized by a transition to the categorial forms of language, and we find the emergence of the subject in the actualized realm of representation. Deleuze cites with approval in this regard Schelling's theory of potentials, which Schelling himself understood to be understood in terms of the myth of the fall.[65] The key differences between

Kierkegaard and Deleuze relate to the transition between innocence and representation. As Tournier shows, the path for Deleuze to innocence is one that can occur through a deliberate project of stepping back from a site of representation. The aim is a methodological solipsism.[66] As well as Robinson, we can see models in Artaud's poetry and formulation of the body without organs, and the 'crack-up' of Fitzgerald or Lowry. For Kierkegaard, innocence is something that cannot be regained. Once we are in a state of knowledge, we cannot even conceive of innocence except as already understood in categorial terms.

Ironically, this emphasis of Deleuze's on solipsism as the basis for philosophy falls away when we move beyond what we might call his juvenilia. While *Difference and Repetition* attempts to develop an imageless thought, Deleuze's later works with Guattari instead aim to replace the arborescent image of thought with the model of the rhizome. Here, as Bogue notes, Kierkegaard's analysis of the possible receives a more positive treatment, as Kierkegaard's thought is seen as one that develops novel ways of living, even if it does so in relation to a moment of transcendence. Here, a move from depths to relations allows a movement beyond the solipsism of Deleuze's early work and opens up the possibility of projects such as Deleuze's later collaboration with Guattari that rely on a new relation to the other, rather than its annihilation. Deleuze finds himself in agreement with Kierkegaard, writing now, with Guattari, that philosophy 'invents modes of existence or possibilities of life'.[67]

Notes

1. I am indebted to Jeff Bell and David Ventura for their helpful comments on an earlier draft of this piece.
   William James, 'On Some Hegelisms', in *The Will to Believe and Other Essays in Popular Philosophy* (London: Longmans Green and Co., 1912), 292.
2. Gilles Deleuze, *Cinema 1*, trans. Hugh Tomlinson and Barbara Habberjam (London: Athlone Press, 1986), 233. In the essay on Tournier, Deleuze simply gives the quotation (Gilles Deleuze, *The Logic of Sense*, trans. Mark Lester with Charles Stivale, ed. Constantine Boundas (London: Athlone, 1990), 318). The story appears in *Cinema 1*. There is a mistranslation in the English edition that attributes the quotation to *The Concept of Anxiety* rather than *The Sickness Unto Death* (*Traité du désespoir*) as it is in the original French.
3. Ronald Bogue, 'The Art of the Possible', *Revue internationale de philosophie* 3, no. 241 (2007): 273–86, suggests the quote may be a mistranscription of the following passage from *The Sickness Unto Death*: 'but when someone wants to despair, then the word is:

Get possibility, get possibility. . . . A possibility – then the person in despair breathes again, he revives again, for without possibility a person seems unable to breathe' (Søren Kierkegaard, *The Sickness Unto Death*, trans. Howard V. Hong and Edna H. Hong (Princeton, NJ: Princeton University Press, 1980), 38–9). This is certainly plausible, though references to possibility run throughout Kierkegaard's work.
4   James, 'On Some Hegelisms', 279.
5   Maurice Merleau-Ponty, *Phenomenology of Perception*, trans. Donald A. Landes (London: Routledge, 2012), 342.
6   Søren Kierkegaard, *The Concept of Anxiety*, trans. and ed. Reidar Thomte with Albert B. Anderson (Princeton, NJ: Princeton University Press, 1980), 81.
7   Ibid., 81–2.
8   G. W. F. Hegel, *Hegel's Philosophy of Nature*, ed. and trans. M. J. Petry (London: Allen and Unwin Ltd, 1970), §250.
9   Gilles Deleuze, *Difference and Repetition*, trans. Paul Patton (London: Athlone, 1994), xix.
10 Deleuze, *The Logic of Sense*, 318.
11 Michel Tournier, *Friday*, trans. Norman Denny (Baltimore: Johns Hopkins University Press, 1997), 40.
12 Ibid., 40.
13 Ibid., 172.
14 Ibid., 90.
15 Tournier quoted in Susan Petit, *Michel Tournier's Metaphysical Fictions* (Philadelphia: John Benjamins Publishing Company, 1991), 18.
16 Deleuze, *Logic of Sense*, 303.
17 Ibid., 313.
18 Ibid., 315.
19 Ibid., 316.
20 Constantin V. Boundas, 'Foreclosure of the Other: From Sartre to Deleuze', *Journal of the British Society for Phenomenology* 24 (1993):1, 32–43, notes the importance of Merleau-Ponty and Sartre here, though focuses on Sartre. His article provides a more sympathetic reading of Deleuze's critique of Sartre than the one offered here.
21 David Ventura, 'The Intensive Other: Deleuze and Levinas on the Ethical Status of the Other', *The Southern Journal of Philosophy* 58, no. 2 (2020): 329–30.
22 Petit, *Michel Tournier's Metaphysical Fictions*, 17.
23 Deleuze, *Logic of Sense*, 366.
24 Ibid., 307.
25 C.f. Jean-Paul Sartre, *Being and Nothingness*, trans. Hazel E. Barnes (New York: Pocket Books, 1978), 250: 'Human-reality remains alone because the other's existence has the nature of a contingent and irreducible fact. We encounter the Other; we do not constitute him'.

26 Deleuze, *Logic of Sense*, 318.
27 Ibid., 305.
28 Ibid.
29 Ibid.
30 Ibid.
31 '[F]or all of us the presence of other people is a powerful element of distraction, not only because they constantly break into our train of thought, but because the mere possibility of their doing so illumines a world of matters situated at the edge of our consciousness but capable of any moment of becoming its centre' (Tournier, *Friday*, 38 quoted in Deleuze, *Logic of Sense*, 305).
32 C.f. Merleau-Ponty, *Phenomenology of Perception*, 74.
33 Deleuze, *Logic of Sense*, 308.
34 Ibid., 309.
35 Ibid., 320.
36 'It will be noted that the earth and air act less as particular elements than as two complete and opposed figures, each one, for its part, gathering the four elements. The earth, however, holds and subsumes them, contains them within the depth of bodies, whereas the sky, with the light and the sun, sets them in a free and pure state, delivered from their limits, in order to form cosmic surface energy – being one and yet characteristic of each element. There is therefore a terrestrial fire, water, air, and earth, but there is also an aerial or celestial earth, water, fire, and air' (Deleuze, *Logic of Sense*, 302). The 'figures' here correspond to the two multiplicities Deleuze discusses throughout his work, and principally in his work on Bergson. These figures would map on to the discrete multiplicity (the earth), which understands the world in terms of discrete bodies occupying a homogeneous space, and the confused multiplicity (sky), which for Bergson is determined by duration, seeing the world in terms of process and change independent of substances undergoing those changes. For Bergson, discrete and confused multiplicities are both ways of understanding the structure of the world, with the discrete multiplicity being a well-founded illusion that maps onto a world of duration in order to allow us to engage with it, while at the same time falsifying its nature.
37 Deleuze takes Descartes's focus on the 'everyman' to be a paradigmatic example of a philosophy founded on the perspective of the other, since it ignores the singularity of the individual. C.f. Deleuze, *Difference and Repetition*, 129–34.
38 Cf. Deleuze, *Difference and Repetition*, 211–14. Bergson's original critique of the notion of possibility is found in Henri Bergson, 'The Possible and the Real', in *The Creative Mind*, trans. Mabelle L. Andison (New York: Philosophical Library, 1946).
39 Immanuel Kant, *The Critique of Pure Reason*, trans. Norman Kemp Smith (London: Macmillan and Co. Ltd, 1929), A599 / B627.
40 Gilles Deleuze, 'Immanence: A Life', in *Pure Immanence: Essays on a Life*, trans. Anne Boyman (New York: Zone Books, 2001), 29.

41 Deleuze, *Logic of Sense*, 312.
42 Deleuze here seems to be deliberately inverting Sartre's criticism of Bergson: 'There is no non-conscious for Bergson; there is only consciousness in ignorance of itself. There is no opacity that is opposed to light and receives it, constituting thus an illuminated object. There is pure light, phosphorescence, without illuminated material, though this pure light, everywhere diffused, only becomes occurrent by being reflected on certain surfaces that serve at the same time as screens for the other luminous zones. There is a sort of inversion of the classical comparison: instead of consciousness being a light that goes from the subject to the thing, it is a luminosity that goes from the thing to the subject' (Jean-Paul Sartre, *The Imagination*, trans. Kenneth Williford and David Rudrauf) (London: Routledge, 2012, 42).
43 Deleuze, 'Immanence: A Life', 25.
44 Tournier, *Friday*, 203.
45 Ronald Bogue, 'Speranza, the Wandering Island', *Deleuze Studies* 3, no.1 (2009): 125.
46 Kierkegaard, *Concept of Anxiety*, 54–5.
47 Merleau-Ponty, *Phenomenology of Perception*, 71.
48 Merleau-Ponty makes this point that the other is not to be reduced to the human most explicitly in *Eye and Mind*: 'Inevitably the roles between him and the visible are reversed. That is why so many painters have said that things look at them. As André Marchand says, after Klee: 'In a forest, I have felt many times over that it was not I who looked at the forest. Some days I felt that the trees were looking at me, were speaking to me. . . . I was there, listening. . . . I think that the painter must be penetrated by the universe and not want to penetrate it. . . . I expect to be inwardly submerged, buried. Perhaps I paint to break out' (Maurice Merleau-Ponty, 'Eye and Mind', in *Primacy of Perception*, ed. James M. Edie (Indianapolis: Northwestern University Press, 1964), 167.).
49 Merleau-Ponty, *Phenomenology of Perception*, 72.
50 Ibid., 370.
51 Gilles Deleuze, 'We Invented the ritornello', in *Two Regimes of Madness*, trans. Ames Hodges and Mike Taormina (London: MIT Press, 2006), 380. Deleuze is clear in his early work that the position of the philosopher should be solipsistic. He contrasts this with Descartes's method, where the *cogito* rests on the assumption that 'everybody is supposed to know implicitly what it means to think' (Deleuze, *Difference and Repetition*, 131). As such, Descartes operates with concepts that are already defined in terms of the other. Ultimately, the philosophical method of Descartes presupposes, for Deleuze, the pre-philosophical field of representation determined by the other: 'In this sense, conceptual philosophical thought has as its implicit presupposition a pre-philosophical and natural Image of thought, borrowed from the pure element of common sense' (Deleuze, *Difference and Repetition*, 131). In his later work, Deleuze does introduce a place for dialogue, but such

dialogue involves a violent rejection of normal forms of discourse: 'Conversation is something else entirely. We need conversation. But the lightest conversation is a great schizophrenic experiment happening between two individuals with common resources and a taste for ellipses and short-hand expressions' (Deleuze, 'We Invented the ritornello', 380).

52 It hardly needs to be mentioned that the silence of Kierkegaard's Abraham as a necessary incongruity with others fits poorly with Tournier's example of the shared world of the sailors on the *Whitebird*.

53 'I have been in all my Circumstances a Memento to those who are touched with the general Plague of Mankind, whence, for ought I know, one half of their Miseries flow; I mean, that of not being satisfy'd with the Station wherein God and Nature has plac'd them; for not to look back upon my primitive Condition . . . and the excellent Advice of my Father, the Opposition to which, was, as I may call it, my ORIGINAL SIN; my subsequent Mistakes of the same Kind had been the Means of my coming into this miserable Condition' (Daniel Defoe, *Robinson Crusoe* (Oxford: Oxford University Press, 2007), 164).

54 Tournier, *Friday*, 205. Robinson explicitly relates this to the story of Adam, describing it as a 'return to the lost innocence which all men secretly mourn' (Tournier, *Friday*, 107).

55 Deleuze, *Logic of Sense*, 310.

56 Kierkegaard, *Concept of Anxiety*, 38.

57 Ibid., 49.

58 Ibid., 42.

59 In his early lectures on grounding, Deleuze writes: 'Kierkegaard's theme will be: we can never conclude sin from sinfulness. It also implies a qualitative leap. Sin is the brute apparition of a new quality. Sin must then be thought and related to anxiety, which is the relation of consciousness with the absolutely different' (Gilles Deleuze, *What Is Grounding?* trans. Arjen Kleinherenbrink (Grand Rapids: &&& Publishing, 2015), 70).

60 Innocence here has a structure similar to writing for Derrida where we can distinguish between a conception of innocence (immediacy) as opposed to guilt (mediacy), but also a primary account of innocence which is prior to incorporation into a structure of categorial opposition.

61 Kierkegaard, *Concept of Anxiety*, 42.

62 Ibid., 46.

63 Ibid., 79.

64 Ibid., 85.

65 See Deleuze, *Difference and Repetition*, 190–1 for his approving reading of Schelling on potentiality. Vincent A. McCarthy, 'Schelling and Kierkegaard on Freedom and Fall', in *International Kierkegaard Commentary: The Concept of Anxiety*, ed. Robert

L. Perkins (Macon, GA: Mercer University Press), 1985), sets out Schelling's reading of the Fall in terms of this account.
66 C.f., for instance, Deleuze, *Difference and Repetition*, 282: 'As a result, in order to rediscover the individuating factors as they are in the intensive series along with the pre-individual singularities as they are in the Idea, this path must be followed in reverse so that, departing from the subjects which give effect to the Other-structure, we return as far as this structure in itself, thus apprehending the Other as No-one, then continue further, following the bend in sufficient reason until we reach those regions where the Other-structure no longer functions, far from the objects and subjects that it conditions, where singularities are free to be deployed or distributed within pure Ideas, and individuating factors to be distributed in pure intensity. In this sense, it is indeed true that the thinker is necessarily solitary and solipsistic'.
67 Gilles Deleuze and Félix Guattari, *What Is Philosophy?* trans. Hugh Tomlinson and Graham Burchell (New York: Columbia University Press, 1994), 72.

III

Possibility and freedom

6

On being educated for the possibility by *The Concept of Anxiety*

Jakub Marek

This chapter aims to interpret Kierkegaard's pseudonymous *The Concept of Anxiety* as a text whose purpose is *education for possibility*. In other words, Vigilius Haufniensis is intended to show how the individual human being can discover and relate to possibility. But what is the possibility in question? And, what is the nature of the education that reveals this possibility?

The answer to the first question is both extremely simple and extremely difficult. The possibility at stake is the restoration of man's relationship to God. In other words, this possibility is Christianity, or rather Jesus Christ as the one who offers humanity grace and gives the possibility of salvation. The sense of the possibility that Kierkegaard is after, thus formulated in essence theologically, is infinitely more difficult to express ontologically. What is this possibility? I admit that I cannot satisfactorily address the question of the ontological sense of possibility in Kierkegaard's work in this short text. However, I will consider this problem at least in a small way.

Education for possibility is therefore a kind of education for Christianity. Admittedly, this is how the entirety of Kierkegaard's work can be framed, especially the first phase of his work as defined by the publication of *Either/Or* and the *Concluding Unscientific Postscript*. Kierkegaard himself, however, does not speak of education, but of that communicative strategy which he calls indirect communication, or links the path to Christianity with the genre of the *Upbuilding Discourses*.

I will therefore proceed as follows: in the first part I will try to conceptually address the problem of possibility and education in *The Concept of Anxiety*. The key message here will be that education takes on the shape of educative anxiety and that freedom is at the heart of the effect that education is supposed to have. In the second step, I will tackle the genre and formal specificity of *The Concept of Anxiety*, where I should first of all distinguish it from the genre of the *Upbuilding Discourses*, and, at the same time, delineate *The Concept of Anxiety* against Kierkegaard's pseudonymous (or 'aesthetic') writings. However, the real result of the analysis in the second part will be the thesis that Kierkegaard's *The Concept of Anxiety* investigates the ways in which one conceals or represses one's own consciousness of sinfulness. This 'phenomenology of sinful consciousness' will be related in the third part of this chapter to its precursor, which is Hegel's *Phenomenology of Spirit*. I will try to clearly demonstrate that the similarity between Hegel's and Kierkegaard's text is profound, and the point of contact is precisely the notion of education. In both, it is the movement of consciousness, which both authors understand as education. In the concluding fourth part I will develop a more sustained interpretation of the notion of education as belonging, together with the upbuilding, to what Kierkegaard calls a dialectic of the single individual. I will provide a preliminary analysis of the radical view of the possibility in Kierkegaard and finally, in a postscriptum, point out the specific genre of *The Concept of Anxiety*: deliberation.

The Concept of Anxiety and the project of educating for possibility

What follows can be understood as a commentary on one curious statement from *The Concept of Anxiety*: '[A]nxiety is freedom's actuality [*Virkelighed*] as the possibility [*Mulighed*] of possibility [*Muligheden*].'[1] The book itself, written under the pseudonym of Vigilius Haufniensis, investigates the idea of the original sin, for which Haufniensis discovers the necessary subjective condition in anxiety. Without anxiety, Adam could not have sinned. It is anxiety which provides freedom's actuality. Adam, through anxiety, sins of his own accord, freely, so that he can also be held accountable. Adam, however, uses the actuality of freedom *to sin*. His ignorance cannot be taken for an excuse; this is not a failure to understand what is right. Adam is not a Socratic character who only commits transgressions out of ignorance.[2] Adam chose to sin and chose freely.

In the final chapter, Haufniensis explicitly connects possibility, freedom and anxiety, and brings them together under a new point of view: education. 'Anxiety is freedom's possibility, and only such anxiety is through faith absolutely educative [*dannende*], because it consumes all finite ends and discovers all their deceptiveness.'[3] What is this absolute education of anxiety? A few more pages later Haufniensis comments on the lightness of actuality and heaviness of possibility. It is possibility which educates absolutely inasmuch as it deprives finitude and finite reasons of persuasiveness. 'Only in this way can possibility be educative', writes Haufniensis.[4] But, let me ask again: What is the necessary connection between anxiety, possibility and freedom? How exactly are anxiety and possibility educative?

In the first chapter of *The Concept of Anxiety*, Haufniensis connected freedom, possibility and anxiety in the narrative of Adam's fall. By sinning, Adam fell from grace and, to put it differently, deprived himself of *the possibility*. He no longer has the possibility of grace, of eternal blessedness, his existence is – after the fall – without possibility. I wish to argue that looking at *The Concept of Anxiety* from this point of view, the book takes the form of an investigation into exactly the possibility of having *the* possibility (*Muligheden*).

The category of possibility can be seen as a true ontological centrepiece of Kierkegaard's work. I will, in what follows, try to show that Kierkegaard understands possibility radically. His understanding of possibility clearly differs from two common senses associated with possibility in the context of his works:

First, Kierkegaard discusses the Romantic idea of self-creation through poetic construction, the existence of the Romantic poet. The existence of such poet is the continuous desire for a new shape, new form, new content, it is the mirage of infinite possibilities – the sum of all possibilities (*Indbegreb af al Mulighed*)[5] at the poet's disposal.[6] This poetic, aesthetic notion of possibility is primarily burdened by fantasy and remains a mere chimera.

Nor does Kierkegaard understand possibility in the sense in which Aristotle relates possibility (*dynamis*) to its realization (*energeia*). In existence, the individual does not realize innate possibilities. In the eschatological framework of hereditary sin man has lost such innate possibility.

The possibility at stake in *The Concept of Anxiety* has the radicality of the incommensurable, of the new, the paradoxical, the absurd. Such radical notion of possibility is then heard in connection with the equally radical notion of freedom: freedom's actuality is the possibility (*Mulighed*) of possibility (*Muligheden*). Possibility here appears in apparent duplication. How are we to understand the unusual formulation: 'the possibility [*Mulighed*] of possibility [*Muligheden*]'?

The duplication is only an apparent one: in the same sentence, Kierkegaard uses the notion of possibility in a double sense. The first possibility (*Mulighed*) is a possibility in the ordinary sense of 'that which can happen'. However, the second time the word possibility is used with a definite article (*Muligheden*), it is a radical possibility that resembles the first only as a homonym. This second possibility – *the* possibility – is what Kierkegaard's work as a whole works towards. This is *the* possibility which Adam had lost. This is *the* possibility which makes human existence ontologically different from the mere being of, say, a potato.[7]

Haufniensis is very peculiar about his choice of words. The actuality of freedom constitutes [a] possibility for [the] possibility. In my reading, Haufniensis distinguishes the first possibility as that which can be achieved by the individual herself, but the second, *the* possibility, is beyond the sphere of human agency. Kierkegaard's later pseudonym, Anti-Climacus, develops a twofold view of the individual's relationship to God. The first stage is what he calls 'becoming a spirit' and it is the preliminary, necessary condition of the second stage. Here, in the second stage, it is Christ 'who from on high will draw all to himself'.[8] This drawing to himself represents *the* possibility, which lies beyond the humanly possible.[9]

In all simplicity, it can then be argued that the fifth chapter of *The Concept of Anxiety* provides the focus and perspective for the entire book, and that it gives a clear answer to the question of what the intention or purpose of the text is in the first place. *The Concept of Anxiety* identifies anxiety as that friendly power which educates the individual to true, radical possibility and thereby, in other words, educates, prepares and forms him for the freedom which is the possibility for [the] possibility itself.

A phenomenology of sinful consciousness

The Concept of Anxiety is undoubtedly an unusual literary work – and that even for Kierkegaard's standards. First, it has been well documented that the pseudonym Vigilius Haufniensis replaced Kierkegaard's own name as an afterthought.[10] Kierkegaard had originally thought of printing *The Concept of Anxiety* under his own name, but then changed his mind.[11] This last-minute alteration might seem like a superficial change, but in the overall structure of Kierkegaard's so-called first authorship (*Either/or* through *The Concluding Unscientific Postscript*), the difference between publishing under his own name or under a pseudonym has a crucial meaning.[12] The puzzling idea being that the only works Kierkegaard published under his own name were the upbuilding discourses. But then, by tearing the front page of the clean draft of the manuscript in half and writing the new author in ink, Kierkegaard changed *The Concept of Anxiety* from a work published under his own name into a pseudonymous one. The two obvious possible interpretations are: perhaps Kierkegaard deviated from the overall structure of his work and *The Concept of Anxiety* constitutes a different genre, one similar to his dissertation *On the Concept of Irony*. This theory could be supported by the fact that Kierkegaard originally did call his book *On the Concept of Anxiety*.[13] The second possible interpretation takes the structure of Kierkegaard's authorship seriously and wonders: could it be that *The Concept of Anxiety* had originally been meant to belong with the upbuilding literature?[14]

The first possibility would posit *(On) The Concept of Anxiety* outside of Kierkegaard's authorship, making it a stand-alone scientific work (i.e. similar to the status of *On the Concept of Irony*). This is still a plausible hypothesis, but the strongest argument against such reading lies in the consistency and coherence Kierkegaard clearly strived for. The similarity to *On the Concept of Irony* underscores another issue with this reading: Why not use his own name? His changing of the title (striking out the 'On') indicates that Kierkegaard wanted to avoid the confusing position of his book in between the pseudonymous and upbuilding works.

The second hypothesis struggles against different obstacles: *The Concept of Anxiety* clearly represents a different style or authorial strategy than the upbuilding discourses published parallel with pseudonymous works. In Johannes Climacus's words, it is 'somewhat didactic' (*lidt docerende*), perhaps because its task consists of a 'communication of knowledge' that takes place 'before a transition could be made to inward deepening [*Inderliggjørelse*]'.[15] In other words, Climacus later describes *The Concept of Anxiety* as an almost academic, explanatory and analytical text. This being the case, according to Climacus, the little book by Haufniensis nonetheless belongs into the whole of the authorship. Climacus ascribes it the function of a stepping stone on the overall journey towards becoming a Christian. Along this journey, Climacus explains, one needs to have necessary information, be educated in a way. It is in this sense that the role of *The Concept of Anxiety* could remind one of an informational leaflet, or of an informed consent form to be signed before the operation (the 'inward deepening') begins.

Formal and structural aspects aside – What does *The Concept of Anxiety* accomplish? What is its scope, goal and subject matter? Is it, in this sense, upbuilding, edifying (*opbyggelig*)? Vigilius Haufniensis does not seem to 'edify' his reader inasmuch as the 'essence and scope [of edification] is to elevate and console'.[16] Yet such definition of the upbuilding (or edifying) seems to be reductive and superficial. It is true that Haufniensis appears to be eminently interested in anxiety rather than in elevating or consoling his readers. But what effect does anxiety have? Does it not, after all, provide consolation of sorts?: '[H]e who passes through the anxiety of the possible is educated to have no anxiety, not because he can escape the terrible things of life but because these always become weak by comparison with those of possibility.'[17] The final chapter of *The Concept of Anxiety* very explicitly formulates the task of learning anxiety in the right way as having learned the ultimate,[18] which is, in a way, a consolation.

But there is more to anxiety than only consolation: anxiety is also terrifying (*forfærdelig*), terrifying in the sense of the upbuilding: 'What exactly is the upbuilding? The first answer to this', writes Kierkegaard in the *Christian Discourses*, 'is what the upbuilding is at first: it is the *terrifying*'.[19] It would seem that by design *The Concept of Anxiety* represents the upbuilding qualities of both being terrifying as well as consolatory: one needs to learn anxiety, allow anxiety to 'ransack everything' [*ransager Alt*],[20] learn to love it as a serving spirit.

The connection to the upbuilding literature seems to exist, yet at the same time the genre and literary style of *The Concept of Anxiety* radically deviates from the upbuilding discourses. The latter have a clear structure including a dedication to Kierkegaard's father and an 'invocation' of the missing 'single individual', whom the discourses seek to find. In all of the stylistic aspects the difference between *The Concept of Anxiety* and the upbuilding discourses could not have been greater.

What then are we to make of *The Concept of Anxiety*? How does it relate to the upbuilding discourses and what place does it have among the pseudonymous production?[21] In order to pursue the question further, we turn to the last chapter of Haufniensis's work. Here, too, Kierkegaard deviated from his earlier plan and, after having written the first four chapters and being done with his book, he later decided to add a final chapter.[22] And it is an exceptionally interesting piece.

In Chapter V, titled 'Anxiety as Saving through Faith', Haufniensis employs a new concept of anxiety. Upon close reading one realizes that in Chapter V Haufniensis suddenly identifies anxiety with – *education* (*Dannelse*).[23] For Haufniensis, education invokes 'formation' or, rather, transformation of the individual. Very much like in the Grimms's fairy tale, one needs to learn fear – albeit not fear as fear of something concrete and external, but *anxiety* which one produces oneself. Learning how to 'be anxious in the right way' is 'the ultimate', Haufniensis ascribes to anxiety the absolute formative role – '[a]nxiety is freedom's possibility, and only such anxiety is through faith absolutely educative [. . .]'.[24]

This should in fact strike us as unusual. Not only does Haufniensis shy away from the word education (*Dannelse*) in the previous four chapters of the book,[25] but so does Kierkegaard the author shy away from the concept of education in the whole of his production. Kierkegaard's continuous critique aims at 'those educated' (*Dannede*), or cultivated. Education and culture seem to be impediments and obstacles of Christianity,[26] or in Climacus's words, 'as understanding and culture and refinement (*Dannelse*) increase, sustaining the passion of faith becomes more difficult'.[27] Kierkegaard advocates against this refinement or cultured education, against this apparent cultural *Philisterei*. He also strongly dislikes the notion of education as drill, which is nothing more than 'a mask which hides the inner emptiness and closes itself off from the human element'.[28]

Haufniensis understands anxiety's education differently. The Danish word *Dannelse* is a loan from German, a translation of the word *Bildung*.[29] More than that: it is a loan of the concept of education. *Bildung* is formative education, 'personal formation or self-cultivation',[30] cultivation in the sense of shaping, building oneself. However, this notion of education is burdened by the Romantic tradition of poetic production. Education here relates to the individuality of the educated as a work of art, which he or she freely constructs and completes.

However, education in *The Concept of Anxiety* hardly resembles poetic production and we have already discussed Kierkegaard's disdain for this Romantic idea; education rather takes the form of 'original experience'. To be educated means to experience something originally, as in '[a] maidservant genuinely in love is essentially cultured [dannet]',[31] which is to say that education relates to 'primitive' experience.[32] This conception of education taken from the *Literary Review* strongly resonates with the view of Haufniensis.

We have already discussed that *The Concept of Anxiety* investigates the original sin in connection with anxiety as its subjective condition. Haufniensis presents his anthropological view that for every later individual the principal situation – the human condition – remains the same. Just like Adam, later individuals sin in anxiety. The principal difference between Adam and the later generations is hereditary sin, understood by Haufniensis as a 'more' of anxiety. In my interpretation, Haufniensis suggests that later individuals live in a state of repression and denial of their sinfulness.

I wouldn't hesitate to understand *The Concept of Anxiety* as a study of man's relationship to sin and its transformations. The goal is to re-acquire a 'primitive relationship to sin'.[33] This is particularly obvious in Chapter 3, where reading seems to be focussed on the first part, the famous discussion of the instant and the analysis of the time–eternity synthesis of man. The emphasis of the chapter, however, lies elsewhere. Haufniensis studies different ways in which individuals react to their sinfulness, how one avoids confrontation with the consciousness of sinfulness, the three main forms being spiritlessness, fate (or the Greek standpoint) and guilt (or the Jewish standpoint). The three reactions are false representations, appearances of truth, which need to be overcome and set aside. The chapter is titled, 'Anxiety as the Consequence of that Sin which Is Absence of the Consciousness of Sin' and accordingly one should arrive at consciousness of sin. The original relationship to sin is covered-up, our sin-consciousness is repressed.[34]

Based on such deliberation, I am convinced that what we have in *The Concept of Anxiety* is a study of the development and constitution of consciousness of sin. The education of anxiety points to the fundamental, primitive, original experience. More precisely, Haufniensis does not actually develop a notion of sin, that remains to be the task of Climacus and Anti-Climacus. What Haufniensis seems to have accomplished is a study of sinful consciousness. Haufniensis holds the view that anxiety itself is the muted or disguised expression of the spirit. Similar to other existential moods, anxiety is an accumulation of the spirit, an accumulation or concentration aimed at expressing the spirit, giving it form and awareness. But fails to be expressed and made clear, transparent to itself. Similarly, in a particularly unusual passus, Judge William inquires about depression (*Tungsind*).

> What, then, is it? It is hysteria of the spirit. There comes a moment in a person's life when immediacy is rime, so to speak, and when the spirit requires a higher form, when it wants to hold of itself as spirit. As immediate spirit, a person is bound up with all the earthly life, and now spirit wants to gather itself out of this dispersion, so to speak, and to transfigure [*forklare*] itself in itself; the personality wants to become conscious in its eternal validity.[35]

'Then the spirit masses within him like a dark cloud; its wrath broods over his soul, and it becomes an anxiety (*Angst*) that does not cease even in the moment of enjoyment.'[36]

Let me rephrase the argument in much fewer words: what Haufniensis attempts is a *phenomenology of sinful consciousness*, a study of the forms in which the spirit appears, manifests itself. The manifestations presented in *The Concept of Anxiety* are different forms of suppression of the sinful consciousness, different ways of concealing the truth or the fundamental condition of the self.

In order to assess such claim, I propose now, with our principal question about the idea of *The Concept of Anxiety* being a work educating towards possibility in mind, to discuss the implicit source of such phenomenology, Hegel's *Phenomenology of the Spirit* (*Phänomenologie des Geistes*).

Education in Hegel's *Phenomenology*

Hegel's *Phänomenologie* is a science of 'appearance' (*Schein*), a science (*Wissenschaft*) dedicated to the study of the appearance of knowledge (*Wissen*) and awareness (*Wissen*). In the course of the *Phenomenology* we follow the dialectical development of natural consciousness. The point of *Phenomenology* is then to demonstrate the essential and necessary steps undertaken by consciousness on its path to knowledge. Hegel construes an ideal history of such development of consciousness or, which is the same, knowledge (*Wissen*). Even though ideal, this history is embedded in the actual history of humanity, in the achievements of the Greeks, in the new experience of Christianity, in the failed and renewed ethos of Enlightenment. It is a history of the spirit. A history in which the spirit gives itself form, understands itself, learns of itself. Shortly, in Hegel's own words: 'The series of configurations [*Gestaltungen*] which consciousness goes through along [*durchläuft*] this road is, in reality, the detailed history of the education [*Geschichte der Bildung*] of consciousness itself to the standpoint of Science.'[37] Unfortunately, much is lost in this translation.

Hegel's word for 'education', *Bildung*, often gets translated as 'formative education'. *Bildung* ought to be understood as the 'building up' of a personality, of a culture or of the spirit. Yet heavens forbid we understand education as edification, as upbuilding, 'philosophy must beware of the wish to be edifying',[38] or such '[i]deal entities and purposes of this kind are empty, ineffectual words which lift up the heart but leave reason unsatisfied, which edify, but raise no edifice.'[39]

A formative education presupposes incompletion; it is a process of perfection or constitution. In this sense the natural consciousness becomes educated formatively, becomes instructed and fundamentally transformed by the instruction. This is Hegel's notion of experience: '[t]he Science of this pathway is the Science of the experience which consciousness goes through [. . .]'.[40] Experience in this sense is far from theoretical insight, far from a 'represented object',[41] experience is the process of 'realization of the Notion.'[42]

Natural consciousness – intelligent life – that is the subject of this 'realization', necessarily starts at a lower and mistaken standpoint. In order to realize the

Notion in its truth, the individual natural consciousness must lose its own truth on this way. It is, in Hegel's words, 'the pathway of doubt [*Zweifel*], or more precisely, [. . .] the way of despair [*Verzweiflung*]'.⁴³

Natural consciousness which becomes educated, despairs and doubts; it becomes, in the course of this formative education, split in two, split between conflicting demands, ideas, notions, desires. This internally torn consciousness is the product of the first four chapters of the *Phenomenology* and by the end of Chapter 4 (Self-consciousness) acquires the title of the 'unhappy consciousness' (*das unglückliche Bewusstsein*). Unhappy consciousness is the product of earlier education. Not of education in the sense of school education, but rather in the sense of crucial formative moments that have shaped the natural consciousness. It experiences loss, defeat, negativity and in this sense Hegel speaks of education by work: the slave consciousness works and 'work forms and shapes'⁴⁴ (*sie bildet*) – formatively educates.⁴⁵

Hegel's *Phenomenology*, understood as such education, can then

> be regarded as the path of the natural consciousness which presses forward to true knowledge; or as the way of the Soul which journeys through the series of its own configurations as though they were the stations appointed for it by its own nature, so that it may purify itself for the life of the Spirit, and achieve finally, through a completed experience of itself, the awareness of what it really is in itself.⁴⁶

Natural consciousness, or as the plot thickens: the unhappy consciousness, seems to be an abstraction, a sort of idealized subject of history. In principle this is true, but Hegel's agenda is not that of writing a history. Hegel's *Phenomenology* constitutes and provides foundation of his Science by wriggling truth out of its earlier manifestations, by writing a book which provides awareness of such knowledge (*Wissen-schaft*).⁴⁷ Now we, the readers, usually adopt different standpoints and have inadequate notions. *It is us who need to be educated, instructed – transformed.* 'The task of leading the individual from his uneducated standpoint to knowledge had to be seen in its universal sense, just as it was the universal individual, self-conscious Spirit, whose formative education had to be studied.'⁴⁸

We are to be educated very much like the natural consciousness, consciousness in the vast space of world-history, needed education. The development of the individual mirrors the development of the species, of art – *Gattung*. To quote Hegel one last time: 'The single individual must also pass through the formative stages of universal Spirit so far as their content is concerned, but as shapes which Spirit has already left behind, as stages on a way that has been made level with toil.'[49]

Kierkegaard's dialectic of the single individual

The connection between Haufniensis and Hegel, between the *Phenomenology of Spirit* and *The Concept of Anxiety* that perhaps was not crystal clear at first, should have become apparent by now. For both, the ontogenetic development follows in the footsteps of the phylogenetic history. We, the later individuals, are – 'like' Adam (*lige/som Adam*), our personal history repeats the fundamental stages of mankind, we must individually pass through the formative stages required of man.

There are crucial differences, such as, most importantly, that Hegel's goal is to proceed from difference to identity and, in other words, the unhappy consciousness becomes eventually whole in the notion of conscience, whereas Kierkegaard insists on the opposite direction of development: the direction leads from identity to difference, and the *education*[50] in principle consists of uncovering, more and more profoundly, the fundamental contradictoriness of existence.[51]

To return to an earlier quoted passage: 'Anxiety is freedom's possibility, and only such anxiety is through faith absolutely educative [*dannende*], because it consumes all finite ends and discovers all their deceptiveness.'[52]

The education of possibility seems, in the light of the reasoning I just presented, to consist of a backward movement of dispelling finite securities or positivities. Possibility towers over all the actualities like an unobtainable ideal, it pierces through the individual illusions and, as an inquisitor, it interrogates everything the individual had taken for true, valuable and solid, eventually not leaving a stone unturned.

'Whoever is educated by anxiety is educated by possibility, and only he who is educated by possibility is educated according to his infinitude. Therefore possibility is the weightiest of all categories.'[53] Let me make this point even clearer: being educated by possibility introduces the absolute demand, the absolute respect and earnestness; it qualifies existence. Without such education existence fails to understand the dubious value of finitude. In finitude, or in the mundane, in temporality, one believes to find possibility. But what possibility is it? What is possible in the world? The worldly possibilities provide only conditional and limited agency. What is it that I 'can'? From the existential point of view only very little. My agency is non-essential. It is, in other words, futility vis-à-vis the flux of time rendering all my doings null and void. Exactly compared to the finitude of the world, accentuated and contrasted by it, there manifests itself possibility as such: the fundamental possibility of being able. Being able to do what? To do what matters. I am using such vague formulations to steer away from the strictly religious phrasing of the possibility as the possibility of eternal blessedness. But being educated by possibility does involve a radical turn away from the possibilities of the world, a movement of transcendence reaching beyond the temporally possible. It is in this sense that I distinguish 'radical possibility' in Kierkegaard from ordinary possibilities. This capitalized possibility with the definite article (*Muligheden*) acquires a different ontological status. It is possibility in the sense of possibly resting, possibly remaining in oneself. Temporal existence, on the other hand, renders such resting and fullness false. In time everything changes. Haufniensis provides the ontological exposition of the temporal aspect of existence in the third chapter of *The Concept of Anxiety*. Its point is to present the concept of the moment (*Øieblikket*) as the ontological category of individual existence (the moment is identified with the spirit) uncovering possibility. In the moment that, which should be lost in time, persists and becomes eternally valid.

Returning to our main problem, I have continuously argued that Haufniensis writes his *The Concept of Anxiety* with the intention of educating the reader for possibility. The work lays down foundations for a transformation which unlocks such possibility. This kind of education happens in anxiety or through anxiety, by means of anxiety. Heidegger will understand anxiety similarly to this educative effect of anxiety as a suspension of the world in total, a suspension of mundane meaning.[54] In Kierkegaard, the education of anxiety brings about an analogous suspension but also posits the absolute demand of the other, capitalized, Possibility. In anxiety one experiences the actuality of freedom in the form of the possibility of the true Possibility. Anxiety is this reality of freedom, which is the opening up of the possible Possibility. It might be the case that I really could have this Possibility. What if it really were possible? Anxiety expresses this profound question. Anxiety is the actuality of a possibility for the Possibility in this sense. As an actualized relation to one's fundamental Possibility. The freedom involved here is not the bravado of 'we can do it' or I can do it but the consuming uncertainty of possibly having the Possibility. But what makes this anxiety of freedom consuming is the absolute certainty of the demand placed on me, the demand of embracing this freedom of trying.

The backward movement of anxiety/education is a deconstruction of mundane securities. Haufniensis says, 'So when the individual through anxiety is educated unto faith, anxiety will eradicate precisely what it brings forth itself.'[55] One has to give up on worldly hope/possibility in order to have possibility. In *The Sickness Unto Death* Anti-Climacus associates the deficit of possibility with trivial existence of the bourgeois.[56] Spoken from the perspective of the world, such existence has all the possibilities. It can become successful in the world, yet it misses the radical possibility which transcends worldly ends.

* * *

We have so far understood *The Concept of Anxiety* as a coherent stepping stone in the overall project of Kierkegaard's first authorship. It is not an upbuilding work. Yet it somehow stands apart from the other pseudonymous works. What is then its genre? My proposition for a solution is to integrate the notion of education (*Dannelse*) in Haufniensis's sense with the notion of the upbuilding (*Opbyggelse*) into what Kierkegaard calls the 'dialectic of *the single individual*'.[57] The dialectic of the single individual describes the overall transformation and development of the individual, which Kierkegaard understands as the goal of his literary production. The *terminus ad quem*, endpoint of this development, is to become a Christian. The dialectic is a complex inward movement, inward deepening, a fundamental change expressed by Kierkegaard by the adoption of new existential standpoints: aesthetic – ethical – religious – Christian. In a more analytical sense, Kierkegaard frames the dialectic by positing specific extremes or ideals of the development. In this sense, the dialectic takes place between the extremes of the individual and the general, between the finite and infinite extremes of the concrete single individual.

Education relates to the finite side of personality, to immediacy, non-essentiality, whereas upbuilding pertains to the universal.[58] Education elucidates or pierces through the individual idiosyncrasies, through the appearance of truth peculiar to the individual. There is nothing universal in spiritlessness, in fate or guilt; they are particular manifestations, appearances in the sense of fallacies (*Schein*). The task of education is to unveil such illusions. 'What then is education [*Dannelse*]? I believe it is the course the individual goes through in order to catch up with himself, and the person who will not go through this course is not much helped by being born in the most enlightened age.'[59]

Education is the first step, the foundation stone of further development. In various other expressions, Kierkegaard repeatedly writes about the need of re-education, a re-constitution.[60] Instead of education, one would better talk of re-education – *Omdannelse*. Especially those educated are deeper embedded in the finite, in the individual, and they 'first have to be reconstituted in order to be built up'.[61]

Education thus complements or rather allows for the upbuilding. It is education in the sense of simplification (cf. Paulsen, 43) in order to level with the simpleminded (*den Eenfoldigere*), in order to return to a lost originality and primitiveness of self-relation. Kierkegaard's insistence on this simple-mindedness, concentration and so on is known well enough, but less so is the role of education (*Dannelse*) as the preparatory step in the dialectic of the single individual. Only then does one proceed with being built up.

Another point I wish to make is that the relationship between education and upbuilding is dialectical as well.

> In true cultivation [*Dannelse*], one never outgrows edification as something a person needs less and less, but rather grows into edification as something one needs more and more; through edification one can be cultivated [*dannes*] in the absence of all other cultivation; without edification, all other cultivation is, understood eternally, malformation [*Misdannelse*].[62]

True education remains a propaedeutic to the process of upbuilding, without the next step of the upbuilding education loses all meaning. Also, education is only needed in order to get rid of education, in order to wash away the cultural sediments and diversions. Understood correctly, education belongs in the overall process of transformation within the dialectic of the single individual. Upbuilding is the necessary and fundamental step in this dialectic, whereas education remains a preliminary and – in some cases – unnecessary step.

Hegel's *Phenomenology* presents a prospective perspective, a movement forward, towards higher and better understanding, towards perfection and completion. Haufniensis on the other hand presents a phenomenology, where one has to walk backwards, in an unwinding movement. Haufniensis writes about the quantitative difference between individuals, quantitative in the degree to which they become entrapped by the constructs of anxiety. 'There are stories about human beings whom mermaids or mermen have subjected to their power with their demonic music. To break the spell, so says the story, it was necessary for the person under the spell to play the same piece backward without making a single mistake.'[63]

But what is the real point of such dialectic of the single individual? We have seen that it consists of two interconnected parts: first, the backward movement of re-educating oneself; and second, of the upbuilding, prospective movement of committing to the cause of Christianity. The movement of education is necessary for those, who are overcomplicated, committed to finite causes, distracted from the fundamental task. Education here is accomplished through the work of anxiety. Anxiety drives out the finite hopes and commitments, scares away the fleeting possibilities in order to uncover *the Possibility*. Precisely this is the point of education as presented in the final chapter of *The Concept of Anxiety*: the education of *the* Possibility.

Postscriptum: The genre of *The Concept of Anxiety* and of the *Upbuilding Discourses*

Let me one last time tackle the curious question of the relationship between *The Concept of Anxiety* and the upbuilding literature. We have already seen the difference between education and upbuilding. The genre of *The Concept of Anxiety* really somehow stands apart from the rest of Kierkegaard's writings. And, very inconspicuously, in a journal entry, Kierkegaard sorts out the difference between the upbuilding (edifying) and what he calls a deliberation. Since this might be the most important piece of my argument regarding the genre of *The Concept of Anxiety*, I quote the entry in full:

> A deliberation does not presuppose conceptual definitions as given and understood; therefore, it must not so much touch, relieve, [and] convince as awaken and prod ppl. and sharpen their thinking. The moment of deliberation is thus prior to action, and therefore what matters is to set all the elements properly into motion. The deliberation must be a 'gadfly'; its tone is thus quite different from that of an edifying discourse, which reposes in a mood, while the deliberation must have a mood that is, in the good sense, impatient, fiery. Irony is necessary here, and the comic is an even more significant ingredient. One may indeed laugh once in a while, as long as the idea becomes more clear and striking. An edifying discourse on love presupposes that ppl. essentially know what love is, and it then seeks to win them over to love, to move them. But this is truly not the case [here]. Therefore the 'deliberation' must first haul them up off the cellar stair, call upon them, and turn their easy thought process upside down, using the dialectic of truth.[64]

Among other skills, a student of Kierkegaard should master the art of reading subtitles. As it is, *The Concept of Anxiety* does have a subtitle: 'A simple psychologically orienting *deliberation* on the dogmatic issue of hereditary sin' (my emphasis). The genre of *The Concept of Anxiety* is that of a deliberation and its goal is to prepare action (inward deepening), it explains and prepares the fundamental conceptual framework necessary in the upbuilding stage of the dialectic of the single individual. Also, unlike other similar works (e.g. *The*

Sickness unto Death), Vigilius Haufniensis writes with much irony, in sharp contrast to the solemnness and seriousness of say Anti-Climacus.

So no, *The Concept of Anxiety* is not an upbuilding work. Its role is that of educating the reader for the Possibility by guiding him or her out of the labyrinth of his or her misconceptions.

Notes

1. Søren Kierkegaard, *The Concept of Anxiety*, ed. and trans. Reidar Thomte in collaboration with Albert B. Anderson (Princeton, NJ: Princeton University Press, 1997), 42 / *SKS* 4, 348.
2. Here, I refer to the major point Søren Kierkegaard puts forth in *Philosophical Fragments* and *Johannes Climacus*, ed. and trans. Howard V. Hong and Edna H. Hong (Princeton, NJ: Princeton University Press, 1985).
3. Kierkegaard, *The Concept of Anxiety*, 155 / *SKS* 4, 454.
4. Ibid., 156 / *SKS* 4, 455.
5. See Søren Kierkegaard, *Either/Or* II, ed. and trans. Howard V. Hong and Edna H. Hong (Princeton, NJ: Princeton University Press, 1988), 17 / SKS 3, 25.
6. See Søren Kierkegaard, SKS 317f / *Concept of Irony*, ed. and trans. Howard V. Hong and Edna H. Hong (Princeton, NJ: Princeton University Press, 1989), 87f / SKS 3, 24 / *Either/Or* II, 15.
7. Cf. Søren Kierkegaard, *Concluding Unscientific Postscript to* Philosophical Fragments', vol 1, ed. and trans. Howard V. Hong and Edna H. Hong (Princeton, NJ: Princeton University Press, 1992), 330f / *SKS* 7, 301f.
8. Søren Kierkegaard, *Practice in Christianity*, ed. and trans. Howard V. Hong and Edna H. Hong (Princeton: Princeton University Press, 1991), 198 / *SKS* 12, 197.
9. Cf. Jakub Marek, 'Anti-Climacus: Kierkegaard's "servant of the word"', in *Kierkegaard´s Pseudonyms Kierkegaard´s Concepts. Kierkegaard Research: Sources, Reception and Resources*, vol. 17, ed. Jon Stewart and Katalin Nun (Farnham: Ashgate Publishing, 2015), 46f.
10. The best point of reference here is the commentary on the history and genesis of *The Concept of Anxiety* (Tilblivelseshistorie) in the 'text description' (Tekstredegørelse) commentary provided by the Danish editors of the Søren Kierkegaard Skrifter. Cf. 'Tilblivelseshistorie (Begrebet Angest)', in *Søren Kierkegaards Skrifter*, vol. K4, ed. Niels Jørgen Cappelørn, Joakim Garff, Johnny Kondrup, Jette Knudsen and Alastair McKinnon (Copenhagen: Gads Forlag, 1998). An online version is available at http://sks.dk/BA/txr.xml (accessed in July 2022).
11. Cf. Lee C. Barrett, 'Vigilius Haufniensis: Psychological Sleuth, Anxious Author, and Inadvertent Evangelist', in *Kierkegaard's Pseudonyms. Kierkegaard Research: Sources,*

Recourses, Reception, vol. 17, ed. Katalyn Nun and Jon Stewart (London/New York: Routledge, 2015), 260f.

12   Søren Kierkegaard himself reflects on the nature of his authorship in a series of works collected in *The Point of View for My Work as an Author*, ed. and trans. Howard V. Hong and Edna H. Hong (Princeton: Princeton University Press), 1998.

13   Again, cf. 'Tilbliveseshistorie (Begrebet Angest)'.

14   Cf. Gregory R. Beabout, *Freedom and Its Misuses: Kierkegaard on Anxiety and Despair* (Milwaukee: Marquette University Press, 1996), 22–31. To my knowledge Gregory Beabout is the only author, who noticed this peculiar aspect of *The Concept of Anxiety*. Also see here note 23.

15   Kierkegaard, *Concluding Unscientific Postscript*, vol 1, 269f / SKS 7, 245.

16   Cornelio Fabro, 'Edification', in *Some of Kierkegaard's Main Categories. Bibliotheca Kierkegaardiana*, vol. 16, ed. Niels Thulstrup and Marie Mikulová Thulstrup (Copenhagen: C.A. Reitzels Forlag, 1988), 156.

17   Kierkegaard, *The Concept of Anxiety*, 157 / SKS 4, 456.

18   Cf. Ibid., 157 / SKS 4, 454.

19   *Christian Discourses: The Crisis and a Crisis in the Life of an Actress*, ed. and trans. Howard V. Hong and Edna H. Hong (Princeton, NJ: Princeton University Press, 1997), 96 / SKS 10, 108.

20   Kierkegaard, *The Concept of Anxiety*, 159 / SKS 4,458. I am diverging from Thomte's translation to allow for the more radical metaphor of 'shaking up' of everything instead of Thomte's 'searching out everything'.

21   Gregory Beabout discusses Vigilius Haufniensis in detail. According to him, *The Concept of Anxiety* is 'essentially different from the other pseudonymous works that comprise the aesthetic literature' (Beabout, *Freedom and Its Misuses*, 23). Strangely enough, Beabout explicitly points to the fact that *The Concept of Anxiety* lacks an accompanying upbuilding discourse, that the balance between the aesthetic and upbuilding production maintained by Kierkegaard since *Either/Or* seems to have been invalidated. Eventually, Beabout offers a discussion of the (possible) upbuilding quality of *The Concept of Anxiety*. 'Is *The Concept of Anxiety* essentially upbuilding?' (ibid., 28). Beabout suggests that Haufniensis should not be considered an aesthetical, but rather religious author. What then is the difference between the upbuilding and pseudonymous production? Beabout writes: 'The purpose, then, of *The Concept of Anxiety* is to be an educative deliberation that answers questions raised by Christianity, but not to deal with precisely Christian issues – dogmatics – for that would entail methodological confusion' (ibid., 29). The interpretation presented in this paper diverges from Beabout's in several important aspects, though. Most importantly, the author's understanding of education seems to be very limited: '*The Concept of Anxiety* is different from the other aesthetic works primarily in that it is explicitly educative. It seeks to clarify a concept which is crucial for understanding human being and the Christian notions of sin and

original sin' (ibid., 30). Neither does this paper concur (ironically, mind you) with the assessment: 'Vigilius's speculation is not the grandiose philosophizing of a Hegelian' (ibid., 31).
22 Cf. 'Tilblivelseshistorie (Begrebet Angest)'.
23 I have found only one commentary on the role of education in *The Concept of Anxiety* in Gregory Beabout's *Freedom and Its Misuses*. As I have commented in a previous note, I find Beabout's interpretation of education in *The Concept of Anxiety* somewhat one-sided. This presentation offers a different reading of the meaning of education (*Dannelse*) in *The Concept of Anxiety*.
24 Kierkegaard, *The Concept of Anxiety*, 155 / SKS 4, 454.
25 In the previous four chapters, Haufniensis uses the verb 'at danne' exclusively in the sense of 'creating', 'forming' as in 'As for the latter synthesis, [. . .] it is formed [*dannet*] differently from the former' (ibid., 85 / SKS 3, 388).
26 Cf. Kierkegaard, *Concluding Unscientific Postscript*, vol. 1, 383 / SKS 7, 349; Gabriel Guedes Rossatti, 'Culture/Education', in *Kierkegaard's Concepts. Tome II: Classicism to Enthusiasm. Kierkegaard Research: Sources, Recourses, Reception*, vol. 15, ed. Steven M. Emmanuel, William McDonald, and Jon Stewart (London/New York: Routledge, 2014), 120.
27 Kierkegaard, *Concluding Unscientific Postscript*, vol. 1, 510n / SKS 7, 550f.
28 Anna Paulsen, 'Education', in *Kierkegaard and Human Values. Bibliotheca Kierkegaardiana*, vol. 7, ed. Niels Thulstrup and Marie Mikulová Thulstrup (Copenhagen: C.A. Reitzels Forlag, 1980), 43.
29 Cf. Guedes Rossatti, 'Culture/Education', 116.
30 Søren Harnow Klausen, *Søren Kierkegaard: Educating for Authenticity* (Cham: Springer, 2018), 4, cf. Joakim Garff, 'Formation and the Critique of Culture', in *The Oxford Handbook of Kierkegaard*, ed. John Lippit and George Pattison (Oxford: Oxford University Press, 2013).
31 Søren Kierkegaard, *Two Ages: The Age of Revolution and the Present Age: A Literary Review,* ed. and trans. by Howard V. Hong and Edna H. Hong (Princeton, NJ: Princeton University Press, 1978), 61 / SKS 8, 60.
32 Ibid., 98 / SKS 8, 93.
33 Kierkegaard, *The Concept of Anxiety*, 26 / SKS 4, 333.
34 Cf. Ibid., 109 / SKS 4, 411.
35 Kierkegaard, *Either/Or*, vol. 2, 188f / SKS 3, 183.
36 Ibid., 186 / SKS 3, 181; cf. John W. Elrod, *Being and Existence in Kierkegaard's Pseudonymous Works* (Princeton, NJ: Princeton University Press, 1975), 83–5.
37 G. W. F. Hegel, *Phenomenology of Spirit* (Oxford: Oxford University Press, 1977), 50; cf. Wolfgang Bonsiepen, 'Einleitung', in *Phänomenologie des Geistes*, ed. G. W. F. Hegel (Hamburg: Felix Meiner Verlag, 1988), xxx.
38 Hegel, *Phenomenology of Spirit*, 6.
39 Ibid., 234.

40 Ibid., 21.
41 Ibid., 19.
42 Ibid., 49.
43 Ibid.
44 At this particular point A. V. Miller translates rather one-sidedly. The sentence reads: 'Work, on the other hand, is desire held in check, fleetingness staved off; in other words, work forms and shapes the thing' (Hegel, *Phenomenology of Spirit*, 118). In original: 'Die Arbeit hingegen ist *gehemmte* Begierde, *aufgehaltenes* Verschwinden, oder sie *bildet*' (G. W. F. Hegel, *Phänomenologie des Geistes* (Hamburg: Felix Meiner Verlag, 1988), 135). Not only does the translation disregard Hegel's italics (or rather letter-spacing [*Sperring*]); more importantly, Hegel uses the verb '*bilden*' intransitively, not indicating 'what' is being shaped and educated. In Hegel's thought, the process always pertains to the subject as well as to the object – both are affected and transformed. It is the consciousness which is educated, shaped in the process of giving form to the object.
45 Hegel, *Phenomenology of Spirit*, 118.
46 Ibid., 149.
47 Cf. Alexandre Kojève, *Introduction to the Reading of Hegel: Lectures on the Phenomenology of Spirit* (Ithaca: Cornell University Press, 1980).
48 Hegel, *Phenomenology of Spirit*, 16.
49 Ibid.
50 N.B. *not* of edification/upbuilding.
51 Cf. Kierkegaard, *Concluding Unscientific Postscript*, vol. 1, 421 / SKS 7, 383 / Jakub Marek, 'Contradiction', in *Kierkegaard's Concepts. Tome II: Classicism to Enthusiasm. Kierkegaard Research: Sources, Recourses, Reception*, vol. 15, ed. Steven M. Emmanuel, William McDonald and Jon Stewart (London/New York: Routledge, 2015).
52 Kierkegaard, *The Concept of Anxiety*, 155 / SKS 4, 454.
53 Ibid., 156 / SKS 4, 455.
54 Cf. Martin Heidegger, *Sein und Zeit* (Frankfurt am Main: Vittorio Klostermann, 1977), §39, 40.
55 Kierkegaard, *The Concept of Anxiety*, 159 / SKS 4, 458
56 Cf. Søren Kierkegaard, *The Sickness Unto Death: A Christian Psychological Exposition for Upbuilding and Awakening*, ed. and trans. Howard V. Hong and Edna H. Hong (Princeton, NJ: Princeton University Press, 1980), 41 / SKS 11, 156.
57 Kierkegaard, *Point of View*, 115 / SKS 16, 95
58 Cf. SKS 27, 453–5, Papir 382 / KJN 11 / I, 154–6.
59 Søren Kierkegaard, *Fear and Trembling* and *Repetition*, ed. and trans. Howard V. Hong and Edna H. Hong (Princeton, NJ: Princeton University Press, 1983), 46 / SKS 4, 140.
60 Translated e.g. as http://sks.dk/nb15/txt.xml?hash=ss16&zoom_highlight =omdannelse 'transformation' in Kierkegaard, *Concluding Unscientific Postscript*,

vol. 1, 581 / SKS 7, 529; SKS 23, 16, NB5:13 / KJN 7, 12 or 'reformation' in SKS 23, 186, NB17:33 / KJN 7, 188.
61 *SKS* 4, 494 / *P*, 32; cf. Christian Fink Tolstrup, 'Jakob Peter Mynster: A Guiding Thread in Kierkegaard's Authorship?', in *Kierkegaard and His Danish Contemporaries. Tome II: Theology. Kierkegaard Research: Sources, Reception and Resources*, vol. 6, ed. Jon Stewart (London/New York: Routledge, 2009).
62 SKS 27, 454n., Papir 382 / *KJN* 11 / I, 155n.
63 Kierkegaard, *Either/Or*, vol. 2, 164 / *SKS* 3, 161; cf. Grethe Kjær, 'The Role of Folk and Fairy Tales in Kierkegaard's Authorship', in *Kierkegaard on Art and Communication*, ed. George Pattison (Berlin: Springer Verlag, 1992), 85n. Also in a formulation from the papers: 'Al sand Religieusitet er derfor i en Forstand Tilbagegang, ɔ: ikke ligefrem Fremgang. Som Barn mener jeg at være Gud nærmest; jo Ældre jeg bliver, jo mere opdager jeg, at vi ere uendelig forskjellige, jo dybere føler jeg Afstanden – og in casu: jo mindre forstaaer jeg Gud, ɔ: jo mere tydeligt bliver det mig, hvor uendelig ophøiet han er' (*SKS* 23, 346n., NB19:27 / *KJN* 7, 353).
64 *SKS* 20, 211, NB2: 176 / *KJN* 4, 210.

7

Isaac I cannot understand
Sacrifice and the possibility of radical intersubjectivity

Tatiana Chavalková Badurová

What exactly is the structure of the *sacrifice* of Isaac? What role does it have in Abraham's famous leap of faith? How does his role contribute to our understanding of sacrifice, and faith, as an *impossible gift*? We build on a hypothesis that focusing on Isaac could be the key to a new ethical reading of the sacrificial story, to the possibility of a radical intersubjectivity. With this goal in mind, we will revisit Kierkegaard's *Fear and Trembling* through the prism of sacrificial gift and the problem of the other presented by Jacques Derrida in *The Gift of Death*.[1] Our analysis will follow three lines of inquiry: the relation between a gift and a sacrifice as problematized by Derrida; Abraham's relation to Isaac and Isaac's relation to Abraham, and a possibility of radical intersubjectivity brought about by the sacrifice.

The sacrifice of Isaac

Interpretations of the *Fear and Trembling* aiming at an ethical reading are predominantly, although unsurprisingly, preoccupied with Abraham's relation to God. This holds true to the extent that Isaac is almost completely omitted from the equation, usually portrayed in a passive manner – a promised son who is given to Abraham, taken to Mount Moriah, a son to be sacrificed, and finally a son given back on a deeper level. Those interpreters who do not completely ignore Isaac use him more or less as an instrument to support their own analyses – and do lose track of Isaac eventually. It is perhaps Isaac's terrible fate to be sacrificed again and again, this time for the higher good of various religious and ethical interpretations of *Abraham*'s story.[2]

Simmons,[3] for example, suggests that we look more closely at Isaac to better understand the ethics Kierkegaard presents in *Fear and Trembling*. Unless we get completely blinded by the absolute relation of Abraham to God, we can see that Isaac, by the sheer power of his singularity and particularity, is 'the very condition for Abraham's "ordeal", and without him there would be no ethical problem in the first place'.[4] Through the promise of Isaac and the faith of Abraham, their mutual relationship is not grounded within the ethical (father–son relation), but within God's call, within the religious. This implies that 'the relationship to God heightens the responsibility to love the other person while the relationship to the other person makes the relationship to God tremble in its paradoxicality'.[5] It is Abraham's relation to God which turns murder into sacrifice, and fatherly love into subjective devotion of the other person. Therefore, Abraham's relation (or Abraham's faith) to God was powered by his relation to Isaac, while at the same time, Abraham's relation to Isaac was powered by his relation to God. This, for Simmons, is yet another level to Abraham's deepened interiority and subjectivity at the moment of the leap of faith. Even though Simmons's text bears the title *What about Isaac?* we state that yet again Isaac *per se* is not analysed. We learn nothing about how Isaac *qua* singularity and particularity might relate to Abraham and God, whether, parallel to Abraham, he too takes the leap of faith or not. However, in a sense, Isaac's position might be even more difficult (and interesting) than that of Abraham, for contrary to Abraham, there is no God's command addressed directly to him to give him some context as to why his own father has brought him to Mount Moriah to sacrifice him there. And yet, Isaac does not protest, nor does he weep, but allows himself to be bound and laid on the altar.

Timothy P. Jackson wonders whether Abraham's relation to Isaac is at all compatible with the commandment to love one's neighbour: 'Does de Silentio's Abraham love Isaac in a way that the author of *Works of Love* could endorse? My answer in this essay is: No.'[6] The attempts at harmonizing the two rather conflicting demands of love (*agape*) are doomed to end in failure, as the eternal love Kierkegaard propagates does not allow for the killing of innocent Isaac, that is, *unless* we understand God's demand to sacrifice Isaac as *ironic*, as Jackson suggests. In such a case, the dissonance of the commands (and we would not shy away from calling it a dissonance within Yahweh) is not meant to tear Abraham apart, but to 'school Abraham *away* from infanticide' as Abraham, at the moment of the crisis of conscience, discovers a new dimension of divine love. A dimension that gets fully expressed on the cross, as Jesus sets the model for the harmonization of love of God and love of neighbour through self-sacrifice.

But it is hard to picture Isaac calmly lying on the altar waiting for the trial to finally end, holding his fingers crossed for Abraham. He too endures the road to Mount Moriah, knowing even less about the nature of the trip than Abraham. This is why we welcome Mitchell J. Gauvin's inquiry into Isaac's position when he ponders the possibility of Isaac's forgiveness to his father.[7] The very fact that Isaac was able to descend the mountain together with Abraham without ever reproaching his father for the dreadful ordeal he, Isaac, had undergone (at least Genesis gives no account of this) is of significant philosophical interest. Gauvin suggests that Isaac must have 'accomplished a difficult and profound, although not a praiseworthy, act of love by refusing to give into the moral demand to resent his father – if such resentment had threatened to arise for Isaac. Without the brashness of his father's act, Isaac has also fulfilled God's command and demonstrated with little fanfare or notice a remarkable act of love'.[8] Isaac has all the power of the ethical to bring his father to justice or to at least demand Abraham to apologize, but he never does that, because he loves Abraham unconditionally to the point of being able to forgive the unforgivable. Gauvin's reading might imply that there are actually two knights of faith, but only one gets noticed.

Our preoccupation with Abraham often lets us completely forget that Isaac, ethically speaking, nearly became the victim of Abraham's faith. Just as de Silentio repeatedly reminds us that we should not hastily jump into the jolly finale of the story and must instead be continually attentive to the anxiety Abraham faced, so too we must be constantly aware of the fact that Isaac nearly lost his life. Moshe Halbertal offers the following critique: 'Though Abraham had to overcome his moral conviction, the real victim of the story is Isaac, not Abraham. Isaac would have been slaughtered in the end. More generally, when morality is depicted as a temptation to be surmounted in the name of a higher goal, it is always someone else who pays the price.'[9] Forgetting about Isaac or – which amounts to the same thing – understanding Isaac as the demand of the ethical which must be suspended if the religious is to be attained leaves the door open to interpretations with gruesome consequences. For example, Halbertal notes that the binding of Isaac was commonly referred to by Jewish parents killing their children to prevent forced conversion to Christianity during the Crusades.[10] Therefore, if Kierkegaard's *Fear and Trembling* is not just an obscure religious text with hidden messages accessible only to the initiated or a manual of fanaticism, the problem of Abraham's relation to Isaac *and* Isaac's relation to Abraham must be carefully examined or at least given explicit attention.

Gift and sacrifice: The gift of death

The basic overview of some of the very few texts that attempt at thinking Isaac, however, demonstrates that the problem of Isaac has not been adequately thematized. In this chapter, we argue that Isaac indeed is philosophically interesting and that focusing on the intersubjective aspect could provide us with yet another level of understanding of *akedah*. As our own interpretation of the possibility of a radical intersubjectivity is inspired by Derrida, we must first remind ourselves of the fundamental arguments he elaborates.

Derrida builds on Kierkegaard's *Fear and Trembling* to analyse the paradox of Abraham's sacrifice, problematizing the relation of gift and sacrifice, gift as sacrifice and the problem of sacrificial gift. He concludes that the 'absolute duty (towards God and in the singularity of faith) implies a sort of gift or sacrifice that functions beyond both debt and duty, beyond duty as a form of debt.'[11] Teleological suspension of the ethical, the leap of faith, Abraham's absolute relation to God is only possible if Abraham gives Isaac as a *pure* gift. His gift must be *absolute*. The trial of Abraham's faith can thus be read as the trial of Abraham's ability or potential to sacrifice in this radical sense.

And radical it truly is, for our everyday understanding of gift, as Derrida argues, is shallow and hypocritical. We are all too ready to say that gift is different from mere exchange or trade, but at the end of the day our gifts show all marks of trade. So, how do we usually understand 'gift'? Marcel Mauss outlined the basic conditions of everyday gift-giving as follows: the gift must be recognized by the receiver as a gift in the first place, there is a recognition of the giver and an unspoken presumption that the gift will be paid back or rewarded, albeit in a different form. The function of gift is to establish bonds of mutual trust and this trust is confirmed and strengthened every time a gift is repaid by another gift in due time. Any hindrance to reciprocity or to any of the abovementioned conditions severely damages the gift-giving.[12] Hence, every time a gift is given, the receiver is in fact indebted to the giver and can only pay this debt through another gift of approximately the same value or higher, which creates yet another commitment of future reciprocity. Gift-giving, just like language, has its rules that everybody must understand to engage in it; it is a form of communication, form of exchange. As such, gift pertains to the sphere of the universal.

Abraham's sacrificial gift, however, meets none of those requirements. How is it possible that a gift violates the very conditions of possibility of gift, making the gift seemingly impossible? Before we answer this question, let us first pause and remind ourselves of Agamemnon, to whom Kierkegaard often contrasts

Abraham. The bottom line of differences between Agamemnon the tragic hero and Abraham the Father of faith lies in their relation to the ethical. If we read the stories of Agamemnon and Abraham through Derrida's critique of gift, we see that Agamemnon's sacrifice has a very strong reciprocal, even mercantile, dimension. He is to sacrifice his daughter Iphigenia in order for the goddess Artemis to give wind to his fleet. Artemis asks this of Agamemnon as a retribution or a punishment for a deer he had previously killed in her sacred grove. So not only does Agamemnon know very well why this came upon him, he also knows what will certainly happen if he obeys the command – Artemis will provide a favourable wind and free his fleet for sail. We are used to calling the story a sacrifice of Iphigenia, but, as a matter of fact, we can simply say that Agamemnon gave Iphigenia in *exchange* for the favourable wind. The reciprocity is clear and beyond doubt, which is why we can call it a quid pro quo scenario, a trade even. Agamemnon's sacrifice, however dreadful, functions completely within the economics of this ordinary, everyday gift. Anytime we sacrifice something in order to get something else in return we are actually making an *economic* decision, no matter how difficult the decision might be. And we definitely expect or at least hope the sacrifice will pay off – that is what we count on when making a sacrifice in the first place. It is part of 'the deal'. Agamemnon is indebted to Artemis and can only repay the debt by either giving up Iphigenia or by giving up his enterprise in Troy. Agamemnon the tragic hero operates fully within the ethical, the universal, as does the gift or the sacrifice he gives – even if that *quid* which he gives is the best he has. Kierkegaard explains the ethical in terms of the universal, the general, in terms of manifestation, disclosure and language. Now we see that the same ethical has a fundamentally economic dimension to it.

Derrida agrees with Kierkegaard that the story of Abraham is fundamentally different from that of Agamemnon. His reading builds on Kierkegaard's premise that in Abraham's sacrifice a teleological suspension of the ethical, the universal, the rational was only possible because the sacrifice itself transcended the ethical, the universal, the rational – and adds that this sacrifice transcended the ordinary gift with its reciprocity and manifestation. Just as the religious transcends the ethical, so does the absolute sacrifice transcend the economy of ordinary gift. Abraham is fundamentally different from Agamemnon because his sacrifice is fundamentally different from that of Agamemnon, even though both fathers sacrifice their only offspring at the command from the Divine. For the sake of clarity, we use the term pure or absolute gift/sacrifice to distinguish Abraham's sacrifice from ordinary reciprocal gifts. For Derrida, the absolute gift is in fact a gift of death.[13]

Therefore, there must be no hidden exchange economy in Abraham's sacrifice.[14] It must suspend all obligations of the ethical and all obligations of gift-giving. Otherwise, Abraham would be but a despicable tradesman carefully calculating his investments and exchanging his only son with a view of some special favours he might be granted in return. If Abraham is the Father of faith, he must give Isaac without expecting anything in return. He does wish wholeheartedly by the virtue of the absurd that Isaac will be returned to him in this life, but it is not the same thing as expecting to be rewarded. If Abraham made any such calculations, albeit only in his heart of hearts, he would engage in a trade with God and Isaac would serve merely as an object of trade, although a very precious one. A pure sacrificial gift is *outside* of *any* economy, it must not bear a trace of calculative reasoning and the giver cannot even count on the receiver's recognition of the gift and its value. All that should be left is but a pure act of giving.

This going beyond all calculation and/or reasoning for Derrida means going beyond reason as such, that is, beyond that which is explicable or communicable, too. Such is Derrida's strict definition of pure (absolute) sacrifice, that is, a gift of death. The nature of gift *stricto sensu* is thus paradoxical: for there to be a gift, it always must come from one person to another, but at the same time, there must be a complete renunciation of the object of gift, of its purpose and of the giver himself. Even a simple 'thank you' would annul the gift, since it presupposes that the receiver is indebted to the giver.[15] This is the paradox of gift: the condition of possibility of gift is inseparably linked to its impossibility. And yet a genuine gift must be possible or else Abraham is but a merchant and a murderer and not the Father of faith. This radical concept of sacrificial gift is by the virtue of its very nature excluded from the sphere of the ethical, communicable, sharable. It renounces disclosure and embraces hiddenness, intensifies inwardness as opposed to the ex-centric manifestation of the universal as was the case with Agamemnon.

Let us highlight the important structural parallels between Kierkegaard's concept of faith and Derrida's radical concept of gift: both require (i) absolute resignation or renunciation, (ii) overstepping the universal and (iii) unconditional commitment; (iv) they both establish an absolute relation without mediation that the universal provides, (v) and both are characterized by silence and concealment. Both faith and absolute gift require uttermost inwardness. Hence, the nature of the absolute gift mirrors that of the leap of faith. Each is, within a purely finite or immanent framework, impossible, in the sense that each exceeds the operational logic of such a system. This is perhaps one of the reasons why Kierkegaard chose the story of Abraham and why Derrida responded to this interpretation. Unlike the ethical and its urge for manifestation, in both faith and absolute gift the focus is radically shifted from exteriority to interiority. Abraham's sacrifice pertains to the religious and can be thus interpreted within the intentions of faith, indeed, it is difficult to separate faith from gift.

Symmetry and dissymmetry: *tout autre est tout autre*

The necessity of the shift from exteriority to interiority is given by the nature of God's command for a sacrifice. In case of the ethical, the relation between a person and the universal is symmetrical – there is clear exchange or communication between both sides, the requirements of the ethical are transparent and accessible by each and every man through reason, and we all must respond to those requirements in transparent and accountable manner. No exceptions. The symmetry is between Agamemnon and the ethical, but also between him and Iphigenia. This symmetry is the core of ethical responsibility. Although the ethical is interiorized, it builds upon exteriority expressed in the symmetry, in reciprocity. In the case of God's demand, the symmetry is inherently broken – or better to say it never existed. God's demand is addressed to Abraham and Abraham alone; it is strictly personal, a secret between God and Abraham that nobody sees into. And the secret is further enhanced by the fact that Abraham does not know why God demands this sacrifice.

For Derrida, Abraham is in a radically dissymmetrical relation to God from the very beginning.[16] God knows what Abraham feels in his heart of hearts, but Abraham does not know what God is playing at. This dissymmetry is the essence of *mysterium tremendum*, which Abraham experiences. As God and Abraham are in a dissymmetrical position, there is no way Abraham can negotiate with God. Negotiating means reasoning, arguing, explaining, calling upon the ethical; it means breaking away from this absolute, direct and exceptional, yet dissymmetrical, relation to God and immersing back into the homogeneity and symmetry of the universal. This secret that is the core of dissymmetry is the core of interiority, too. Up to this point, Derrida strictly sticks to Kierkegaard's reading of the akedah.

As is so typical of his texts, Derrida expresses this dissymmetrical relation using a wordplay: *tout autre est tout autre*. 'Every other (one) is every (bit) other [*tout autre est tout autre*], everyone else is completely or wholly other.'[17] Due to this dissymmetry, the Other is wholly other to me. For Derrida, this holds true both for God *and* Isaac. The rules of the ethical are universal to everybody (and anybody), which is why they are of no use to me in this exceptional and unique situation. In face of the absolute Other, in face of his private demand addressed to me and me only, I find myself in absolute solitude. In this dissymmetry, the other is not communicated to me through the medium of the universal. The other is not communicated to me at all, he is completely unknown, inaccessible, alien, shrouded in mystery, absolutely Other, *tout autre*. In face of such a demand, I only have two options. I can either break from this dissymmetry by disclosing the secret, by talking, by translating the absoluteness down into the terms of the general or decide to respond in absolutely singular manner, maintaining this dissymmetry, opting for a radical sacrifice where I give and do not expect anything in return, not even consolation. I transcend the ethical which, as a consequence, requires a radical redefinition of who I am, of who the Other is and what responsibility means. Not only the relationship to Isaac but the relationship to the whole is implicated in Abraham's act, since Isaac is not only son but also the symbol of a covenant with the Divine, suggesting God's presence and favour through the promise of a future nation of Israel. The possibility involved in the act of sacrifice then is also a renunciation of the whole understanding and calculation of what it is to be in relation to God. It is a movement away from one's own understanding to the recognition that, as Kierkegaard writes in *The Sickness Unto Death*, 'God is that all things are possible.'

The dread and horror of absolute sacrifice lies in the fact that I am required to respond with no exterior (i.e. ethical, universal) grounds to give me support. Abraham is not responding to God's command as a father or a king, or any other function or role that can help him decide what to do and thus help lift some of the weight off of his shoulders. The knight of faith cannot shield himself with some ethical ideal valid for everyone. Abraham is standing here *qua* Abraham, as this unique irreplaceable singularity that is called to respond, to decide. As such he has no exterior support and yet he must act and take full responsibility for his actions. There is no universal to guide him, he cannot appeal to any ethical ideal. The only support there is for him lies in his faith, in the leap of faith he takes. And the absolute sacrifice is the realization of this leap of faith. The leap of faith brings about a complete transformation. He is reborn, redefined as this interiority he is. He is absolute singularity, expressed outside of the universal. This transformation brings about the transformation of his relation to God, too. No longer an impersonal, universal principle, somewhat known but distant, God is now close to him in his absolute otherness. Abraham is in an absolute relation to God.

Nevertheless, Abraham responds not only to God but also to Isaac. Abraham's relation to Isaac is not based within the ethical, within the universal. His love for Isaac is more than a father's love for a son. His love to Isaac is exceptional, incomparable to Agamemnon's love to Iphigenia. Kierkegaard is very clear on this point.[18] One can have many sons, many heirs, many treasures, but there is only one Isaac. For Abraham, Isaac is singular and unique, which requires Abraham to respond to Isaac as to this unique singularity which cannot be grasped within the intentions of the ethical. The dilemma is there because both God *and* Isaac address Abraham *qua* singularity. This implies that Abraham cannot speak because that would mean not only breaking up the unique relation he has with God but also breaking up this unique relation he has with Isaac. Giving reasons pertains to the universal, whereas Abraham's relation to Isaac does not.

We suggest that Isaac, who was all too familiar to Abraham as his son, as his heir, as the most precious, as the ethical obligation a father has towards his son, is now seen as this absolute Other as well. There is only one Isaac in his absolute otherness. Abraham´s responsibility to Isaac is now that of one singularity towards another singularity; it is strictly personal. Thus, Abraham gives the gift of death to God and simultaneously gives a gift of death to Isaac. Abraham is in a dissymmetrical relation to both God *and* Isaac. Derrida's definition of absolute gift renders the possibility of Abraham's relation towards Isaac as to the absolute Other. Absolute sacrifice is thus the founding stone of the possibility of new intersubjectivity.

When within the universal, we constantly give up our singularity, our absolute otherness for the sake of being manifested, for the sake of being able to participate in symmetrical exchange. Everybody is required to do the same. As a result, we also approach others only through the medium of the universal, meaning we only come to contact with that which is translatable, shareable and manifestable about others. Our perception of others is flat and reduced, shallow even. We ourselves act from this flat and reduced position. Our obligations to every other, as a consequence, are equal to the limit where we actually have moral obligation or responsibility towards the universal, towards abstract principles. One might object that we do not approach everyone in the same manner – for example, my relation to my mother is different to my relation to the postman. Surely, but why is that? The obvious responses at hand – she is *my mother*, I *owe* her for my life and upbringing, she knows me the best, she always wants the best for me, she is always there for me and so on – tell a lot about my expectations, needs, commitments. Yet they tell absolutely nothing about this very unique person she is. I cannot tell why I love (or hate) her, and the minute I offer reasons for that, I am giving an account of my intimately reciprocal relation to her. I simply do not know who my mother really is beyond all these attempts at description. My very own mother *is* in fact wholly *other* to me. And so is any other person.

It is in and through the absolute gift that I find my interiority, my own true subjectivity, irreplaceable and unique. And it is in and through the absolute gift, by radical refusal of the universal (mercantile) exchange that I am able to perceive and value others as interiority, as their own true subjectivity, as the absolute Other. Completely unknown to me, but all the closer to me. This is what we call, in this chapter, 'radical intersubjectivity', for it is radically different from the intersubjectivity where our interactions with others are mediated through the ethical, the universal, in a form of gift-giving we never admit is mercantile, because reciprocal.

Isaac I cannot understand

With this perspective on the radical gift and the Other that Derrida provides, let us look more closely at Isaac. Kierkegaard does not examine, beyond the brief treatment in the 'Attunement', what the sacrifice might mean for Isaac himself – Johannes de Silentio keeps silent and so does Derrida. And yet, Isaac too endures the three-day journey to Mount Moriah and must understand with frightening clarity that it is *him* his own father is about to sacrifice. Abraham carries the knife and fire; Isaac carries the wood. Isaac asks only once where the sacrificial lamb is and then he asks no more. He does not speak anymore; he endures the road silently just like Abraham. Parallel to Abraham, he does not understand the reasons behind *his* sacrifice, he knows not that this is 'only' a trial. Even worse, he does not even know that God commanded it. Still, he lets his father bind him and lay him on the altar. Iphigenia cries, weeps, tries to persuade her father to help her evade her horrible fate. Isaac, on the other hand, does none of that. He does not protest; he does not try to appeal to Abraham's fatherly love or duties, he does not fight for his life. Isaac I cannot understand. There is nothing understandable about Isaac's behaviour. Isaac either takes it as his duty as a son to obey his father and carries out this duty to the point of self-destruction and self-alienation. This still does not explain why he never pleads for mercy, never challenges Abraham's fatherly duties, nor prays to God for help. Or, he presumes *his* sacrifice is meant to please Abraham's God, which, again, does not explain why Isaac does not at least challenge Abraham's determination and trust in a god who first materializes his promises to Abraham in him, Isaac, and then, out of a sudden, demands his life. Isaac questions neither Abraham's love and commitment nor God's intentions. This leads us to a third option – just like Abraham has faith in God the Father, so does Isaac have faith in his father Abraham. Isaac's silence and trust in Abraham are analogous to Abraham's silence and trust in God. He believes, by the power of the absurd, that the same father who is right about to sacrifice him, will at the same time spare his life. Abraham gives Isaac as an absolute sacrificial gift to God, Isaac gives himself as a pure sacrificial gift to Abraham. If faith and absolute sacrifice amount to the same, then Abraham is not the only one to take the leap of faith. Isaac takes one, too. Isaac I cannot understand.

We previously demonstrated that Abraham is in a dissymmetrical relation both to God and to Isaac. Now we see that also Isaac is in a dissymmetrical relation to Abraham. Isaac's relation to Abraham transcends the ethical, the universal, the manifestable. This is expressed through Isaac's silence, through his trust and love to Abraham *qua* Abraham. If Isaac related to Abraham through the ethical, he would have acted like Iphigenia. He must love Abraham beyond the scope of son's love to a father to be able to give himself to Abraham absolutely, beyond all duties and reciprocity. Isaac's behaviour bears no trace of calculative reasoning, which means he makes the absolute sacrifice to Abraham, he gives Abraham the gift of his own death.

Isaac is a miraculous child, a living proof of Abraham's trust in God and a proof that God fulfils his promises. He is Abraham's heir, a beloved son, a guarantor of the future of Abraham's lineage. We argue that prior to sacrifice, Isaac is primarily a personification of the mutual commitment between Abraham and God. He is a function of Abraham's relation to God. However, at the moment of sacrifice, the situation dramatically changes. Isaac is no longer an object of reciprocal exchange between Abraham and God. He now emerges as subjectivity, as an irreplaceable unique singularity that has his own absolute value outside any reciprocal commitments.

The sacrifice on Mount Moriah is generally interpreted as a test, a trial of Abraham's faith. Kierkegaard develops his own analysis in these intentions, especially when he speaks about the temptation by the ethical.[19] Exegesis aside, what if God's demand to sacrifice Isaac was not a trial at all?[20] What if this terrible ordeal was not meant to test Abraham's faith, but to make him learn something essential about himself, God and Isaac, too? What if the goal of the sacrifice was for both Abraham and Isaac to discover the absolute otherness in God and in each other? What if the goal of the sacrifice was not to establish

Abraham's absolute relation to God but to establish the absolute, unmediated relation between Abraham and Isaac? After all, Isaac is the very first son of Abraham's offspring to which God gives his blessing upon the new covenant on Mount Moriah.

The essence of the possibility of this new intersubjectivity *stricto sensu* lies in the way one relates to the other. Kierkegaard himself provides a hint when he says: 'for he who loves God without faith reflects upon himself, he who loves God believingly reflects upon God.'[21] Faith (or absolute gift) is the game changer that enables man to transcend the circle or cycle of constant self-reflection, self-relation or self-centredness and instead reflect upon the Other, be it God, Abraham or Isaac. For Kierkegaard, reflecting upon God and reflecting upon a fellow human are two different things, but for Derrida the other person, in fact, is just as other as God. Derrida, thus, would not shy away from re-formulating it as follows: 'he who loves the Other without faith reflects upon himself, he who loves the Other believingly reflects upon the Other'.

Tout autre est tout autre can also be read in the sense that every other is just as absolutely other as the absolute Other. The unshareable, hidden, innermost core of other man is just as heteronomous to me as God is. God and Isaac are equally wholly other to Abraham. When Abraham was about to sacrifice Isaac, he was not ready to give up an article of trade, communicable and somewhat replaceable by definition, but this unique, secret, sacred, irreplaceable otherness of Isaac. Derrida explicitly repeats that Abraham was sacrificing one other for another other. One incommensurable otherness for another. Therefore, we dare say that if faith and gift *stricto sensu* have the same structure, then Abraham at the moment of the sacrificial gift did not make the leap of faith only with regard to God but also with regard to Isaac. Our own reading shows that Abraham is wholly other to Isaac. Isaac was giving himself, his own unique otherness, to Abraham *qua* unique, secret, secret, irreplaceable otherness. He was sacrificing one other (himself) for another other. He gave the best he had, his very life, to the absolute otherness of Abraham.

The possibility of radical intersubjectivity

The sacrifice on Mount Moriah is complicated, of course, for there are three others involved – God, Abraham, Isaac. Our intersubjectivity argument is easier to follow if we isolate it into three dyads, God–Abraham, Abraham–Isaac and Isaac–Abraham.[22] Transcending the ethical through faith or sacrifice enabled

Abraham to establish a new relationship with the other (or the Other), reaching beyond the rational, communicable and the pragmatic. The same movement was performed also by Isaac. Let us not forget that this new relationship, this new intersubjectivity, could not be born without dread, without anxiety – the dread Kierkegaard constantly reminds us of when retelling the story of Abraham. We add that the same dread was borne in solitude and silence also by Isaac.

To relate to the other through faith or sacrifice means to be in a constant state of paradox, suspending the universal, the ethical. It is a leap of faith in the direction of this otherness, otherness which is always fundamentally hidden and unknown to me. The burden of such relationship is great and announces a new dimension of responsibility, where one cannot rely on the soothing element of reason or the support of the society, just like Abraham could not weep and be soothed by Sara and just like Isaac could not cry and be calmed by Abraham. To make radical sacrifice, to take the leap of faith, both Abraham and Isaac, each of them separately, must transcend the universal, all the roles they live in the society, they must transcend everything they understand and know. Abraham and Isaac must emerge *qua* Abraham and Isaac for themselves, but also for each other.[23] The consequences of this new subjectivity and the new relationship to other, of this new intersubjectivity are grave and far-reaching.

Our focus on Isaac helped us uncover within Kierkegaard the possibility of radical intersubjectivity. Despite all the analogies between Abraham and Isaac that we showed and analysed, there remains one fundamental difference. Abraham speaks to God, hears his call, responds to the *Divine* command. Isaac, however, speaks and responds only to a human being. A provocative question arises: Is it even possible to take a leap of faith towards a human being? The reading we offer does suggest so. If, together with Derrida, we understand the leap of faith as the absolute gift outside reciprocity, that is, outside the universal, the ethical, if, in the leap of faith, we approach the other as unique singularity, the hidden, the secret, unknown, unmanifested and ineffable otherness, then yes. *Tout autre est tout autre* with all the dread, fear and trembling the possibility of such intersubjectivity and responsibility implies.

Derrida reminds us that Kierkegaard ends *Fear and Trembling* by saying: 'God sees in secret and knows the distress and counts the tears and forgets nothing.'[24] 'God sees in secret' is a clear reference to Mathew 6 explaining that one should pray, fast and give without others knowing it – even my own left hand should remain unaware of what the right one is doing. Once again, the symmetry produced by reciprocity is thus required to be cancelled in all respects. 'God who sees in secret' sees inside of me, knows my true intentions and the deepest motivation of my actions even if I am not consciously aware of them or even if I try to hide them from myself. To put it differently, God knows about my deeds even if others do not know about them. If I only pretend to give an absolute gift, there is always God who knows about my hypocrisy. And if I give purely, outside of any economy, there is God who sees the sincerity of my heart. This is the true meaning of fear and trembling, of *mysterium tremendum* between me and God, between me and God who sees in secret. God knows whether my relation to the other is one pertaining to the ethical or whether I relate to the other as *tout autre*.

Matthew promises that God who sees in secret and counts my tears will grant me a celestial reward. The reward, of course, is not one of equal exchange within a circular economy but rather that of 'absolute surplus value, heterogeneous to outlay or investment',[25] since 'God the Father, who sees in secret, will pay back your salary, and on an infinitely greater scale'.[26] Derrida spots in these lines two separate economies – an earthly economy of reciprocal and symmetric exchange, and a heavenly economy that only God takes count of and which, however, is characterized by dissymmetry, non-reciprocity and secrecy. And just as one gets exactly what he gives according to the earthly economy, the heavenly economy rewards one infinitely more generously, stacking up the treasures in heaven. To put it differently: giving pure gifts without expecting any reciprocity brings one a genuine reward in heaven. Note that when Abraham gets Isaac back, both are changed. As John Lippitt proposes, this '"getting back" which faith provides is something I cannot bring about myself. To view someone or something (Isaac, or life itself) under the aspect of "gift" is radically to transform my view of it – and myself'.[27]

From Abraham's perspective, sacrificing Isaac without any calculative expectations brought about the very reward in the form of Abraham's absolute relation to the Absolute (Is there anything greater than that?), Abraham's transformation into the Father of faith (i.e. the transformation of his subjectivity) and an absolute relation to Isaac, too. Isaac's absolute sacrifice to Abraham brought about the reward in the form of the transformation of his subjectivity and an absolute relation to Abraham.

Once again, this 'getting back' does not function in reciprocal manner, though. It is a heavenly reward for those capable of genuine sacrifice, that is, for those who give without expecting any reward at all.[28] Even though Abraham and Isaac undoubtedly loved each other from the very beginning, we suggest that prior to the sacrifice, they perceived each other through the prism of a father–son relationship, that is, within the discourse and economy of the ethical, the universal. However, the leap of faith on Mount Moriah re-established their mutual relationship beyond the ethical. It is in and through their respective faith and radical sacrifice that Abraham truly receives Isaac and Isaac truly receives Abraham. Such is the paradox of gift and faith: in expecting nothing, I receive everything. I receive myself, God and the Other. This is why God can now fulfil his promise and seal the covenant with Abraham and with his offspring.

Conclusion

We demonstrated that the absolute gift founds a possibility of intersubjectivity, where we do not see the other as either a partner or an object of trade but as a person worthy in themselves, thus absolutely transcending the rational, universal, ethical, communicable, sharable and justifiable. The problem of the sacrificial gift does not lie in our inability to give everything but in our inability to give anything without expecting a reward. In our inability to not instantly turn the other into a means of attaining our goals and so to deny the radical possibility in the encounter with the other. We might go so far as to claim that genuine intersubjectivity exists only where there is genuine, absolute gift – and that all the other human interactions are but learnt ways of either satisfying one's own physical, social or mental needs, or the needs of the society. In these interactions, the innermost and hidden part of ourselves that is strictly individual remains untouched, if not completely ignored. Yet, in Derrida's concept of gift, in Abraham's and Isaac's sacrificial gift, this hidden part manifested itself in secrecy, beyond the universal, beyond all earthly calculation, communication and abstraction.

As a singularity, as *I* that reaches beyond any function and role, my responsibility means taking decisions which effectively translate as sacrifices. Whenever I make the choice of helping or responding to one particular other, I am at the same time saying no to all the other others as I am a limited and finite being with limited and finite possibilities. Every time I make a decision, I in fact sacrifice the otherness of the other. Derrida is fully aware of this aspect and identifies the fear and trembling which is inherently present in every such decision/sacrifice as each such decision/sacrifice is unjustifiable.[29] My decision or sacrifice is unjustifiable, yet I must take full responsibility for it. I cannot explain why I am sacrificing Isaac to God, why I chose to respond to God as wholly other and not to Isaac as wholly other, because that would mean finding support in reason, calling upon the understanding of others, limiting Isaac to a set of reasons. It would mean that I am not responsible on a deeply subjective level (i.e. as a unique irreplaceable singularity), but as a role within the universal that responds to some abstract idea of the Good, as both Kierkegaard and Patočka point out.[30] I cannot rationalize my decision either prior to acting it out or post factum. I can never understand Abraham just as Abraham can never himself really understand *why* he decided to sacrifice absolute otherness of Isaac for the absolute otherness of God. He can only state he made the decision and is ready to be responsible for it.

Derrida explains that Abraham's story is relevant even today and argues that each decision we make is in fact an Abrahamic dilemma.[31] Again, we repeat that we must not forget about Isaac as it is important to analyse also what possibilities there are for those others impacted by such decision. After all, sometimes we are Abrahams – and at other times in life we are Isaacs. Our reading showed Isaac is not powerless, helpless, lost, sacrificed. He is not a passive recipient of whatever fate has been assigned to him. In fact, he does have the power of his own to make his own decision. The subtlety of his decision, the quietness of his love and the modesty of his absolute sacrifice disclose the hidden possibility of radical intersubjectivity.

The definition of intersubjectivity based on the sacrificial gift is indeed radical. It seems radical because we are all too used to acting within the sphere of the universal, the ethical. We can understand the sacrifice of Iphigenia, we might be even welcoming of the fate of Agamemnon, but the sacrifice of Isaac is too strange, too distant. What can we learn from this new concept of responsibility and intersubjectivity? How does one relate to such a demand personally, and how, if at all does it translate to the level of the social or political? When Patočka writes about two concepts of responsibility, a Platonic and a Christian one, he recurs to the question of the meaning and identity of Europe, concluding that Europe proclaims to be Christian, while in fact remains within Platonism.[32] In other words, we declare our responsibility is devoid of any economic dimension, while in fact our gifts do count on earthly reward. Such is the reality. But now, at the height of tremendous political changes, the question is posed anew by the demand of the Other: can our politics transcend the realm of 'prudent calculations'[33] and embrace a radical possibility?

Notes

1 Jacques Derrida, *The Gift of Death,* trans. David Wills (Chicago: University of Chicago Press, 1996).

2 This is implicitly demonstrated, for example, in John Lippitt's overview of interpretations of *Fear and Trembling*. See *The Routledge Guidebook to Kierkegaard's Fear and Trembling* (New York: Routledge, 2016), 146–206. However, the list is much longer than that. To name a few: Daniel Conway, *Kierkegaard's Fear and Trembling. A Critical Guide* (Cambridge: Cambridge University Press, 2015); Robert Stern, *Understanding Moral Obligation. Kant, Hegel, and Kierkegaard* (New York: Cambridge University Press, 2012); John Llewelyn, *Margins of Religion: Between Kierkegaard and Derrida* (Bloomington: Indiana University Press, 2009); Marius-Timmann Mjaaland, *Autopsia: Self, Death and God after Kierkegaard and Derrida* (Berlin: Walter de Gruyter, 2008). None of those lengthy publications deal with Isaac as worthy of particular interest.
3 J. Aaron Simmons, 'What About Isaac? Rereading *Fear and Trembling* and Rethinking Kierkegaardian Ethics', *The Journal of Religious Ethics* 35, no. 2 (2007): 319–45.
4 Ibid., 321. Although Simmons uses the term 'singularity' very much in Derrida's sense, he makes no explicit reference to Derrida.
5 Ibid., 336.
6 Timothy P. Jackson, 'Is Isaac Kierkegaard's Neighbour? *Fear and Trembling* in Light of William Blake and Works of Love', *The Annual of the Society of Christian Ethics* 17 (1997): 97–119.
7 Mitchell J. Gauvin, 'Can Isaac Forgive Abraham?', *Journal of Religious Ethics* 45, no. 1 (2017): 83–103.
8 Ibid., 97.
9 Moshe Halbertal, *On Sacrifice* (Princeton, NJ: Princeton University Press, 2012), 74.
10 Ibid., 61.
11 Ibid., 63.
12 Marcel Mauss, *The Gift: Forms and Functions of Exchange in Archaic Societies* (London: Cohen & West, 1966a).
13 'It is finally in renouncing life, the life of his son that one has every reason to think is as precious as his own, that Abraham gains or wins. He risks winning; more precisely, having renounced winning, expecting neither response nor recompense, expecting nothing that can be *given back* to him, nothing that will *come back* to him (when we once defined dissemination as "that which doesn't come back to the father" we might as well have been describing the instant of Abraham's renunciation), he sees that God gives back to him, in the instant of absolute renunciation, the very thing that he had already, in the same instant, decided to sacrifice. It is given back to him because he renounced calculation. Demystifiers of this superior or sovereign calculation that consists in no more calculating might say that he played his cards well. Through the law of the father economy reappropriates the *an* economy of the gift as a gift of life or, what amounts to the same thing, a gift of death' (Derrida, *The Gift of Death,* 95–6).

14 Ibid., 72.
15 Derrida points out that *merci* derives from a Latin word *merces*, wages. A simple *merci* for a gift received is not only an expression of gratitude, but also a form of paying back for the gift (ibid., 107, 109, 112). Notably: 'To want to be noticed means wanting recognition and payment in terms of a calculable salary, in terms of thanks [*remerciement*] or recompense' (Derrida, *The Gift of Death*, 107).
16 Ibid., 73.
17 Ibid., 68. 'Every other (one) is every (bit) other [*tout autre est tout autre*], everyone else is completely or wholly other' is the translation David Wills provides an English reader with. As a person speaking French, I must only appreciate the efforts and success with which Wills conducted the translation of the whole essay.
18 'Next I would describe how Abraham loved Isaac. To this end I would pray all good spirits to come to my aid, that my speech might be as glowing as paternal love is. I hope that I should be able to describe it in such a way that there would not be many a father in the realms and territories of the King who would dare to affirm that he loved his son in such a way. But if he does not love like Abraham, then every thought of offering Isaac would be not a trial but a base temptation [*Anfechtung*]' (Søren Kierkegaard, *Fear and Trembling*, trans. W. Lowrie (Princeton, NJ: Princeton University Press, 2013), 68–9). For more on the nature of Abraham's love to Isaac, see Troels Nørager, 'Kierkegaard, Love, and Sacrifice. Is There a Solution to Abraham's Dilemma?', *Neue Zeitschrift für Systematicsche Theologie Und Religionsphilosophie* 50, no. 3–4 (2008): 267–83.
19 Kierkegaard, *Fear and Trembling*, 135.
20 Edward F. Mooney toyed with the idea whether Abraham could become the Father of faith even if he decided *not to* sacrifice Isaac. He came to the conclusion that it indeed is possible, 'not by hitting on the right response, but first, by being terribly vulnerable to the full complexity of the dilemma they [Abraham and hypothetical Maharba – T.Ch.B.] face, refusing to falsify in the name of simplicity the intractableness, the darkness, of the struggle they endure; and second, by being open to a groundless but mysteriously empowering assurance and trust. It is a drama of paradoxical demands, inescapable decision, fundamental risk, and enabling hope' (Edward F. Mooney), 'Abraham and Dilemma. Kierkegaard's Ethical Suspension Revisited', *International Journal for Philosophy of Religion* 19 (1986): 23–41 (36).
21 Kierkegaard, *Fear and Trembling*, 77.
22 Surely, we can also identify the relationship between Isaac and God, but the analysis would probably show there is no much difference between Abraham–God and Isaac–God relationship.
23 Patočka is aware of this when he writes: 'The responsible human as such is I; it is an individual that is not identical with any role it could possibly assume' (Jan Patočka,

Heretical Essays in the Philosophy of History, trans. Erazim Kohák (Chicago, IL: Carus Publishing Company, 1996), 107).
24 Kierkegaard, *Fear and Trembling*, 215.
25 Derrida, *The Gift of Death*, 105.
26 Ibid., 107.
27 Lippitt, *The Routledge Guidebook to Kierkegaard's Fear and Trembling*, 56.
28 For more on receiving back (Isaac, oneself) at the instant of sacrifice from both Kierkegaard's and Derrida's perspective, see for example: David J. Kangas, *Kierkegaard's Instant. On Beginnings* (Bloomington, IN: Indiana University Press, 2007).
29 Derrida, *The Gift of Death*, 68–72.
30 Instead of responding to each man as to a unique singularity, irreplaceable subjectivity, I am held accountable to abstract principles void of deeply personal commitment. This is the difference between being responsible in the ethical stage and being responsible in the religious one. Jan Patočka, on whom Derrida's essay also builds, calls these types of responsibilities as one pertaining to Platonism in contrast to a Christian concept of responsibility. Platonic responsibility responds to universal and impersonal idea of The Good, whereas Christian responsibility responds to 'a self-forgetting goodness and a self-denying (not orgiastic) love' (Patočka, *Heretical Essays in the Philosophy of History*, 106).
31 To get a glimpse at the relation between sacrifice, responsibility, violence and the role of law in other texts by Derrida, see Jeffery Hanson, 'Returning (to) the Gift of Death: Violence and History in Derrida and Levinas', *International Journal for Philosophy of Religion* 67, no. 1 (2010): 1–15.
32 Patočka, *Heretical Essays in the Philosophy of History*, 106–7.
33 Kierkegaard, *The Concept of Anxiety*, ed. and trans. Reidar Thomte in collaboration with Albert B. Anderson (Princeton, NJ: Princeton University Press, 1997), 65.

IV

Possibility and hope

8

Just a glance! Kierkegaard's eschatology of the possible

Saitya Brata Das

In a moment, in the twinkling of an eye, at the last trump: for the trumpet shall sound, and the dead shall be raised incorruptible, and we shall be changed.
— 1 Cor. 15.52[1]

The argument

To begin with, let me put what I wish to do in the form of a hypothesis: that Kierkegaard's idea of possibility is a profound reflection of time and eternity which effectively interrupts the mythic law in history, and places existence in radical freedom. Pauline in inspiration, especially a reflection of Corinthians and Philippians, the question of possibility – which for Kierkegaard is basically that of possibility *of* freedom, or possibility *in sight of* freedom – unworks, in a deconstructive gesture, any system of necessity to open up existence to the outside of totality. The result is a *kenotic* political eschatology that puts into question the worldly order of *nomos* and frees us towards new singularity to come. This gesture, very close to later Schelling's thinking, influences thinkers like Franz Rosenzweig in fecund ways that have profound significance for our time.

Glance

It is just a glance!
    Kierkegaard writes in *The Concept of Dread*:

    Nothing is so swift as the glance of the eye, and yet it is commensurable with the content and value of eternity.[2]

Just a glance, a blink, a lightning flash, a sudden and momentary arrest of time – for the world to pass away, and eternity to break through the fabric of time. That with which time, in all its endlessness, is incommensurable suddenly becomes commensurate in the twinkling of the eye, in the swiftness of the glance – with eternity itself, suddenly crossing over the abyss of distance that separates one from the other and the other from the one: 'In a moment, in the twinkling of an eye, at the last trump: for the trumpet shall sound, and the dead shall be raised incorruptible, and we shall be changed.'[3]

What an impossible thought, a vertigo of knowledge, a paralysis of worldly sagacity! The human, all-too-human thinking comes here to standstill; and our glance, having to see the impossible in the gleam of the lightning flash, comes to a point of arrest. The logic of the possible and of possibility, as we understand it in our human, all-too-human understanding, comes here to its peril: *aporos* is this passage or non-passage (*a-poros* means 'non-passage') through which and in which the impossible *advents*, arrives, comes. It is as if, as it were, the non-passage is the condition of possibility of all arrival, of all that comes, in true sense of the term, that is: the advent of the impossible. *Only the impossible truly advents, comes, arrives.* Without this *adventure of the advent* there is no *event* of the (im)possible, that is, the impossible letting itself be possible. This (non)passage is not the dialectical passage of the concept; it is not the passage of the speculative proposition that Hegel propounds in the very first pages of *Phänomenologie des Geistes*, which converts nothing into being by the sheer power of the negative.[4] The concept assumes here the force of the law (we will speak more of this in what follows), while the 'twinkling of the eye' in both St Paul and Kierkegaard is the eschatological suspension of worldly *nomos*.

Let us take an analogy to understand this: in the way that the true love is the love of the unlovable, and true forgiveness is that of the unforgivable, so the true event of the *possible* has to pass through the (non)passage of the impossible, tearing the constituted order of things that we call the 'world', and making manifest – in the twinkling of the eye, in the gleam of the sudden the unapparent. What is unapparent – what refuses dialectical mediation and transition – suddenly, in a lightning flash, arrests the gaze, and transfixes the constituted order of totality, and in a moment, of rapture and rupture, the vast abyss of distance is crossed. How to understand this enigma of manifestation where all 'doxa' comes to its 'para', where all knowledge is immediately (i.e. without mediation and without transition) transformed into *para-doxa*? Yet, precisely this may happen – in this *adventure* of the *advent* – that, in the twinkling of the eye, the end may suddenly come to copulate with the beginning in the most monstrous way possible. This is a monstrosity that is un-demonstrable in the human, in all-too-human understanding: to understand here is to be offended; to think is to suffer vertigo; to see is to be blind. Yet, this scandal of the event – the very event of the impossible making itself possible, the unapparent manifesting itself – constitutes the very heart of Christianity, 'an offense to understanding', 'a scandal to the Jews and foolishness to the Greeks'[5] to which Christendom itself could not remain faithful in its two-thousand-year history. This paradox lies in the inaugurating moment of Christianity itself: God can reveal Himself as human, the glance of the eye can commensurate itself with eternity. What inaugurates Christianity cannot be exhausted and cannot become assimilated in the two-millennia-long history of the world-politics. In relation to the constituted order of totality, it is an *excess*, and two thousand years could not approximate what is made proximate in the twinkling of the eye, in the glance of the moment, in the flash of lightning. Thus, Christ Himself – in his very self-revelation – could not be recognized as 'Christ'. In more than one place, especially in his *Training in Christianity*, Kierkegaard insists on the invisibility of the Christian God – the *Deo Absconditus* – despite the self-manifestation of the Christ-event: a paradox that may be called Kierkegaard's 'negative theology':

> And now in the case of the God-Man! He is God, but chooses to become the individual man. This, as we have seen, is the profoundest incognito, or the most impenetrable unrecognizableness that is possible; for the contradiction between being God and being an individual man is the greatest possible, the infinitely qualitative contradiction . . . the unrecognizableness of the God-man is an incognito in the fact that it is so almightily maintained that He Himself suffers under His unrecognizableness in a purely human ways.[6]

Thus the ground of all apparitions – the inapparent itself – cannot be exhausted in what it gives rise to (the manifest in the light of world-historical politics); and it thus remains, as such, something excessive, offensive and indemonstrable in the visible order of the world-historical politics. The ground of all that is possible – the impossible itself – cannot be exhausted in all that it gives rise to: the paradox of the impossible as the ground of the possible is the heart of Kierkegaard's political eschatology.

Possibility

First of all, we must be able to distinguish as rigorously as possible – in the Kierkegaardian spirit – the probable from the possible.[7] When the question of the possible is reduced to probability, then the paradox disappears. Christianity's thought of the possible is tied to the paradox – and here is Christianity's scandalous character and its foolishness – insofar as the ground of the possible is nothing other than the impossible itself (namely, *der Abgrund* – the abyss – of freedom). Historical Christendom, on the other hand, has *come to be* based upon the thought of the probable and not on the possible, forgetting the offensive and scandalous spirit of eschatology which inaugurates Christianity vis-à-vis the pagan world. Thus Paul's *Epistle to the Romans* (to give just one example) exhorts us to put the stake of our existence elsewhere than just the normative obligations to the Roman Empire and the blood relations of family ties.[8] Here what is found to be offensive and scandalous is the immense problematic of *eschaton* that finds in St Paul its most effective voice. Here is Paul from 1 Cor. 15.52, a verse Søren Kierkegaard himself does not fail to quote: 'in a moment, in the twinkling of an eye, at the last trump: for the trumpet shall sound, and the dead shall be raised incorruptible, and we shall be changed'.

What is radical about this eschatological spirit is that it brings into question the logic of the probable that constitutes the law of the world as we generally understand it. This bringing into question does not mean just the linguistic mode of 'questioning' the world, but rather that of bringing it into *judgement*, or before (eschatological) judgement. Immediately here we should be able to make this Pauline distinction, crucial to us as much as to Kierkegaard himself: this is the distinction between the sort of judgement which is associated with the worldly *nomos;* and on the other hand, the true judgement, the divine judgement that comes to pass in the name of eschatological justice. Thus when Paul speaks of the disappearance of the worldly order 'in the twinkling of an eye', it is this eschatological problematic of divine judgement that he means. What happens in this 'twinkling of an eye' does not belong to the order of the probable, but nevertheless it is possible, in the sense of the acute eschatological intensity that is peculiar to Paul's theology. Paul is in a hurry: there is no time to waste, for eternity is *not* a long time ahead of us: 'The night is far spent, the day is at hand.'[9] It is this eschatological spirit, eighteen-hundred years later, that moves the spirit of Søren Kierkegaard against the secular pantheism of the nineteenth-century idea of progress, which conceives eternity as a long time ahead of us.[10] This critique of historical reason is based upon the qualitative distinction that Kierkegaard makes, in the spirit of early Christianity, between history in general (*Weltgeschichte*) and the salvation/sacred history (*Heilsgeschichte*).[11]

To understand this, however, it is necessary to hold onto this distinction, which would be crucial for Kierkegaard himself.[12] When the world is understood to be governed by the law of the probable, then the question of its judgement (and consequently, the question of eschatology) does not arise, and then the world of the probable may exist inoffensively and un-scandalously. The law of the world that is governed by the logic of the probable is the *mythic* world; on the other hand, *religion* (in the sense that Christianity is to be understood by Kierkegaard) disrupts the mythic continuum, and places us *in sight of* freedom.[13] Now this 'in sight of' is precisely the *temporality* of the possible which is not – unlike Hegel's categorial-conceptual transition – a movement of categories on the scale of empty eternity: it is the *leap* whose presupposition is a qualitative disjunction.

It is this qualitative disjunction that nevertheless is crossed – in the twinkling of the eye, in the glance of the sudden, in a flash of lightning – which makes Christianity *paradoxical*: in other words, offensive, scandalous and foolish. What for the worldly order of the probable takes a very long time to reach, Christianity envisions (the Kingdom of God) coming in a twinkling of the eye, in the suddenness? of the glance, in a flash of lightning: 'the dead shall be raised incorruptible, and we shall be changed'. What can be more offensive to the human understanding than this? Yet, this impossible idea of Paul – that the impossible, truly speaking, may be the possible, but on the other hand, the improbable never *becomes* possible – an idea we know to be the very essence of Pauline eschatology, lies at the heart of Kierkegaard's own *kenotic* eschatology. What follows in the following pages is a rough outline of the eschatological problematic as Kierkegaard himself would understand it; and we will see that the consequences of this eschatology are political in nature; that is, it evokes the claim of the divine itself to strike the constituted order of the world as it exists, thereby opening the world to something like divine, eschatological justice.

Christianity of the apostolic era understands itself always *in sight of* the *eschaton* which *temporalizes* the world in an un-thinkable way: here *temporalization* is to be understood in the sense of the verbal infinitive, thereby distinguishing it from the understanding of time in the sense of 'noun' (i.e. on the basis of 'space'). If one takes this view, then the future becomes the origin of the *temporality*, which constitutes the essentially *historical* character of the world: the future here is the eschatological possibility that attunes the Christian spirit in a radical hope in the *coming* of the Kingdom. To understand the world eschatologically is to see it in its transiency (passing away), thus making the world like an open wound, rendering the world receptive to the *arrival* of eternity in 'the twinkling of the eye'. This *temporalization* (against the spatial worldly order of the mythic-pagan) is to be understood in terms of a new *Oikonomia*: this *Oikonomia* is not to be understood in the old sense of the family ties, but as the *Oikonomia* of the *Heilsgeschichte* (salvation history).[14] *Oikonomia* – which ordinarily means economy of the household – is transformed into Christian *theologoumenon*, implying the salvation history (*Heilsgeschichte*) as the work of providence. The thought of the *possible* (which is not the probable, as we have seen) – which is only to be understood in the blazing eschatological light of *Heilsgeschichte* – is always the question of the possibility *of* freedom, that is, the freedom that is to be actualized, and is now a not-yet. This 'of' (the possibility 'of' freedom) is the *historical* and *temporal* sense that is implied in the *Oikonomia* of *Heilsgeschichte* (thus it is to be distinguished from the mythic-pagan). When in *The Concept of Anxiety* Kierkegaard speaks of the possible as the possibility *of* freedom, it is meant that freedom is *not yet* actual, for when where freedom becomes *actual*, then possibility is annihilated. This is, then, the paradox: the ground of the possible is otherwise than the possible. It is towards this 'otherwise' that possibility is always 'in sight of'; as the otherwise than the possible – the impossible is the annihilation of the possible. The annihilation of the possible is *der Abgrund* of freedom which, when it manifests itself as actual, annihilates possibility. The history *towards* this *eschaton* is a divine economy (*Oikonomia*): history, understood Christianly (i.e. eschatologically), is this 'toward' of being placed and established in radical freedom. This 'toward-ness' *singularizes* us, *each one* alone and *each one* with *each other*, by making everyone into an 'each one' (i.e. an irreducible singular being), *temporalizing* us *in sight of* eternity. It is in this light that Kierkegaard's insistence on the singular human being before God is to be understood, that is, *in sight of* the radical freedom which is inaugurated when the mythic law is suspended by the paradoxical event of God dying on the Cross. When the mythic law of the world is suspended, everyone is potentially transformed into *each one*: the individual is now released from being a mere particular instance of the universal (the genus, the species, the race, the state, the family and the Roman Empire) and from the law-positing violence of the natural existence; rather now, she truly *comes* to be (a self); she is displaced from the mythic order of 'being' into her 'be-coming' (Christian), thus *freed* and absolved from the older ontological status of mere instantiation of the universal, from the mere one among the many. In other words, she is now placed in *possibility*, which is always the possibility *of* freedom, by being displaced from the constituted order of the probable. Having been placed before the eschatological judgement, she becomes a 'self', into 'each one' and not merely one among 'everyone' she becomes a non-number, an uncountable something, the self that is un-assimilable to the 'crowd', an indigestible remnant, an offensive self before the world who nevertheless does not take offense in the God becoming man. It is this possibility of becoming a non-number, the possibility of *becoming* at all (in other words, this possibility of becoming a self before God) which produces the anxiety, for this becoming demands a radical interruption of the constituted order of phenomenality (the state, the family, the empire, the crowd, genus, race etc.) wherein we otherwise find consolation and a foothold – the constituted order wherein the finite consciousness recognizes its normative obligations to the worldly order of *nomos*, to the state and to the family now suddenly – in the sudden of the leap, in the glimpse of the moment, in the glance of the eye – discloses itself as the order of nothing (in the sense of *non-thing*). It is in confrontation with this *non-thing* that *die Grundstimmung* of anxiety comes to us in all its ambivalence, where freedom which is desired and longed for now appears simultaneously as something repulsive: in other words, Kierkegaard's 'psychological' analysis of anxiety moves within the fundamental eschatological spirit of Christianity that welcomes (and yet is repulsed by that) the claim of the divine to strike the worldly order of *nomos* in an incalculable moment with something like a divine, eschatological violence.[15] This point needs elaboration.

The anxiety before the non-thing (before the non- or un-constituted) may be a wilful, demoniacal refusal to retreat from the normative obligations to the already constituted order of worldly *nomos*: then the self does not *come to be*; it does not then come to see itself established in the groundless actuality of freedom. Because the moment (in a lightning flash, in the glance of the eye, in the leap of the sudden) the constituted, mythic order of worldly *nomos* is suspended for the self, and the self comes to assume this very interruption as the task of its own existence, then all our normative obligations to the worldly order of *nomos* get relativized; the absolute character of these normative obligations loses its absolute binding force. It is this *un-binding* from normative obligations to the world-historical powers and *re-binding* to the offensive God-man, it is this eschatological essence of *Christianity* that Kierkegaard conjures up against a secularized *Christendom* (paganism in the Christian world, as Kierkegaard says) that inverts the eschatological spirit (*un-binding* from the offensive and scandalous Christ and *re-binding* to the worldly values of power and force), and thereby takes away the eschatological 'thorn in the flesh'. It is this Pauline 'thorn of the flesh', especially the Paul of the *Romans*, that forms the background of Kierkegaard's own kenotic eschatology.[16] Kierkegaard's own peculiar, idiosyncratic 'psychological' analysis of anxiety can thus be best understood against the eschatological background of Pauline political theology. This is why the following footnote from *The Concept of Anxiety* is crucial:

In the New Testament there is a poetical paraphrase of the instant. Paul says that the world will pass away 'in an instant, in the twinkling of an eye'. By that he also expresses the thought that the instant is commensurable with eternity, because the instant of destruction expresses at the same instant eternity.[17]

Paul's messianic paradox – that the instant can be commensurate with eternity – intimates Kierkegaard's eschatological paradox: they displace our normative obligation to something and somewhere other than to the world-sovereign authorities in the profane order: 'be not conformed to this world'.[18] The constituted order of the world is the order of *passing away*, of utter transiency and even the order of nature – not just us – is groaning for redemption: 'for we know that the whole creation groaneth and travaileth in pain together until now'.[19] We find a similar political–theological idea in Walter Benjamin's politics of world-nihilism. Here for Benjamin, as much as it is for Paul and Kierkegaard, such passing away becomes the very task of our existence: 'to strive after such passing, even for those stages of man that are nature, is the task of world-politics, whose method must be called nihilism'.[20]

By introducing the problematic of the instant, Kierkegaard thus renews the old Pauline political eschatology. While Paul introduces the problematic of the instant against the Hellenistic (essentially Platonic) notion of the sudden (which, with Hellenism, is a backward-looking glance), Kierkegaard renews the Pauline thought of the instant against the secular pantheism of immanence, which finds its expression in Hegel's nineteenth-century theodicy of history.[21] It is in this eschatological light that the following words from Kierkegaard acquire a remarkable theologico-political resonance:

> Thus understood, the instant is not properly an atom of time but an atom of eternity. It is the first reflection of eternity in time, its first effort as it were to bring time to a stop. For this reason Hellenism did not understand the instant; for even if it comprehended the atom of eternity, it did not comprehend that it was the instant, did not define it with a forward orientation but with a backward, since for Hellenism the atom of eternity was essentially eternity, and so neither time nor eternity has true justice done it.[22]

What is important to recognize here is that by introducing the problematic of the instant, Kierkegaard introduces the question of possibility as against the probable: this thought of the possible cannot be understood as a speculative-dialectical transition of concepts, but as the eruption of the paradoxical event that can only be affirmed by virtue of the absurdity of faith, because its glance is forward-looking. Kierkegaard understands it in this way because the very notion of Pauline eschatology he renews here (in his polemics against the eighteen-hundred years of Christendom as much as against the Hegelian pantheistic theodicy of history) is not a thought of transition or mediation on a homogenous plane of world-history. Between the two aeons, the unredeemed state of nature on the one hand and the redeemed-messianic condition, there is no mediation or transition, but a leap, an interruption, an *Abgrund*. Only the instant, in the glance of an eye, may bring to proximity that which is separated by an abyss of an infinite distance; only the instant, in the twinkling of the eye, brings to a 'monstrous copulation',[23] which are qualitatively disjunct. It is this scandalous, impossible idea of a possibility which could be thought neither by backward-looking Platonic thought nor by the speculative investment of Hegelian theodicy. This is why Paul is necessary for Kierkegaard; and by that same measure, it is also necessary for us to understand Kierkegaard in light of the eschatological spirit that moves Pauline political theology.

Eschatology

We have seen above that in Kierkegaard's political eschatology – which is Pauline in inspiration – the question of the possible is raised in the eschatological light of judgement and redemption. It is in this eschatological light that Kierkegaard's deconstruction of nearly two-millennia-old Christendom acquires a radical political intensity. What I have called elsewhere Kierkegaard's 'political eschatology' or 'political theology'[24] is nothing other than an attempt to think the possible (which is not the probable) eschatologically as radical displacement from the mythic order of immanence into the freedom of the divine *Oikonomia*. Understanding this 'displacement' as qualitatively opposed to the speculative-dialectical *mediation* of concepts (as in Hegel's speculative dialectics of mediation), I try to show the proximity of the later Schelling's Positive Philosophy of the 'actuality without potentiality' to Kierkegaard's political eschatology, which takes up the thought of possibility as the very possibility *of* freedom. In both cases, it is always the attempt to think the possible as the non-categorial, or non-conceptual leap.

This is because the leap is not a concept but an *event*: aleatory, incalculable and irreducible to knowledge. There cannot be a *concept* of the leap, because the concept does not *leap*. This is why any system of concepts ineluctably mirrors, as metaphysical expression, the mythic immanence of pantheism.[25] The leap is the eschatological interruption of any mythic immanence. This is why in the very 'Introduction' to his *The Concept of Anxiety* Kierkegaard qualitatively distinguishes between the speculative system of immanence (Hegel's dialectical system of concepts) and, on the other hand, the transcendence of the becoming, of the leap, of movement, of Reality:

> In logic every movement (if for an instant one would use this expression) is an immanent movement, which in a deeper sense is no movement, as one will easily convince oneself if one reflects that the very concept of movement is a transcendence which can find no place in logic. The negative is the immanence of movement, it is the vanishing factor, the thing that is annulled (*aufgehoben*). If everything comes to pass in that way, then nothing comes to pass, and the negative becomes a phantom.²⁶

The leap is un-assimilable to the conceptual order of immanence: it is an offence to the concept, and a scandal to the system. For the conceptual system of immanence, the glance is just an annulled moment (in that sense, it is already always past – a *passé*), a spectre of the accidental, an ephemeral instance of one transition among others. For Kierkegaard, on the other hand, the leap is rigorously thought in the light of the *eschaton*, hence as a radical transcendence of qualitative dialectics. The event of the leap is *the event of history* (hence, it is not a historical event, in the sense that it does not belong to the 'history in general') itself on account of which Kierkegaard distinguishes the historical (in the sense of the event) presupposition of Christianity against the mythic immanence of pagan philosophy as much as from the conceptual immanence of the Hegelian theodicy. The leap of the instant 'appears now as strange being', reads an important footnote from *The Concept of Anxiety*, 'which lies between movement and repose, without occupying any time'. Far from being a 'transition' of a concept, the instant is the leap:

> Now, if logic is willing to affirm that there is no transition in it . . . then it will become clearer that the historical sphere and all the knowledge which reposes upon a historical presupposition has the category of the instant. This category is of great importance as a barrier against the philosophy of paganism and the equally pagan philosophy in Christianity.²⁷

In his *Negative Dialectics* (1981) Theodor Adorno shows the innermost connection between the logical operation of the concept and the operation of the law that is at work within a legal order: the concept is *posited*, as much as the law, within an order of immanence. The metaphysical violence of the concept (*Begriff*: formed from *greifen*) as much as the mythic violence of the law (*Gesetz*: formed from *setzen*) lies in the positing (*setzen*) act of the concept that seizes (*greifen*), that is, subsumes the differential multiplicity of the non-identical under the force of the law, under the unitary power of the concept. The 'each one' is reduced into the mere life of 'everyone' or the 'All'. It is this power of the concept that is posited as immanent movement when Hegel's speculative dialectic violently transforms the movement itself into something essentially conceptual. The gaze of the law transfixes – and this is its metaphysical violence – the singularity of the 'each one' (who, each time, is singularized by the *possibility* of freedom) into the universality of 'everyone' (the state, the crowd, the mass, the empire, the race, the species); the *possibility* of freedom is thus annulled and is violently subsumed within the constituted order of necessity and unfreedom. The totalitarian order of the concept is thus the mythic-immanent order of determination where everyone is posited and *transfixed* in a *fixed* order of succession: the *gaze* of the sovereign power is everywhere (*pan*) as the God (*Theos*) of the law (*nomos*). It is against this pantheistic-mythic order of immanence that the *glance* of the *eye* is to be affirmed in the Christian faith: this is why the glance is always lacking in the mythic order of necessity. In the constituted world of necessity everyone is transfixed by the *gaze* of the sovereign power; Christianity transforms the *gaze* of the mythic law of necessity into the freedom of the love, which is expressed in the divine *glance*. It is not for nothing that the Goddess of the law, as she appears in the court of the worldly legal order, often appears as blindfolded. The divine love, on the other hand, whose judgement is passed in sight of redemption of life for the sake of life itself, the divine is presented as an *eye* with a *glance*. The following brief footnote from *The Concept of Anxiety* is again revealing:

> It is noteworthy that Greek art culminates in statuary, in which it is precisely the glance that is lacking. This, however, has its deep reason in the fact that the Greeks did not in the profounder sense comprehend the concept of spirit, and therefore did not in the profoundest sense comprehend the sensuous and the temporal. How striking is this contrast that in Christianity God is pictorially represented as an eye.[28]

This glance is the glance that sees the *possibility* of freedom. Without freedom – without this possibility of freedom – there is no life. It is in the divine love that such life in its purity is to be found. This is why St Paul regards the sovereign order of worldly *nomos* as the regime of death. The law violently grasps and subsumes life as mere-being-alive, but to merely be alive is not life in its purest possibility. In the *gaze* of the *law*, the *glance* of *life* is lacking! This is why Kierkegaard could say that with God everything is possible, 'or that everything is possible is God'.[29] By this he means nothing other than that the impossible is possible only in God: only in God can death be transformed into life, the *gaze* into a *glance*, the dead can be raised incorruptible and we may be changed in the twinkling of the eye.[30] It does not take a long time, but just a glance. For 'nothing is so swift as the glance of the eye, and yet it is commensurable with the content and value of eternity'.[31] Against the patience of the (Hegelian) concept ('the seriousness, the suffering, the patience, and the labour of the negative',[32] Kierkegaard invokes the impatience of prayer: 'Thy Kingdom come.'[33] With prayer, the violence of the concept is abandoned.

It will be a worthwhile task to write a phenomenological account of Kierkegaard's prayers. The essence of prayer lies in the hastening of eternity as nearly as possible to us. But this possibility would not be possible if there were no instant. Without the instant, the Kingdom of God will always be far away, and thus eternally the Kingdom does not come.[34] For the Kingdom to come, the nearest must not be simply passed over. This possibility is thus to be distinguished from the other meaning of 'possibility' in the sense of human 'capacity'. In fact, in prayer, the legitimacy of the human as the sovereign master of the world and of its own destiny is abandoned: 'He must increase; I must decrease'.[35] Kierkegaard devotes a profound and a beautiful upbuilding discourse to this Johannine saying.[36] With the renunciation of violence that emanates from the worldly *nomos*, the human for the first time *becomes* human: *each one* in her singularity, absolved from the tyranny of the anonymous totality, faces God who, out of incomprehensible love for us, assumes the impossible and makes the impossible possible. The paradox of this possibility is the mystery of divine love who is Love Himself.

Notes

1 Scripture quotations from The Authorized (King James) Version. Rights in the Authorized Version in the UK are vested in the Crown. Reproduced by permission of the Crown's patentee, Cambridge University Press.

2 Søren Kierkegaard, *The Concept of Dread*, trans. Walter Lowrie (Princeton, NJ: Princeton University Press, 1957), 78.

3 1 Cor. 15.52.

4 Hegel thus says: 'Death, if that is what we want to call this non-actuality, is of all things the most dreadful, and to hold fast what is dead requires the greatest strength. Lacking strength, Beauty hates the Understanding for asking of her what it cannot do. But the life of Spirit is not the life that shrinks from death and keeps itself untouched by devastation, but rather the life that endures it and maintains itself in it. It wins its truth only when, in utter dismemberment, it finds itself. It is this power, not as something positive, which closes its eyes to the negative, as when we say of something that it is nothing or is false, and then, having done with it, turn

away and pass on to something else; on the contrary, Spirit is this power only by looking the negative in the face, and tarrying with it. This tarrying with the negative is the magical power that converts it into being' (G. W. F. Hegel, *Phenomenology of Spirit*, trans. A. V. Miller (Oxford: Oxford University Press, 1977)).

5 1 Cor. 1.23.
6 Søren Kierkegaard, *Training in Christianity*, trans. Walter Lowrie (New York: Vintage Books, 2004), 116.
7 In *Judge for Yourself*, Kierkegaard writes: 'Here is the infinite difference from the essentially Christian, since Christianly, indeed, even religiously, the person who never relinquished probability never became involved with God. All religious, to say nothing of Christian, venturing is on the other side of probability, is by way of relinquishing probability' (Søren Kierkegaard, *For Self-Examination; Judge for Yourself*, trans. Howard Hong and Edna Hong (Princeton, NJ: Princeton University Press, 1991), 99–100).
8 See Jacob Taubes, *The Political Theology of Paul*, trans. Dana Hollander (Stanford, CA: Stanford University Press, 2003).
9 Rom. 13.12.
10 In a manner similar to Kierkegaard's critique of the nineteenth-century philosophy of history, which is based on the ideology of progress, Franz Rosenzweig deformalizes the quantitative view of world-historical temporality (which assumes in Hegel's thought the resolute form of a theodicy), and opposes it to the messianic intensification of time in the light of eternity, which is a not a long time ahead. Rosenzweig's messianic critique of historical Reason inevitably reminds us of Kierkegaard's critique of the same, elaborated in his *Training in Christianity*. Thus Rosenzweig writes: 'Eternity is not a very long time, but a tomorrow that just as well could be today. Eternity is a future, which, without ceasing to be future, is nevertheless present. Eternity is a today that would be conscious of being more than today' (Franz Rosenzweig, *The Star of Redemption*, trans. Barbara E. Galli (Madison, WI: Wisconsin University Press, 2005), 241). Rosenzweig could thus speak of eternity – which he rigorously distinguishes from the quantitative idea of infinite progress (of the world-historical politics) – only because, like Kierkegaard, he posits a paradoxical idea of the instant of a qualitative leap where the furthest can be nearest in the most unforeseeable ways:

> if the Kingdom grew only with mute, obscure, impulsive drives and did so nonstop until the infinity of time, advancing interminably with an end before it, located only in infinity, then the act would be paralyzed, and since the furthest distance would be infinitely out of sight, that which is nearest and the nearest person would be inaccessible to it. But where the Kingdom advances in the world with unforeseeable steps and where every moment would be ready to receive the plenitude of eternity, the furthest distance is that which is expected

at the nearest moment, and so that which is nearest, that which is always only the placeholder of the furthest, of the highest, of the whole, becomes accessible at every moment. (Ibid., 245)

Without the instant – that is, without the event of the possible – the Kingdom of God would always recede, at every moment of time, into an infinite distance: the Kingdom of God would thus remain, without the instant, a philosophical concept of empty formality, an ethical principle without being the event of 'breaking-through' of eternity into our existence. Without the instant, the historical Reason of world-politics would either be confounded with the Kingdom of God (as in Hegel's theodicy, a theodicy that ends up in an apology of the world as it exists); or eternity would be the infinite goal which will never come (as in Kant). The instant, on the other hand, by de-formalizing the empty infinity of homogenous moments – which Walter Benjamin calls 'homogenous empty time' (Walter Benjamin, 'Theses on the Philosophy of History', in *Illuminations*, trans. Harry Zohn (New York: Schocken Press, 1968), 253–64 (261)) – makes the impossible possible (the furthest can be the nearest; God can become man): this is the paradox that Kierkegaard alludes to.

11 Kierkegaard writes: '"history", says faith, has nothing whatever to do with Christ. As applying to Him, we have only sacred history (qualitatively different from history in general), which recounts the story of His life under the conditions of his Humiliation, and reports moreover that He himself said that He was God. He is the paradox, which history can never digest or convert into a common syllogism. In His humiliation He is the same as in His exaltation – but the 1,800 years (or if there were 18,000 of them) have nothing whatever to do with the case. The brilliant consequences in world history which well neigh convince even a professor of history that He was God – these brilliant consequences are surely not His return in glory!' (Kierkegaard, *Training in Christianity*, 25).

12 See Kierkegaard, *The Concept of Dread*.

13 The mythic is the closed order of totality which takes nature – in its eternal return to the same – as its modal; decision, freedom, existence etc., cannot be thought within such an immanent order of totality whose fundamental *arché* is *Kosmos*. The fusion of the God and the world – which is the pantheistic-mythic system – must be interrupted for freedom to be rescued and for existence to be freed from the closure of totality. Thus Christianity does not call itself a cosmic religion. In many places in his journals and notebooks, Kierkegaard insists on this point.

14 For an illuminating discussion of the question of *Heilsgeschichte,* see Karl Löwith, *The Meaning in History: The Theological Implication of the Philosophy of History* (Chicago: Chicago University Press, 1957) and Oscar Cullmann, *Christ and Time: The Primitive Christian Conception of Time*, trans. Floyd V. Filson (Westminster: John Knox Press, 1964).

15 In his essay 'The Critique of Violence' Walter Benjamin in a similar way – by an intensification of difference between 'the mythic' and 'the messianic' – speaks of the messianic possibility of a divine violence that *strikes* (which Benjamin distinguishes from the mythic *threat*: while the mythic violence *threatens*, the messianic-divine violence *strikes*) the worldly order of *nomos* in light of *redemption* which he defines as *pure life* (as distinguished from *the mere life* under the grip of the law). See Walter Benjamin, 'Critique of Violence', in *Reflections*, trans. Edmund Jephcott (New York: Schocken Press, 1986), 277–300.

16 Søren Kierkegaard, 'The Thorn in the Flesh', in *Eighteen Upbuilding Discourses*, trans. Howard Hong and Edna Hong (Princeton, NJ: Princeton University Press, 1992), 327–46.

17 See Kierkegaard, *The Concept of Dread*, 79.

18 Rom. 12.2.

19 Rom. 8.22.

20 Benjamin, 'Critique of Violence', 312–13.

21 Along the same lines Kierkegaard also distinguishes the backward-looking 'recollection' from the forward-looking 'repetition' (see Søren Kierkegaard, *Repetition / Philosophical Crumbs*, trans. M.G. Piety (Oxford: Oxford University Press, 2009) and Ibid., *The Concept of Dread*).

22 Kierkegaard, *The Concept of Dread*, 79. This citation alone shows, and there are many more to cite, that Jürgen Moltmann insufficiently understands Kierkegaard's concept of the instant. In his well-known book *Theology of Hope* Moltmann writes: 'In the struggle against the seeming deceit of the Christian hope, Parmenides' concept of God has thrust its way deeply indeed into Christian theology. When in the celebrated third chapter of Kierkegaard's treatise on *The Concept of Dread* the promised "fullness of time" is taken out of the realm of expectation that attaches to promise and history, and the "fullness of time" is called the "moment" in the sense of the eternal, then we find ourselves in the field of Greek thinking rather than that of the Christian knowledge of God. It is true that Kierkegaard modified the Greek understanding of temporality in the light of the Christian insight into our radical sinfulness, and that he intensifies the Greek difference between *logos* and *doxa* into a paradox, but does that really imply any more than a modification of the "epiphany of the eternal present"'? (Jürgen Moltmann, *Theology of Hope*, trans. James W. Leitch (Minneapolis: Fortress Press, 1993), 29). Moltmann's own answer to his question is of course in the negative. If one bothers to go on to read *The Concept of Dread* from this passage on (from the passage that I am citing here, which Moltmann too cites) then one sees that Kierkegaard, in distinction from the Greek conception of eternity ('The Greek eternity lies behind, as the past into which one enters only backwards' (Kierkegaard, *The Concept of Dread*, 80)) posits the pre-eminence of futurity, and thereby posits the whole problematic of the possible and the dread / anxiety: 'the future, the possibility of the eternal in the

individual is dread' (ibid., 81). This is why 'the possible corresponds precisely to the future. For freedom the possible is the future; and for time future is the possible. Corresponding to both of these in the individual life is dread' (ibid., 82). It is in this sense Kierkegaard could say that 'the future signifies more than the present and the past; for the future is in a sense the whole of which the past is a part, and in a sense the future may signify the whole. This is due to the fact that the eternal means first of all the future, or that the future is the incognito in which the eternal, as incommensurable for time, would nevertheless maintain its relations with time. Thus we sometimes speak of the future as identical with eternity: the future life = eternal life' (ibid., 80). Thus it is clear that Kierkegaard posits the idea of possibility in the genuine eschatological spirit as the radical futurity, as his Pauline quotation justly shows. I think Moltmann translates the word 'instant' (*Øjeblikket*) as 'present', thereby confounding the whole eschatological spirit of Kierkegaard's thought with the Greek insistence on 'presence'.

23 Friedrich Hölderlin, 'Becoming in Dissolution', in *Essays and Letters on Theory*, trans. Thomas Pfau (Albany: State University of New York Press, 1988), 96–100.

24 See Saitya Brata Das, *The Political Theology of Kierkegaard* (Edinburgh: Edinburgh University Press, 2020).

25 Greek religion is mythological: God, according to Greek theogony, is the cosmic principle, immanent in the world. The Jewish-Christian God of revelation, on the other hand – and this is the crux of eschatology – is transcendent; He is not the cosmic principle. In regard to the created order, the creative God is free. This freedom of God cannot be mythologically grasped. In the nineteenth-century philosophy of German Idealism, especially in Hegel, the attempt is made to reconcile these two (paganism and eschatology). Kierkegaard shows how this attempted dialectical reconciliation by Hegel (by German Idealism) fails: Hegel's speculative dialectics ends up becoming an immanent system of concepts, unable to think the creative God of decision and freedom. Because of the very nature of the system in Hegel, which is grounded on a speculative logic (where the concept itself is mobilized and is made mobile and processual), God can only be understood as the concept, and not as existence, as life, as reality (which is extra-logical and extra-conceptual): Hegel's system, which is an order of totality, can conceive God only as immanence. As such, it renews the pantheism of mythological thought in the epoch of modernity against which Kierkegaard renews the eschatology of the Christianity via Paul.

26 Kierkegaard, *The Concept of Dread*, 12.

27 Ibid., 75.

28 Kierkegaard, *The Concept of Dread*, 78.

29 Søren Kierkegaard, *The Sickness Unto Death*, trans. Alastair Hannay (London: Penguin Books, 1989), 45.

30 1 Cor. 15.52.

31 Kierkegaard, *The Concept of Dread*, 78.
32 Hegel, *Phenomenology of Spirit*, 10.
33 Mathew 6:10.
34 Like Kierkegaard, Franz Rosenzweig writes of prayer: 'eternity, that is to say, must be hastened, it must always be capable of coming as early as "today"; only through it is it eternity. If there is no such force, no such prayer that can hasten the coming of the kingdom, then it does not come eternally, but – eternally does not come (Rosenzweig, *The Star of Redemption*, 306). And further: 'to hasten the future, to make eternity into the very nearest thing, into the today. Such an anticipation of the future would have to be a true turning of eternity into a today' (Ibid., 307).
35 Jn 3.30.
36 Kierkegaard, 'The Thorn in the Flesh', 275–90.

9

Climate despair from a Kierkegaardian perspective

Asceticism, possibility and eschatological hope

Hjördis Becker-Lindenthal

We are living in a time of massive anthropogenic global climate change, a crisis that humankind has never before experienced on such a scale. In 2019, a group of 11,000 scientists from 153 countries declared a climate emergency, urging governments to take immediate action to mitigate the devastating effects of global warming. And yet, in summer 2021, as I write this chapter, the situation is worse than it was two years ago: the levels of CO_2 in the atmosphere are higher than ever, and the news reports 'record-shattering' heatwaves and wildfires in Australia and the western United States,[1] hurricanes in parts of Asia and Africa, even floods in Germany and the United Kingdom – countries that hitherto considered themselves safe from climate-related disasters. The longer the needed changes of our way of living on Earth are postponed, the more likely the predicted global catastrophe becomes. While time is ticking away, humankind, it seems, is running out of options to mitigate the effects of climate change. The shrinking possibilities on the level of effective environmental action are directly linked to the increasing possibility of a sixth mass extinction, which this time is likely to include humankind as well, at least in the long run. Such bleak prospect for our species does, however, strongly affect the outlook we have on our individual lives right now: the sense of diminishing existential possibilities goes hand in hand with hopelessness and despair.

Psychologists warn of the enormous impact the climate crisis increasingly will have on mental health,[2] and new terms like 'climate despair' and 'eco-anxiety' are now frequently used not only in the academic discourse but also in the media and self-help literature.[3] The climate crisis is related to a variety of psychological phenomena: sometimes it leads to aggressive denial and the 'frenetic activity'[4] of busying oneself in order to forget about the red alert and pretend everything is fine. Many of us live in constant worry about the uncertainty of the future, and sometimes we are paralysed by the impression that it is impossible to avert the catastrophe. Emotionally, cognitively and practically, climate change is overwhelming – we are confronted with a 'hyperobject'[5] that exceeds our frame for understanding causal relations and temporal features. The 'slowfast time of the climate catastrophe', Catherine Keller writes, is 'too fast to prevent irreversible destruction; too slow to make it a top priority even of those who do not deny it'.[6] We might feel guilt and shame, while also feeling unable to make amends when the reduction of one's individual carbon footprint seems inefficient and meaningless. Thus, we experience ourselves as having no agency while at the same time being part of a collective that is, at least in the Western World, responsible for the ongoing destruction of habitats, the extinction of species, climate wars, the suffering of climate refugees and, as a whole, a massive interference with the Earth system – summed up in the recent declaration of a new epoch called the Anthropocene.[7]

The psychological effects of such immense change, of witnessed and experienced hardship and of responsibility combined with helplessness are not merely fleeting emotions or short phases of mental distress. Rather, they affect the whole person, our sense of self. As J. Aaron Simmons points out, 'in the face of losing hope, one faces losing oneself'[8] – one's agency, the meaning that one has given to one's life so far, the expectations of how one's life will continue. Unsurprisingly, then, hope is another concept that has strong currency in contemporary ecological discussions. How the role of hope is perceived, however, varies widely. On the one hand, hope is presented as the ultimate condition for action in an unprecedented crisis like the one we are currently facing. Catriona McKinnon defines hope as aiming 'at an objective which exists in the future, is valued by the hoper, and is desired by the hoper in virtue of this evaluation', furthermore as involving 'the belief that the future in which its objective exists is logically, conceptually, and nomologically possible', and she emphasizes that 'without it, the small window in time remaining for us to tackle climate change is already closed'.[9] Diametrically opposed to such a definition is the view that hope is preventing action that will induce change. For instance, the environmental policy technologist Matt Frost calls for resolve, not hope. For him, the latter is linked with the moralization of climate change, which he condemns as ineffective. Thus, 'the first step . . . must be to reduce the moral content of previous climate mitigation efforts, wherever possible replacing it with engineering challenges' like solar panels and nuclear reactors.[10] The eco-critic and environmental writer

Andrew McMurry counters views like this: the idea to solve the climate crisis with investments in renewable energy sources – a 'more-of-the-same-only-smarter approach' – is a red herring, because 'the climate system is already loaded with so much inertia that we could reduce the human carbon footprint to zero tomorrow and we would still undergo catastrophic warming over the next century'.[11] McMurry agrees, though, with the negative assessment of the role of hope. In his view, hope often is misused as 'the power-bringing magic word that helps make the bad stuff go away',[12] and apocalyptic novels and films only serve to keep the status quo: 'The appeal to hope is simply the growth machine voicing through us its impossible, reckless vision of limitless expansion, another ruse by which our suicidal culture asserts its authority over our imagination and robs us of our ability to come to grips with its perverse trajectory.'[13]

Hence the appeal to 'rethink what it means to have hope', as for instance Jonathan Franzen in his intensely debated New Yorker essay *What If We Stopped Pretending?* proposes.[14] His suggestion to stay hopeful *and* 'accept that disaster is coming' resonates with the climate psychologists' recent call to a 'radical hope', that is, the belief 'that meaningful action can make a difference, which is rooted in the reality of the crisis rather than a belief that it might not be as bad as we think'.[15] The distinction between different kinds of hope has a rich theological and philosophical tradition, with prominent contributions in the last century by Ernst Bloch, Gabriel Marcel and Jürgen Moltmann, not to forget Terry Eagleton's recent account of 'hope without optimism' and Jonathan Lear's analysis of the 'radical hope' of Plenty Coups, Chief of the Native American Crows, who were confronted with the collapse of their culture and identity.[16]

One author, however, is rarely mentioned in the context of hope in the face of the climate crisis: Søren Kierkegaard (1813–55).[17] In the following, I will argue that even though Kierkegaard might not be the obvious choice when it comes to a detailed account of humankind's relationship with nature,[18] his unique analysis of despair, particularly in relation to possibility, hope and imagination, can fruitfully be applied to the phenomenon of climate despair, offering new perspectives on hope in the Anthropocene. After an analysis of Kierkegaard's account of despair and selfhood with particular regard to possibility and an application to contemporary forms of despair (1), I will show how Kierkegaard's idea of asceticism, which can also be described as existential kenosis when it aims at following after Christ (2), offers a way to distinguish between the multiplicity of human possibilities (which bear the risk of hubris) and an infinite divine possibility that exceeds human anticipation, giving rise to a different kind of hope (3). Eschatological hope relates to possibility with humble courage, and, far from advocating detachment from the world, involves an attunement to temporality that fosters (climate) action as a constant beginning, unperturbed by worries about success (4).

Despair and possibility

In *The Sickness Unto Death*, Kierkegaard's pseudonym Anti-Climacus lucidly describes the role of possibility and its counterpart, necessity, for despair. For him, despair is not simply a feeling or a mood, but the loss of the self, or rather: failed selfhood, since becoming a self is a life-long task for every individual. How so? Let us look at Anti-Climacus's concept of the self. He defines it as a conscious, reflective relation of a synthesis of opposites.[19] These opposites are the eternal (infinite) and the temporal (finite), and possibility and necessity. The non-despairing self takes a stand towards this relation, for example, accepting the necessities of being born in a specific time (like the Anthropocene), raised in a particular social environment, having certain abilities and lacking others – all the aspects of our existence that we cannot change. At the same time, however, the self acknowledges the chances one has to determine one's life oneself. We are not simply the result of our upbringing or physical endowments, and we transcend the present through our anticipation of the future and our memory of the past. We believe in certain values and shape our lives through the decisions we make. Thus, we would usually agree that our self is more than a socially, historically and physically determined existence, and this 'more', as Leslie Howe puts it, 'is the eternal in us, and it can be represented in us by love, the good, ethical life, or the search for God'.[20] Still, we cannot escape the task of accepting ourselves as we are, which includes accepting that we cannot 'design' our lives from scratch. The non-despairing self 'rests transparently in the power that established it'.[21]

Since climate despair is mainly constituted by the perception that it is impossible for us to avert the climate catastrophe, I will focus on two of the self's constituents, that is, possibility (*Mulighed*) and necessity (*Nødvendighed*). Dominance of one of these aspects is the cause of despair, which, notably, does not have to be experienced as despair by the subject herself. Anti-Climacus distinguishes between possibility's despair and necessity's despair.[22] Possibility's despair is to lack necessity. To get to the core of this, let us first consider why it is important to be able to imagine possibilities at all. The self has – *is* – the continuous task of becoming itself, and 'in order to become itself, it reflects itself in the medium of imagination [*Phantasiens Medium*]'.²³ In such a manner, we can explore different ways to live our life – staying in the city or moving to the countryside and growing our own food, having children or not and so on. But it is not only the big life decisions that are influenced by our ability to imagine an alternative; the small scale is affected too, for example, in daily interactions with other people, envisioning possible ways to be a self, including different ways to evaluate a situation, act and react is essential, as David Gouwens has shown with regard to what he calls the 'ethical imagination'.²⁴

But we need to invest an equal amount of energy in choosing and actualizing *some* of the options, because if we do not, we end up with a series of 'phantasmagoria [*Phantasmagorier*]', which 'follow one another in such a rapid succession that it seems *as if everything were possible*, and this is exactly the final moment, the point at which the individual himself becomes a mirage [*et Luftsyn*]'.²⁵ The result of the copious use of this 'mirror of possibility'²⁶ is exemplified in the case of the so-called 'Aesthete' who is criticized in *The Concept of Irony* for imagining 'a multitude of destinies'²⁷ instead of taking responsibility for the realization of a few particular possibilities in her life. Such a person might seem to be content, but in truth, she is 'building only castles in the air', and even though 'all these imaginatively constructed virtues make it [the self] look splendid' she is in deep despair.²⁸ Applied to the twenty-first century, the life of the 'Aesthete' appears in the online existences we lead in social media and virtual realities, where images and words are suggestive but usually remain without consequences. A contemporary term for the Aesthete's despair could hence be 'escapist's despair'. But the despair of possibility can also be found in the many resolutions we make to reduce our carbon footprint: never fly anymore, boycott fast fashion brands, become vegan, get rid of the car, go plastic-free and so on. But often, we doubt the efficiency of our individual contributions to mitigate global warming, so we do not follow through with these imagined possibilities to save the planet. Such possibilities, therefore, are just fantasies or 'phantasmagoria'. Not only are they detrimental to the planet but also, according to Anti-Climacus, to the self: they turn the self into a mirage as much as a climate action procrastinator.

The contrasting (albeit no less despairing) life view is based on denying possibility. Anti-Climacus calls it *necessity's despair*. It appears in two forms: as fatalistic or deterministic mentality and as philistine-bourgeois mentality (*Spidsborgerlighed, Trivialitet*).²⁹ For the fatalist, every single aspect of life is determined and unchangeable. Denying possibility – one of the essential constituents of the self – she fails to become a self, thus, lives in despair. This form of despair probably represents what is most commonly associated with climate despair, that is, the paralysing belief that whatever we do, either as collective or as individuals, will not have a mitigating effect on global warming. The *Spidsborger*, by contrast, experiences no such mental distress. 'Bereft of imagination [*uden Phantasie*]',[30] he does not envision the worst-case scenario, but simply 'lives within a certain trivial compendium of expectations as to how things go ... what usually happens' and thinks that he 'controls possibility', leading 'possibility around imprisoned in the cage of *probability*' and 'imagining himself to be the master'.[31]

Applied to our current situation, this kind of despair can be found in those who outrightly deny the climate crisis, or those, who do acknowledge it, but apply what McMurry calls a 'schematization of hope': they articulate the unthinkableness of the worst-case scenario in order to disarm it, like 'I cannot believe that the human race will destroy itself'.[32] This attitude often goes together with the belief that soon, geoengineering will be able to offer an easy way out, for instance through stratospheric sulphur injections that deflect solar radiation. The trust in the calculability of technofixes, however, ignores the possible long-term, non-anticipatable side effects of yet another interference with the Earth system. Moreover, Anti-Climacus would emphasize that control over possibility is a hubristic illusion that does not account for the fact that the self, like the whole of Creation, has its source in 'the power that established it'. Hence, the *Spidsborger* fails in becoming a self. Even though he might not suffer, he nevertheless is in deep despair.

Slumbering despair turns into suffering when something extraordinarily bad happens, for instance, when someone's worst nightmare becomes real. Here, imagination plays an important role. Anti-Climacus speaks of the 'horror that a terrified imagination has pictured [*en forskraekket Indbildningskrafts Gysen har forstillet sig en eller anden Rædsel*]', and he stresses that 'at this point, salvation is, humanly speaking, utterly impossible'.[33] To exemplify what Anti-Climacus means, let us consider two cases, an individual and a collective trauma. Assume that someone's partner or child suddenly dies. For this person, then, it does not seem that *anything* could happen that would make life enjoyable again – except for the impossible return of the beloved. A case of collective trauma is the downfall of one's culture, which the Native American Crows experienced,[34] or the destruction of one's home due to climate change. Needless to say, this home can also be 'our common home', as Pope Francis calls the Earth in his previous encyclical letter.[35] When our worst fears are to become true, only the one who has faith does not 'collapse', Anti-Climacus says, for only the believer has the 'infallible antidote for despair – possibility – because for God everything is possible at every moment'.[36]

It appears that for the believer, as much as for the one who suffers from possibility's despair, *possibility is total*. Hence, we seem to be in a deadlock. Furthermore, the imagination at the same time can foster and obstruct becoming an authentic self: On the one hand, the imagination can conjure up possibilities after possibilities, that is, suggest that *everything is possible*, with the consequence that the self turns into a mirage and actualizes none of the possibilities to act (e.g. to reduce one's carbon footprint). On the other hand, it is the imagination that pulls the *Spidsborger* out of the unconscious despair of necessity: 'in order for a person to become aware of his self and of God, imagination [*Phantasien*] must raise him higher from the miasma of probability, it must tear him out of this and teach him to hope and fear – or to fear and to hope – by rendering possible that which surpasses the *quantum satis* [sufficient standard] of any experience'.[37] According to Anti-Climacus, when we complacently trust in the calculability of life and nature, controllable by our machines and statistic models, we are displaying signs of the despair of necessity. By vividly conjuring up the possibility of a planet destroyed by hurricanes, drought, floods and raging civil wars, the imagination helps us wake up from our hubristic lull.

But the imagination appears to succeed only to a certain degree: 'the ingeniousness of the human imagination [*Phantasies Opfindsomhed*], can extend to the point of creating possibility but at last . . . only this helps: that for God everything is possible'.[38] Hence, there is only one way to relate to possibility, and this is in humble faith. The infinite, soothing and assuring idea that everything is possible implies that we need to acknowledge our own limits and, according to Anti-Climacus's theological anthropology, our sinful disposition.[39] Hence, to be able to truly hope, we need to die to our perceptions, beliefs, plans and expectations – in short: to the very idea we have of our dear self.

Asceticism

Commonly, asceticism is understood as abstinence and renunciation of physical indulgence. In the context of the climate crisis, individual measures like turning down the thermostat and forsaking the idea of cheap vacations in popular tourist spots that are easily reached via cheap air travel, appear to be the kind of asceticism we have to endorse, whether we like it or not. Such asceticism is equated with austerity, which is often depicted as the inevitable consequence of the economic, political and individual changes necessary to mitigate global warming. Kierkegaard's understanding of asceticism, however, is different:

his call to die to the world and the self is grounded in a hopeful theological anthropology. Through an asceticism that aims at the core of our very being and not just a few habits, we restore and continue to become the self that we are supposed to be. To overcome despair, 'the cure is simply to die, to die to the world'.[40]

Kierkegaard's concept of dying-to (*hendøen, afdøen*) builds on a long Christian ascetic tradition,[41] and the emphasis on letting go of our mundane, smug and all-too-convenient ways of perceiving ourselves, the world and God occurs in many of his writings.[42] In the most extreme case, this asceticism is part of following after Christ, where it can be described as existential kenosis.[43] Spiritual asceticism restores the self's receptivity to divine possibility and enables a specific kind of hope. Let us now take a closer look at what it means to die to one's self and the world through a reading of the *Upbuilding Discourse* 'The One Who Prays Aright Struggles in Prayer and Is Victorious – in That God Is Victorious' (1844) and the third part of *Practice in Christianity* (1850).

Implicitly referring to Mk 8.35, the *Discourse* describes the process it takes of turning from someone who mundanely prays into someone who is attuned to the divine. In the beginning, the praying person is like most people, and as such, has a 'sensate person's conception' of what it means to pray. He thinks praying is 'a matter of making oneself clear to God, of truly explaining to him what is beneficial for the one who is praying, of truly impressing it upon his mind'.[44] If one accomplishes this, one's wish will be fulfilled. In addition, the praying person has a very specific conception of God, who 'has the heart to feel humanly, the ear to hear a human being's complaint; and even though he does not fulfil every wish, he ... is moved by the struggler's cry'.[45] Furthermore, the praying person confidently understands himself as a true believer, daring 'to testify that he is straining all his understanding to become sufficiently foresighted to spy the remotest hint of the fulfilment, that he is straining every thought to conjure forth from the most insignificant event anything it could be hiding'.[46] Building on mundane sagacity, sensate persons believe they can actively influence God. They regard prayer as a calculable function to guarantee the fulfilment of worldly wishes to get one's 'share in the good things',[47] like a thriving trade, good weather for the harvest, or, applied to our contemporary situation, global warming to stop.

Repeatedly, the praying person is confronted with the failure of such calculating prayers – the wishes remain unfulfilled. After having desired many things, he 'little by little gives up that which according to his earthly conception is less important'.[48] As an astute negotiator, the praying person now concentrates his soul on *one* single wish. But that single wish is not fulfilled either. Finally, the praying person also lets go of this particular wish. Now his desire does not have a mundane object anymore; he asks for 'nothing in the external world, his wish does not centre on anything earthly'.[49] He only asks for an explanation: Why does God not even fulfil that single wish? At this point, he is still not praying properly, Kierkegaard says, because he has neither refrained from adopting a demanding role in his relation to God nor is his soul empty: 'still he is not idle [*ledig*], because he is ruminating, and still he is not passive [*uvirksom*], because he is pondering an explanation'.[50]

The praying person's struggle with God has become inward: day and night, unaffected by the worldly life, his mind is working restlessly. What has happened, he thinks, 'must of course be for the best, the loss and the pain must be efficacious in quite another way than the fulfilment of the one and only wish or of all wishes'.[51] Such a mind, Kierkegaard emphasizes, is still fraught with the concept of efficaciousness, and thus has not entered into a true relation to God: 'Efficacious – yes that is the name of the bridge he wants to throw from his pain across to his blessedness, but alas, the bridge is continually being cut off!'[52] The praying person needs to let go of the wish for an explanation, too. He has to accept that God requires only faith and does not adhere to the rationales of the *Spidsborger* culture. Finally, after 'the external world and every claim on life were taken away from him . . . it seems to him that he is reduced to nothing at all'.[53] And this is exactly the purpose of the process! Only by becoming nothing can the praying person gain the most, that is, being transformed by God: 'Only when he himself becomes nothing, only then can God illuminate him so that he resembles God.'[54] In the painful process of leaving behind all mundane wishes and human sagacity, the praying person has changed. He understands himself differently now, and his prayers now consist of thanking God for this. Finally, the praying person became 'one who prays aright'.

The Upbuilding Discourse about the praying person focuses on the renunciation of mundane desires and the *spidsborgerlig* idea of reason based on calculation, means-to-ends-relations and probability. The third part of *Practice in Christianity*, another work by Kierkegaard's pseudonym Anti-Climacus, additionally considers the role of the imagination, which is why we now take a short look at the story of the young man who tries to actualize an extreme possibility of being a self. He wishes to follow after Christ, that is, 'to suffer approximately as he suffered in this world'.[55]

The young man is under the influence of an *idealized* image because his imagination has created a beautified version of the most extreme existential possibility. This causes some problems, because 'it looks very easy the way the imagination [*Indbildning*] depicts the image [*Billede*]; one sees only the perfection, sees even the struggling perfection only as finished'.[56] Like most of his contemporaries, he holds a convenient 'fantasy picture of Christ [*et phantastisk Billede af Christus*]' that rather focuses on the glory, not abasement, mockery and self-denial.[57] After a while, the adolescent realizes that the imagination has not given him an adequate idea of what it means to actualize his mental image of the Crucified. He realizes 'what this love [of the image of perfection] will cost him, but who knows, he says, after all, better times may come, help will certainly come, and it can still turn out all right'.[58] Again, this is a wrong understanding of what it means to follow Christ. Suffering is not rewarded; it is an illusion to assume one would be able to follow Christ in his loftiness. This experience intensifies the young man's suffering. Still unable to give up the image of the suffering Christ as such, he gives up the all-too-convenient interpretations of it and lets go of his conceited expectations, including the calculations and specific hopes for the intervention of God. Slowly he starts to picture himself differently in relation to the Crucified. Finally, he comes to imitate Christ as much as it is humanly possible: through dying to oneself.[59]

Like the praying person from the Upbuilding Discourse, the young man lets go of the mental image he holds of himself, of his image of God and the specific way God would help him, 'all calculating, all sagacity and probability'.[60] Had he clung to his expectations and specific hopes, he would have fallen into despair.

Divine possibility and eschatological hope

Before we turn to the question of what this can teach us about climate despair, let us first look at what the ascetic process demonstrated by the praying person and the young follower of Christ implies for a revisited concept of possibility. The young man and the praying person both firmly believe in God's omnipotence, but they painfully experience that 'everything is possible for God'[61] is not the same as God fulfilling one's specific hopes and ideas about what is needed in a desperate situation. Absolutely none of the praying person's wishes are fulfilled, and the young man prays in vain 'that help will certainly come'.[62] Instead of lifting the pain, God only helps him further into the suffering. As a consequence, they let go of their images of God as a lenient father who uses His almighty power to fulfil his child's every wish or as a business partner with whom one can negotiate. In the end, they still experience God as loving and almighty, but not in the way they have originally imagined. When they finally surrender, they realize that, indeed, for God everything is possible, but it is totally different from what they thought this meant. Through letting go of the idea of control, calculability and probability, of the belief that they know what is best for themselves, of the mental images they hold of themselves, of the way to imitate Christ and even of God, they experience the spiritual suffering of dying to oneself. Ultimately, the young man gives up his will and thus comes to resemble Jesus Christ who prays in the garden of Gethsemane: 'Father ... everything is possible for you. Take this cup from me. Yet not what I will, but what you will' (Mk 14.36).

The kenotic process restores one's openness to the divine possibility, which is a boundlessly rich, yet abstract possibility. It is the fullness of a divine *that*, and not a ragbag crammed with trivial possibilities of 'whats' and 'hows', subject to human speculation and wishful thinking. Thus, similar to the notion of Christ as *Truth*, one could speak of God as *Possibility*.[63] The believer embraces the dizzying thought that God in His almighty power is able to do everything at any moment, including things she cannot even imagine.[64] Out of this restored sense for Possibility rises a new kind of hope: 'authentic hope' (*sand Haab*, lit. 'true hope'), which is different from what Anti-Climacus identifies as 'the merely human manner of speaking' about hope.[65] Kierkegaard calls it 'earthly hope', which is 'a longing expectation now of one thing, now of another, in short, an expectant person's relationship to the possibility of multiplicity (*Mangfoldiges Mulighed*)'.[66] Moltmann's distinction between *futurum* and *future* (Zukunft) is helpful to shed light on this difference between true hope and its mere shadow: whereas the first is extrapolated from our experiences of the past and the present, the latter is associated with the radically new, with parousia.[67] Kierkegaard defines true hope as 'relating oneself in expectancy to the possibility of the good'.[68]

As Sylvia Walsh observes, this hope is a 'gift of the Holy Spirit that comes only after one has 'died to' the understanding's merely human view of hope'.[69] Furthermore, such hope is a manifestation of continuous humility, recognizing 'the limits of one's imaginative capacity *qua finite creature*'.[70] It is a hoping 'against all hope' (Rom. 4.18), transcending our cognitive and imaginative capacities and the horizon of collective memory. Opening 'a framework by which one's historical possibilities are reconsidered as non-ultimate',[71] this hope is eschatological. But does this mean that one's actions are irrelevant, and all one has to do is blindly trust that a divine miracle will happen, which, in our case, will stop global warming? Moreover, should this shift our attention from the earthly life, for example, our concern for the planet, to salvation in the afterlife?

In the end: Humble courage and infinite striving

Statements like 'there is only one eternal hope on this earth: to follow Christ into heaven'[72] seem to suggest that all that counts is the hereafter, inviting quietism. However, we must not forget that in order to become a true, non-despairing self (i.e. a relation that relates itself to its contradictory elements), one has to develop a synthesis of the possible and the necessary, the eternal and the temporal. Hence, while Kierkegaard admonishes us to give up our idolatrous attachment to worldly values, to hubristic ideas we hold of ourselves as individuals and as a culture (e.g. continuous economic growth), he also reminds us that we need to stay committed to our earthly existence. In the above quote, he defines hope as '*relating oneself* (*forholde sig*) in expectancy to the possibility of the good'[73] – this includes the authentic relation a non-despairing has to itself. Such relation makes us revalue single goods and relate to the many possibilities and necessities in our lives in a new manner. In hope, one 'makes an eschatological stand towards the good in one's life', which 'can only be related to through expectation, since unlike the ethical it cannot be the intentional object of the will. And yet, this good incorporates the ethical; in this sense we should continue to actively strive for it'.[74] Kierkegaard's Lutheran emphasis on unconditional forgiveness as a manifestation of divine goodness does not make human action irrelevant. Even though we must never think that we will be saved by human inventiveness, sagacity and deeds, we nevertheless are encouraged to continue striving.[75] Moreover, the security of being forgiven liberates us to strive in the first place! Kierkegaard emphasizes that 'the fact that I am saved by faith, that as far as that goes, nothing at all is demanded from me, ought to make it possible for me to strive, so that I do not collapse under impossibility but am encouraged and refreshed by the fact that my salvation has been decided'.[76]

How can this be applied to climate despair? As we have noticed, climate despair comes in many forms. It does not only consist in losing hope that there will be a future in which Earth is still home to many species and hospitable to humankind but from a Kierkegaardian perspective, climate despair can also show itself in an idolatrous trust in human efficaciousness or in losing oneself to the many possibilities of individual climate action, with procrastinating effects. Our imagination plays a crucial role, whether we despairingly escape into the realms of science fiction and social media, or whether we lose heart about haunting images of the climate catastrophe which our imagination vividly paints in our minds, enforced by the apocalyptic narratives offered by film and news reports. What would Kierkegaard say about all this? First of all, he would probably emphasize the need to make this despair conscious and face our various despairing strategies by which we try to cope (or rather, evade) the climate crisis. This could lead to even deeper despair, but in the end, it is a chance to be cleansed of inadequate imagery of ourselves, the world and our relation to God.

It is tempting to understand Kierkegaard's attacks on human sagacity, its appreciation of probability and calculability, together with his disapproval of the natural sciences,[77] as a justification to turn our backs to climate sciences and instead solely focus on faith. Obviously, this can get dangerously close to the denial of climate change. Today, the sciences fulfil a role that Kierkegaard did not anticipate: they do not always and not necessarily foster the belief in, nor the justification of, the human mastery of nature. Rather, they make us realize that this belief led to the current crisis in the first place, showing that humankind's interference with natural processes got out of control. According to Kierkegaard, only after we have let go of the various ideas we hold about us being in control (as individual, culture, nation or humankind), of us being able to fully anticipate and successfully plan, breaking possibility down to probability, only when we let go of this mindset, only then are we filled with the gift of true hope: *for God, everything is possible*. Hence, we can expect the good to happen, even though it might not be the good as we currently understand it. Furthermore, humbling ourselves under the thought that it is *God, not us*, for whom all things are possible, we might do good to realize that some things, while they certainly are possible, are not realizable for us. This applies to the large scale of geoengineering as much as the daily routines of our individual lives: of course, it is perfectly possible to get rid of the car and to cycle to work for an hour every day, but one might be too afraid of being exposed to the traffic, or one might simply be lazy. Acknowledging these 'sinful' aspects of our selves, which inhibit us from realizing specific possibilities, and trusting in God's forgiveness, might free us from paralysing guilt, so we can direct our attention and energies to those possible actions that we are actually able to turn into ecological habits.

In addition, the very experience of losing hope in terms of particular hopes for this and that can have a liberating effect, because,

> when we lose the specific hope that we had for the future relative to evidence that makes it no longer reasonable to believe as possible, we also lose the arrogance that we are the key to unlocking the future in a specific way. Far from leading to a life of apathy, quietism or resignation, however, this humbled self-conception allows us to continue to work for particular futures without being crushed by failing to bring them about.[78]

In that vein, many faith leaders and people of faith have joined the climate change movement or created their own activist groups. For instance, Christian Climate Action (CCA) regularly takes part in Extinction Rebellion protests and organizes independent events as well, like vigils for the victims of climate change (so-called 'die-ins' during which activists lie down on public places to represent people killed by climate disasters). The CCA's principles and values express humble resolution: 'we are called to be faithful, not successful: None of us are perfect for tackling the climate emergency, but there is no time to wait until we are. We are called to tell the truth about the emergency we are in and to faithfully act now.'[79] Such faithful activism relies on a firm, but unspecific hope, which implies a specific relation to time. It abstains from the desire to want to know for sure what the long-term future will hold. Instead, it practices 'an attunement to temporality and temporalization that keeps time by keeping it open, absurdly open . . . by virtue of the eternal'.[80] With 'humble courage' (*ydmygt Mod*) one thus continuously tries to realize the good not only during demonstrations and protests but also in small actions and habits, day by day, again and again.[81]

For the believer, Kierkegaard's understanding of despair, hope and possibility is soothing, and helpful to restore the agency of those who are struggling with climate despair. But does one have to be religious to have one's climate despair alleviated by the Kierkegaardian perspective? While it certainly helps to believe in an omnipotent, graceful God who will transfigure us in His likeness and keep His promise to make all things right, a secularized version of Kierkegaard's account of possibility as that which exceeds our rational and imaginative capabilities is also able to instigate hope, that is, hope as a general attitude without the usual specific expectations that can easily be disappointed. In this way, we might have the strength to keep on striving in our efforts to mitigate global warming. Hence, it could be worthwhile to question our instrumental use of reason, our idolization of human sagacity, which reduces possibility to probability and the familiar. Finally, the ecological forms of asceticism called for today and dreaded as austerity, might be viewed in a different light: they help remove attitudes and ways of living that are harmful not only to the planet but also to the selves we could be.[82]

Notes

1 Daisy Dunne, 'Scientists Who Declared Climate Emergency Two Years Ago Say Earth's Vital Signs have Worsened', *The Independent*, 28 July 2021. Available at

https://www.independent.co.uk/climate-change/news/climate-emergency-earth-vital-signs-b1891724.html (accessed 8 August 2021).
2 Cf. the open letter by practitioner psychologists: https://docs.google.com/forms/d/e/1FAIpQLSdU6L3NM12ikT-34ZPlp1yv-6nHcM5aqhmid6nK-M3plZGu3A/viewform?vc=0&c=0&w=1 (accessed 28 July 2021).
3 See for instance Anouchka Grose, *A Guide to Eco-Anxiety: How to Protect the Planet and Your Mental Health* (London: Watkins, 2020); see also Jane Fonda, *What Can I Do? My Path from Climate Despair to Action* (New York: Penguin, 2020).
4 Pope Francis uses this expression in his ecological encyclical letter *Laudato Si'* to describe the reaction to the 'profound imbalance' we experience in our relation to the Earth: Pope Francis, *Encyclical Letter Laudato Si' of the Holy Father Francis: On Care for Our Common Home* (2015), 164. Available at https://www.vatican.va/content/francesco/en/encyclicals/documents/papa-francesco_20150524_enciclica-laudato-si.html (accessed 24 July 2021).
5 Timothy Morton, *Hyperobjects: Philosophy and Ecology After the End of the World* (Minneapolis: University of Minnesota Press, 2013).
6 Catherine Keller, 'Encycling: One Feminist Theological Response', *Syndicate* (online), 23 December 2015. Available at https://syndicate.network/encycling-one-feminist-theological-response/ (accessed 24 July 2021).
7 For a critical perspective see Alf Hornborg and Andreas Malm, 'The Geology of Mankind? A Critique of the Anthropocene Narrative', *The Anthropocene Review* 1, no. 3 (2014): 62–9.
8 J. Aaron Simmons, 'Living Joyfully After Losing Social Hope. Kierkegaard and Chrétien on Selfhood and Eschatological Expectation', *Religions* 8, no. 33 (2017): 1–15 (5).
9 Catriona McKinnon, 'Climate Change. Against Despair', in *Ethics and the Environment*, vol. 19, no. 1, ed. Victoria Davion (Bloomington: Indiana University Press, 2014), 31–48 (34; 45).
10 Matt Frost, 'After Climate Despair', *The New Atlantis. Journal for Technology and Society*, Fall 2019. Available at https://www.thenewatlantis.com/publications/after-climate-despair (accessed 8 August 2021).
11 Andrew McMurry, *Entertaining Futility: Despair and Hope in the Time of Climate Change* (College Station: Texas A&M University Press, 2018), 89.
12 Ibid.
13 Ibid., 93.
14 Jonathan Franzen, 'What if We Stopped Pretending?', *New Yorker*, 8 September, 2019. Available at https://www.newyorker.com/culture/cultural-comment/what-if-we-stopped-pretending (accessed 23 July 2021).
15 Caroline Hickman, member of the Climate Psychology Alliance, as quoted in Jillian Ambrose, '"Hijacked by Climate Anxiety". How Climate Dread Is

Hindering Climate Action', *The Guardian*, 8 October, 2020. Available at https://www.theguardian.com/environment/2020/oct/08/anxiety-climate-crisis-trauma-paralysing-effect-psychologists (accessed 20 July 2021).

16 Gabriel Marcel, *Homo Viator: Introduction to a Metaphysic of Hope*, trans. Emma Craufurd (New York: Harper & Row, 1962 [1945]); Ernst Bloch, *The Principle of Hope*, trans. Neville Plaice, Stephen Plaice and Paul Knight (Cambridge, MA: MIT Press, 1995 [1954]); Jürgen Moltmann, *Theology of Hope on the Ground and the Implications of a Christian Eschatology*, trans. James W. Leitch (London: SCM Press, 1969 [1964]); Terry Eagleton, *Hope Without Optimism* (New Haven, CT: Yale University Press, 2015); Jonathan Lear, *Radical Hope. Ethics in the Face of Cultural Devastation* (Cambridge, MA: Harvard University Press, 2006).

17 I am only aware of one fine paper by Ruby S. Guyatt, 'Kierkegaard in the Anthropocene: Hope, Philosophy, and the Climate Crisis', *Religions* 11, no. 6 (2020): 1–12. While Guyatt focuses on Kierkegaard's understanding of hope in relation to the eternal good and other human beings through love, I approach climate despair and hope through Kierkegaard's account of ascetic selfhood.

18 Usually, the literature with this regard concentrates on Kierkegaard's three discourses on the lilies in the field and the birds in the air (see Søren Kierkegaard, *Upbuilding Discourses in Various Spirits*, ed. and trans. Howard V. Hong and Edna H. Hong (Princeton, NJ: Princeton University Press, 2009), 155–212). For the latest scholarship, see Marius Timmann-Mjaaland, 'Ecophilosophy and the Ambivalence of Nature: Kierkegaard and Knausgård on Lilies, Birds and Being', in *Kierkegaard Studies Yearbook*, ed. Heiko Schulz, Jon Stewart and Karl Verstrynge (Berlin and Boston: De Gruyter, 2021). For an overview of Kierkegaard's account of nature see Will Williams, 'Kierkegaard's Defense of Nature and Theology Against Natural Theology', in *The Kierkegaardian Mind*, ed. Adam Buben, Eleanor Helms and Patrick Stokes (Milton Park: Routledge, 2019), 254–66.

19 Søren Kierkegaard, *The Sickness Unto Death*, trans. Alastair Hannay (London: Penguin Books, 1989), 13 / SKS 11:129.

20 Leslie A. Howe, 'Kierkegaard and the Feminine Self', *Hypatia* 9 (1994): 131–57 (133).

21 Kierkegaard, *The Sickness Unto Death*, 14 / SKS 11: 130.

22 Ibid., 35–42 / SKS 11:151–7.

23 Ibid., 35 / SKS 11:151.

24 David J. Gouwens, 'Kierkegaard on the Ethical Imagination', *The Journal of Religious Ethics* 10, no. 2 (1982): 204–20. See also Ryan Kemp, 'The Role of Imagination in Kierkegaard's Account of Ethical Transformation', *Archiv für Geschichte der Philosophie* 100, no. 2 (2018): 202–31.

25 Kierkegaard, *The Sickness Unto Death,* 36 / SKS 11:152; my emphasis.

26 Ibid., 37 / SKS 11:152.

27 Kierkegaard, *Concept of Irony,* ed. and trans. Howard V. Hong and Edna H. Hong (Princeton, NJ: Princeton University Press, 1989), 282 / SKS 1:317.

28 Kierkegaard, *The Sickness Unto Death*, 69 / SKS 11:183.
29 Ibid., 41 / SKS 11:156.
30 Ibid.
31 Ibid., 41–2 / SKS 11:156f.
32 McMurry, *Entertaining Futility*, 92.
33 Kierkegaard, *The Sickness Unto Death*, 38 / SKS 11:154.
34 See Lear, *Radical Hope*.
35 *Encyclical Letter Laudato Si' of the Holy Father Francis: On Care for Our Common Home*.
36 Kierkegaard, *The Sickness Unto Death*, 39f. / SKS 11:155.
37 Ibid., 41 / SKS 11:156.
38 Ibid., 39 / SKS 11:154. In 'Kierkegaard on Imagination: Hope, Possibility, and the Imitation of Christ', *History of European Ideas* 47, no. 3 (2021): 484–99, I argue that according to Kierkegaard, the imagination cooperates with grace in this transition.
39 It is important to note that according to Kierkegaard, becoming a true Christian implies becoming an authentic self: from the self's adequate relation to the 'power that established it' flows an adequate relation of the self to itself, with a balanced relation of its opposing elements, i.e., eternity and temporality, possibility and necessity. In other words, one cannot be a true Christian without being an authentic self. Whether one can – according to Kierkegaard – be a true self without being a Christian is a different question, as the two parts of *The Sickness Unto Death* show.
40 Kierkegaard, *The Sickness Unto Death*, 6 / SKS 11, 118.
41 See the seminal work by Marie Mikulová Thulstrup, 'The Significance of Mortification and Dying away (to)', in *The Sources and Depths of Faith in Kierkegaard*, ed. Thulstrup, Marie Mikulová (Copenhagen: C.A. Reitzel, 1978), 160–7.
42 Kierkegaard often ridicules physical ascetic practices that in his view are not connected to an inward change of the self; see David L. Coe, 'Ascetism', in *Kierkegaard's Concepts* vol. 15, tome 1 *Kierkegaard Research: Sources, Reception and Resources*, ed. Steven M. Emmanuel, William McDonald and Jon Stewart (Farnham: Ashgate, 2013).
43 David R. Law coined the term 'existential kenoticism': David R. Law, *Kierkegaard's Kenotic Christology* (Oxford: Oxford University Press, 2013), 287. See also Hjördis Becker-Lindenthal and Ruby S. Guyatt, 'Kierkegaard on Existential Kenosis and the Power of the Image: *Fear and Trembling* and *Practice in Christianity*', *Modern Theology* 35, no. 4 (2019): 706–27.
44 Kierkegaard, *Eighteen Upbuilding Discourses*, ed. and trans. Howard V. Hong and Edna H. Hong (Princeton, NJ: Princeton University Press, 1992), 388 / SKS 5, 371.
45 Ibid., 387 / SKS 5, 370.
46 Ibid., 388 / SKS 5, 371.

47 Ibid., 387 / SKS 5, 370.
48 Ibid., 393f. / SKS 5, 375.
49 Ibid., 394 / SKS 5, 376.
50 Ibid.
51 Ibid.
52 Ibid.
53 Ibid.
54 Ibid. On the mystic aspects and the role of the *imago Dei* in this Upbuilding Discourse, see Hjördis Becker, 'Mirroring God. Reflections of Meister Eckhart's Thought in Kierkegaard's Authorship', in *Kierkegaard Studies Yearbook*, ed. Heiko Schulz, Jon Stewart, and Karl Verstrynge (Berlin and Boston: De Gruyter, 2012), 3–24.
55 PC 178 / SKS 12:179. On following Christ in the third part of Søren Kierkegaard, *Practice in Christianity*, ed. and trans. Howard V. Hong and Edna H. Hong (Princeton, NJ: Princeton University Press, 1991), see Sylvia Walsh, 'Standing at the Crossroads: The Invitation of Christ to a Life of Suffering', in *International Kierkegaard Commentary*, vol. 20 (Practice in Christianity), ed. Robert L. Perkins (Macon: Mercer University Press, 2004), 125–60; and Brian Gregor, 'Thinking Through Kierkegaard's Anti-Climacus: Art, Imagination, and Imitation', *The Heythrop Journal* 50, no. 3 (2009): 448–65 (450).
56 Kierkegaard, *Practice in Christianity,* 187 / SKS 12:186.
57 Ibid., 97 / SKS 12:106. Cf. Ibid., 99 / SKS 12, 107.
58 Ibid., 190 / SKS 12:190.
59 Cf. WA 234 / SKS 22: 26. I have explored this argument in more detail in Becker-Lindenthal, 'Kierkegaard on Imagination'.
60 Kierkegaard, *Eighteen Upbuilding Discourses*, 380 / SKS 5, 364. On the paradoxical way in which the follower of Christ is called 'to surrender everything to the grace of God – including, in a certain sense, his will to imitate Christ' see Christopher Barnett, *Kierkegaard, Pietism and Holiness* (Farnham: Ashgate, 2011), 188.
61 Kierkegaard, *The Sickness Unto Death*, 40 / SKS 11:155.
62 Kierkegaard, *Practice in Christianity*, 190 / SKS 12:190.
63 See Søren Kierkegaard, *The Point of View for My Work as an Author*, ed. and trans. Howard V. Hong and Edna H. Hong (Princeton, NJ: Princeton University Press, 1998), 73 / SKS 11:77. Cf. Anti-Climacus comments that 'since everything is possible for God, then God is this – that everything is possible [*saa er Gud det, at Alt er muligt*]' (Kierkegaard, *The Sickness Unto Death*, 40 / SKS 11:155). We find a similar thought in Nicolas of Cusa's *De Apice Theoriae*, including the self-transcending effects this perception has on the self: 'When the mind sees by means of its own capability that Possibility itself, because of its excellence, cannot be grasped, then by means of [this]seeing, it sees beyond its own capability', Nicolas of Cusa, *De Apice Theoriae*, trans. Jasper Hopkins (Minneapolis: Arthur J. Banning Press, 1989 [1464]), 1430.

64 Abraham demonstrates the same in *Fear and Trembling*. His words 'give voice to a trust *that* God will provide while remaining completely indeterminate with respect to *how* God will provide'. Jeffrey Hanson, *Kierkegaard and the Life of Faith. The Aesthetic, the Ethical, and the Religious in Fear and Trembling* (Bloomington, IN and Indianapolis: Indiana University Press, 2017), 191.
65 Kierkegaard, *The Sickness Unto Death*, 38 / SKS 11, 153.
66 Kierkegaard, *Upbuilding Discourses in Various Spirits*, 112 / SKS 8, 214 and Kierkegaard, *Works of Love*, ed. and trans. Howard V. Hong and Edna H. Hong (Princeton, NJ: Princeton University Press, 1995), 250 / SKS 9, 250.
67 See Jürgen Moltmann, *The Future of Creation*, trans. Margaret Kohl (London: SCM, 1979), 29; cf. Ryan A. Neal, *Theology as Hope. On the Ground and Implications of Jürgen Moltmann's Doctrine of Hope* (Eugene: Pickwick Publications, 2008), 27–32. For Moltmann, Zukunft is built on the believer's trust that God will keep his promise to make things right. Moltmann's verdict, however, that Kierkegaard's philosophy lacks hope due to its focus on the 'moment' as present (i.e. not future-oriented) epiphany of the eternal is inadequate; cf. Terrence Sweeney, 'Hope against Hope: Søren Kierkegaard on the Breath of Eternal Possibility', *Philosophy & Theology* 28, no. 1 (2016): 165–84 (175).
68 Kierkegaard, *Works of Love*, 249 / SKS 9: 249.
69 Sylvia Walsh, *Kierkegaard: Thinking Christianly in an Existential Mode* (Oxford: Oxford University Press, 2009), 159. In the Upbuilding Discourse 'Purity of Heart is to Will One Thing', Kierkegaard explicitly demands that all 'earthly hope should be killed, because not until then is one rescued by the true hope' (*Upbuilding Discourses in Various Spirits*, 116 / SKS 8, 217).
70 John Lippitt, 'Kierkegaard's Virtues? Humility and Gratitude as the Grounds of Contentment, Patience, and Hope in Kierkegaard's Moral Psychology', in *Kierkegaard's God and the Good Life*, ed. J. Aaron Simmons and Michael Strawser (Bloomington: Indiana University Press, 2017), 95–113 (107).
71 Simmons, 'Living Joyfully After Losing Social Hope', 7.
72 Kierkegaard, *Upbuilding Discourses in Various Spirits*, 229 / SKS 8: 330.
73 Kierkegaard, *Works of Love*, 249 / SKS 9: 249, my emphasis.
74 Mark Bernier, *The Task of Hope in Kierkegaard* (Oxford: Oxford University Press, 2015), 213.
75 On the dialectics of Lutheran faith, see *Kierkegaard's Journals and Notebooks* vol. 7, 436f. / SKS 23: 428a (NB 20:65a).
76 Ibid., 436 / SKS 23: 428, NB 20:65. Hence, as Roe Fremstedal notes, 'forgiveness makes possible not only salvation, but also the realisation of the Kingdom of God'. Roe Fremstedal, 'Kierkegaard on the Metaphysics of Hope', *The Heythrop Journal* 53 (2012): 51–60 (54).
77 See for instance *Kierkegaard's Journals and Notebooks* vol. 4, 67 / SKS 20: 68 (NB78) or Ibid., 57–61 / SKS 20: 58–62 (NB70).

78 Simmons, 'Living Joyfully After Losing Social Hope', 11.
79 https://christianclimateaction.org/who-we-are/cca-principals-and-values/ (accessed March 2022).
80 Peter Kline, *Passion for Nothing. Kierkegaard's Apophatic Theology* (Minneapolis: Fortress Press, 2017), xcdd 137. In a similar manner, Pattison emphasizes the role of the 'instant' or 'moment' (*Øjenblikket*) and repetition (*Gjentagelsen*) as continuous, infinite beginnings in offering us the experience of 'gracious time', which 'gives us the possibility of hope, even when we are engulfed in the cortices of time's seemingly all-destroying storms'. George Pattison, 'The Grace of Time. Toward a Kataphatic Theology of Time', in *Hermeneutics and Negativism. Existential Ambiguities of Self-Understanding*, ed. Claudia Welz and René Rosfort (Tübingen: Mohr Siebeck, 2018), 145–59 (145).
81 Kierkegaard, *The Sickness Unto Death*, 85 / SKS 11: 199. Cf. Clare Carlisle, 'Humble Courage. Kierkegaard on Abraham and Mary', *Literature & Theology* 30, no. 3 (2016): 278–92.
82 This work has been funded by the Leverhulme Trust and by the Isaac Newton Trust.

10

Hope in the task of forgiveness

John Lippitt

'Expectancy' and 'substantial hope'

This chapter is concerned with one manifestation of possibility: the attitude or stance that we call hope. I will compare the hope that Kierkegaard labels as a variety of 'expectancy' (*Forventning*) with what Philip Pettit has called 'substantial' (as opposed to 'superficial') hope, focusing on the capacity of both phenomena to provide what Pettit calls 'cognitive resolve'. I shall defend both against objections, before going on to apply these thoughts to a specific context: what this might tell us about the role of hope in the task of interpersonal forgiveness.

Kierkegaard's comments on hope, like those on the broader category of possibility, are decidedly mixed. In *Fear and Trembling*, for instance, the pseudonym Johannes de Silentio is dismissive of 'fools and young people' who mistakenly chatter 'about everything being possible for a human being'.[1] Their mistake is to conflate what is possible 'spiritually speaking' (for 'with God all things are possible') with what is possible 'in the finite world', where there is much that is *not* possible. Johannes labels as 'paltry [*usle*] hope' the attitude that says 'One can't know what will happen, it might still be possible',[2] which he dismisses as a mere 'caricature' of faith. 'Paltry hope' sounds like that variety of hope given equally short shrift at the start of *Repetition*, which is associated with youthfulness, cowardice and superficiality and described as 'a beckoning fruit that does not satisfy'.[3] The 'fools and young people' who unquestioningly put their trust in possibility are an echo of the 'naive hopers' referred to in the discourse 'The Expectancy of Faith', more of which shortly.[4]

And yet in *Works of Love*, Kierkegaard contrasts one aspect of possibility with the 'tough slime' of 'practical sagacity' or shrewdness (*Klogskab*).[5] Possibility is 'this marvellous thing' that is 'so infinitely fragile . . ., so infinitely frail . . ., and yet, brought into being and shaped with the help of the eternal',[6] is 'stronger than anything else, *if it is the possibility of good!*'.[7] So it is 'the good' that makes the difference. But 'relating oneself in expectancy to the possibility of the good' has already been given as a definition of *hope*,[8] conceived of as a 'formed disposition' of the person of faith.[9] What Kierkegaard is talking about here, then, is not a one-off instance of hoping, or even a succession of them (even the 'paltry' hoper could manage that), but hopefulness as a disposition. So this is not what *Repetition* dismisses. 'Hope is a new garment', claims Constantine Constantius, 'stiff and starched and lustrous, but it has never been tried on, and therefore one does not know how becoming it will be or how it will fit'.[10] On the contrary, if hopefulness has become a formed disposition, it has been well and truly 'worn in'.

We need to make a distinction, then, between mere possibility, 'paltry hope' and the tendencies of the 'naïve hoper' on the one hand, and that kind of formed disposition that Kierkegaard labels expectancy of the good on the other. On one level, the latter hopefulness can be contrasted with despair. This is not the place for a lengthy discussion of Kierkegaardian despair – investigated many times before, far more commonly than Kierkegaardian hope – but in general I would share Mark Bernier's view that despair is at root the unwillingness to hope.[11] But my main concern here is how such hopefulness, such expectancy, works at a practical level. In what follows, I will argue that helpful light is shed on such a distinction by a comparison with what Philip Pettit has called 'superficial' as opposed to 'substantial' hope. I claim that such a comparison shows how hope – *qua* expectancy of the good – operates at a practical level.

In much recent philosophical writing on hope, the default conception of it is a 'desired possibility', which is neither impossible nor certain. In other words, where the probability of the desired end is somewhere between zero and one – but neither zero nor one. Such an approach conflates hope with the *belief* that some possibility may or may not obtain, and the *desire* that it *does* obtain.[12] There is nothing in this conception that distinguishes hope from the 'paltry' version. Contrast this with Margaret Urban Walker's thought that in order to count as hoping for an outcome, one has to invest some of one's agency in it. Whereas wishing can be a spectator sport, hope engages our agency in a far more significant way.[13] This is key to what Walker calls the 'efficacy' of hope. She puts the point thus: 'In hoping, we become alert to the ways and means by which the hoped-for circumstance could come about. We imagine scenarios in which what is hoped for comes to pass and plays out before us. We create ideas and plans and awaken anticipation, excitement, or pleasure about what its realization and consequences will be like'.[14] This is illustrated in the film *The Shawshank Redemption*. The wrongly imprisoned Andy – the spokesman for hope – has set up a way to access his money and get to Mexico if he is able to escape from jail. His friend Red – who considers hope to be dangerous – has made no such plans.[15] Some sense of agency with respect to the object of hope seems to be what Kierkegaard seeks in talking about 'relating oneself in expectancy' to the possibility of good. Hope, Kierkegaard insists, always pertains to a task – a task for one who has the good as their object.[16] Even when it appears that there is no task, the task can still be to bear the situation with patience, not to abandon patience in waiting.[17] This is one of several ways in which hope might require patience.

In the 1843 discourse 'The Expectancy of Faith', Kierkegaard addresses the thought that our relation to the future is of vital significance for our ability to find meaning in the present,[18] when he claims that we dare to be occupied with the future only when we have 'conquered' it.[19] This is glossed as actively expecting 'victory', a likely reference to Rom. 8.28, sometimes rendered as 'in all things God works for the good of those who love him'.[20] (I take it that this is the sort of thought that inspires Julian of Norwich's famous 'All shall be well; and all shall be well; and all manner of thing shall be well'.) Later in this discourse, Kierkegaard claims that '[e]very time I catch my soul not expecting victory [in this sense], I know that I do not have faith'.[21] I shall argue that the expectancy of faith sounds like a particular version of what Pettit labels 'cognitive resolve'. Granted, Pettit's non-theistic account lacks the reliance on God or 'the eternal' that is central to Kierkegaard's account, as we shall see. But this does not mean that Pettit's account cannot help to illustrate what Kierkegaard's claim amounts to in practical terms. Here's why.

Intuitively, one might understand 'expectancy' in two different ways. One is essentially predictive: to expect something is to anticipate that it will happen. On such a view, to approach expectancy in terms of probability – asking, 'What are the chances?' – is a fair question for practical reason to ask. This sounds like the approach of the figure that Kierkegaard (in 'The Expectancy of Faith') labels the 'man of experience', who sees himself as a rational adjudicator between the excessive claims of the overly optimistic (the naïve hope of youth) and the overly pessimistic ('the troubled person', who brings her past disappointments into each new situation), armed with his all-purpose tool, the phrase 'to an extent' or 'to a certain degree' (*til en vis Grad*).[22] But this is not what Kierkegaard has in mind. In his discussion of the 'patience in expectancy' of the prophet Anna, in waiting for the Messiah (at Lk. 2.36-38), he compares her favourably with the person who 'wastes the power of his soul and the content of his life in calculations and the irascible unwholesomeness of probabilities'.[23] In proposing instead that the practical role played by Kierkegaardian expectancy can be understood by considering how Pettit's substantial hope as cognitive resolve operates, we need to consider two related dimensions of the latter. Substantial hope, claims Pettit, is a way of 'retaining our identity' in the face of uncertainty, and it offers the 'best way of coping with', finding our way through, harsh realities.[24] Let's unpack this.

What is substantial hope?

Pettit's account of substantial hope draws an analogy with precaution. Just as Kierkegaard contrasts fear and hope as different manifestations of expectancy,[25] so Pettit considers precaution as a reaction to a feared, undesirable outcome and substantial hope as a reaction to a desired outcome. Suppose I have an intense aversion for a possible outcome: Pettit's example is a serious cost overrun on a building project. To avoid this danger – and the danger of my own action leaving me unprotected against it – I adopt the strategy of acting as if it *will* occur or as if there is a *good chance* that it will occur, as the best method available of protection.[26] So I set aside additional funds as a kind of insurance policy.

Substantial hope for a desired possibility works by analogy to this. It amounts to acting as if there is reason to be moved to act as if the desired prospect *will* obtain, or as if there were a *good chance* that it will obtain.[27] How might this be rationally defensible?

Precaution makes sense if the level of confidence that I have 'for the feared prospect's materialising is too low to guard against the danger of being unprotected'.[28] Even if one lives in a comparatively safe area, it still makes sense to insure against being burgled. The parallel for hope is if the level of confidence that the agent has for the desired prospect is too low to guard against another kind of danger: namely, that 'the agent loses heart and ceases to exercise agency effectively'.[29] If the desired prospect is assigned a low probability, this might cause me to give up. 'What's the point?', I ask myself: despair, in the most everyday sense. But such loss of heart can lead us to give up on prospects that are within our influence. An example familiar to many an experienced teacher is the student who drops out of university in the face of one disappointing set of grades. It might thus be that I *have* to hope if I am to be able to keep going. This gives us one reason why hope may often be pragmatically rational. Such hope helps 'lift us out of the panics and depressions to which we are naturally prey and to give us firm direction and control'.[30] Without hope, we are not capable 'of asserting our agency and of putting our own signature or stamp on our conduct'. Faced with the possibility of collapsing in despair and uncertainty,

> Hope in this scenario can be our one salvation as agents and persons, *our only way of remaining capable of seeing ourselves in what we do*. . . . In many circumstances, hope represents the only way of retaining our identity and selfhood and of not losing ourselves to the turmoil of brute, disheartening fact.[31]

The second, related reason is that hope may also offer us the best way of coping with those harsh realities and of finding our way through them.[32] A commonly cited example concerns hope in the face of illness. There is a weight of empirical evidence which suggests that hope helps people cope better with such diagnoses.[33] More broadly, in facing bad news, the hopeful often succeed in overcoming obstacles that might otherwise have brought them down. As Walker puts it, the human capacity for hope 'can be astonishing, like weeds that can grow up through the smallest cracks in slabs of concrete. Hope, too, is a kind of growth towards the light'.[34] Now, people get rightly suspicious about some of the more outlandish claims made in this sort of context. ('If you only believe in yourself, there is nothing you cannot achieve!') But Pettit claims that '[t]here need be no magic involved here'. On his account, to hope involves investing the scenario with 'a level of confidence' that may *exceed* the confidence of 'my actual *belief* in the prospect'.[35] As Nancy Sherman has noted, an attitude of hope 'redirects attention, desire, and imaginative planning' to possibilities that a more 'fact-processing, probability-assessing, evidence-seeking mentality'[36] – what Kierkegaard often calls 'sagacity' or 'shrewdness'[37] – would likely reject. But this should not thereby be dismissed as irrational, wishful thinking. As Pettit nicely puts it,

> Forming the hope that a particular scenario will eventuate, or at least eventuate in the event of your taking a certain initiative, is a way of handling the hurly burly of belief. It frees you from the bleakness of beliefs that wax and wane unpredictably in level of confidence. . . . To have hope is to have something we might describe as *cognitive resolve*.[38]

Hope as cognitive resolve is a way of facing up to the anxiety introduced by doubt.[39] Such cognitive resolve and the attitudes and actions it inspires distinguishes such hope from idle wishing, wishful thinking and 'paltry hope'. This, I submit, is how hope as expectancy functions on a practical level.[40]

One obvious objection to this is that Kierkegaard's expectancy, Pettit's substantial hope, or both, involve self-deception. Surely – so the objection goes – if I am to be reasonable, I should proportion my hope to the evidence?

A possible response to this is that of William James, in his example of the climber in the Alps who becomes trapped in a position from which the only possible escape is by a great leap. This attempt can only be made by a hope or confidence in his ability that outstrips the evidence for that ability. James argues that if we assume that choices can only be made between options that have certain or highly probable outcomes, then such dilemmas cannot be resolved.[41]

But it is Pettit's own response to this that I find especially interesting. He argues that rationality 'does not always support such detached processing of fact in the cases where hope is relevant'.[42] Such an assumption reckons without the kind of creatures we are: not mere probability-calculating machines, but creatures subject to being swamped by feelings of anxiety, desolation, failures of confidence and so on, which can radically undermine our capacity for agency. Crucially, substantial hope need not involve any illusion as to how things actually are. When the hopeful person acts 'as if things were otherwise than the evidence suggests' or 'as if they were more firmly established than the evidence shows', this can be done quite openly and honestly, their being willing to admit to themselves and others that 'for very good, pragmatic reasons . . . they are refusing to expose themselves to the low or unstable tide of evidence; for current practical purposes, they are investing their confidence in a firmer, more encouraging prospect'.[43]

Allow me a personal example. My father died in 2019. In the face of a terminal cancer diagnosis the previous year, which gave him up to three years to live, Dad some time thereafter got the news that one key part of his treatment had ceased to be effective, which reduced the prognosis to twelve months. This meant that he was by now already living on borrowed time. One evening, over a pub meal with his loyal friend Eddie, they started discussing the idea of taking the ferry over to Ireland for a holiday, two old widowers together. This conversation, probably a month or so before Dad's eventual death, looks from one angle absurd. Even at the time, many would have dismissed it as wishful thinking. But I think Pettit enables us to see it as something else. The prospect of this kind of possibility was a hope that kept Dad going, which a detached weighing of the probabilities would have snuffed out. I don't believe my Dad ever believed that this trip was *likely*, but it was *possible*, and in entertaining it, discussing it seriously as a potential future project, he chose to view it after the fashion of Pettit's hope as cognitive resolve, 'investing . . . in a firmer, more encouraging prospect'. Although Pettit acknowledges that there is 'an element of make-believe in hope', he insists that 'make-believe does not amount to self-deception'.[44] How so? Well, hope displays *some* facets reminiscent of self-deception: 'If I set out to act on a certain hope, for example, I may tell you that I do not want you to take me through this or that litany of evidence and fact.' However – and this is the key point – 'I may recognize that this is so, and in refusing to listen to the full recital of presumptive evidence, I do not tell myself a lie. I can be utterly undeceived about what I am doing.'[45]

That, I believe, is what my Dad was doing. And I concur with Pettit that, far from being dismissed as self-deception, such hope can be a pragmatically rational attitude to take.[46] I would add that, insofar as it enables one to avoid despair and to go on, it may even be a work of proper self-love. This is in part because, as Walker suggests, 'There is a special poverty of spirit, sometimes an unendurable emptiness, in the loss of important hopes'.[47]

My claim has been that on a practical level, hope as cognitive resolve is more or less how Kierkegaardian expectancy works. It is not – at least not necessarily – that I force myself to believe against the evidence, but that I adopt a hope for a desired prospect that is able to keep me going even in the face of doubt, in the face of the waxing and waning of the strength of my belief.[48] I now turn to the question of how this might play out in the context of interpersonal forgiveness.

Hope in forgiveness

Consider the above thoughts in relation to two rich memoirs of interpersonal forgiveness. The first is the Icelandic playwright Thordis Elva's extraordinary *South of Forgiveness*, about the lengthy struggle of a victim of date rape to forgive her rapist. The second is an instance of third-party forgiveness: that expressed by Sister Helen Prejean in her attitude towards the convicted Death Row inmate Elmo Patrick Sonnier in her compelling *Dead Man Walking*.[49] Both memoirs illustrate that the hope involved in forgiveness is at least twofold: hope as oriented towards others (for instance, hope for the wrongdoer's willingness to repent and their ability to reform) and hope as oriented towards oneself (for instance, in one's ability to begin and continue on the path of forgiveness).[50] Both also manifest forms of social or political hope, though here I'll focus on the interpersonal dimension. Both illustrate the importance of hope as requiring the investment of one's agency, as opposed to just idly wishing. Thordis Elva corresponds by email for years with Tom Stranger, the Australian ex-boyfriend who raped her, each of them eventually flying half-way across the world to South Africa for the week-long meeting that gives the memoir its focus. Prejean devotes her life to the fate of Death Row inmates, the battle for the lives and souls of those to whom she offers spiritual counsel becoming all-consuming.

I believe that the hope that such forgiveness manifests can reasonably be described as a work of love. (Love, Kierkegaard claims, 'takes upon itself hope, hoping for others, as a work',[51] as a task.) How so? Prejean's attitude to Sonnier, and Thordis's towards both Tom and her initially angry and damaged self is, I suggest, an illustration of 'normative hope', in Adrienne Martin's sense of that term: an aspiration we hold on behalf of ourselves or a good we hold out for another person, in the hope that they will aspire to it.[52] The idea here is that in some versions of hoping for others, 'part of the point of addressing others with hope is that the recipients might take up the values or principles deemed worthwhile and aspired for on their behalf', such that hope can 'scaffold' their normative change.[53] It is this that *Dead Man Walking* shows as succeeding in the case of Sonnier (but failing in the case of a second inmate, Robert Willie). Some writers on forgiveness have seen resentment towards another as a call-and-response kind of reactive attitude, 'an address to another that we are holding him to account'.[54] Such normative hope is also a call-and-response attitude, one that issues a challenge (sometimes indirectly) that the wrongdoer should take responsibility for their actions, repent and attempt to reform.[55] Normative hope is 'an aspiring attitude with regard to worthwhile ends we set for ourselves or others'.[56] Hope's attitude towards possibility – that possibilities are open – is a prospect that can 'galvanize energy . . . stabilize focus and fortify resolve'.[57] This can be a work of love if it is underpinned by what Nicholas Wolterstorff has labelled 'care-agapism', in which *agapic* love for the wrongdoer is not a justice-ignoring benevolence, but a form of aspiration-setting love that has a concern for justice built into it.[58] In both 'The Expectancy of Faith' and *Works of Love*, Kierkegaard makes the surprising claim that genuine hope cannot be disappointed. While this claim is ultimately about eschatological hope,[59] there is a version of this thought that applies in the context of forgiveness: never giving up on, never despairing over, the one for whom you hope (Prejean for Sonnier; Thordis for both Tom and, in battling her own demons, herself). Kierkegaard urges his reader to '[h]ope all things: give up on no human being, since to give up on him is to give up on your love for him'.[60] Such love allows one to hope in a way that 'sagacity' or 'shrewdness' cannot.[61]

Two objections considered

Let me address two possible objections here. First, what we might call the 'something particular' objection. In 'The Expectancy of Faith', Kierkegaard is critical of hope that is for 'something particular' (*noget Enkelt*): 'the person who expects something particular can be deceived in his expectancy, but this does not happen to the person of faith [*den Troede*]'.[62] I see this not as the embrace of what David Kangas has labelled the 'absolute future' as opposed to the future as represented.[63] Applied to the context of forgiveness, that would come uncomfortably close to the embrace of *any* eventuality, which would be to fail to acknowledge the wrongness of the action and the legitimacy of negative reactive attitudes towards it, which risks failing to distinguish forgiving from condoning or excusing.[64] And there is at least one way in which this hoped-for future must be represented if it is to count as an instance of hope at all: namely, represented *as good*. It is rather that we should not seek to specify too determinately in advance what form that good will take. This amounts to resisting the terms of doubt's challenge to faith, namely that '[a]n expectancy without a specified time and place is nothing but a deception'.[65] (This is how the phrase 'something particular' is first introduced in this discourse.) Rather than being an unconditional acceptance of the future *qua* future, I think that what is being commended is the acceptance of the future as a manifestation of the good even if we lack the capacity to understand *how* the good will be manifested.

(I am not sure how great a difference there ultimately is between Kangas's position and mine on this point. His discussion oscillates between talk of 'representable' and 'determinately representable'.[66] The latter term would narrow the gap between his position and mine considerably [perhaps collapsing it]. Maybe all Kangas means is what Bernier describes thus: 'an attitude of *openness* toward possibility, toward the future as such – to see all possibility hopefully, that all possibility stands in relation to the possibility of the good'.[67])

This brings us into the territory of Jonathan Lear's Kierkegaard-inspired notion of 'radical hope', so named because it is 'directed toward a future goodness that transcends the current ability to understand what it is'.[68] Lear's primary example of radical hope is the case of Plenty Coups, the last great chief of the Crow Nation, facing up to the collapse of his culture and the concepts that had given that culture its meaning, and wondering for what he might hope in the face of such cultural devastation. But I suggest that radical hope also has a place in some circumstances where the devastation is not so much of a culture and its concepts as of a life where the furniture of one's universe is radically disrupted by a cataclysmic event. Thordis's rape is such an example. Her memoir makes clear the profound psychological consequences of her ordeal: a multi-year history of 'eating disorders, alcohol, and self-harm';[69] along with ill-judged relationship choices, some of which led to further instances of rape.

Central to Thordis's problems was her inability, for years, to trust, having had that trust so cruelly betrayed. My suggestion is that such an experience can take one to what Lear labels 'the limits of one's understanding'[70] in a different sense from the collapse of one's culture. My question here is as follows. Is what the forgiving person 'substantially' hopes for 'something particular' in the sense to which Kierkegaard objects? If so, then there is a clear disanalogy here with both Kierkegaardian 'expectancy' and radical hope. Or can what is 'substantially' hoped for be sufficiently indeterminate to avoid this worry?

Of course, many instances of 'substantial' hope – Pettit's building project; my father's trip to Ireland – will be hope for 'something particular'. But my proposal is that many instances of hope in interpersonal forgiveness do avoid this objection, and that this helps us to see such hope in a different light from the way it is often portrayed. At first glance, Prejean's or Thordis's hope that Sonnier or Tom would repent and reform also sounds like 'something particular'. But not so fast. First, there is no expectation that this occur in a 'specified time and place'. More significantly, consider Thordis's shifting sense both of what she wants from Tom and of the significance of her rape. Her view of what the hoped-for manifestation of the good looks like changes radically over the course of the memoir. Her initial sense of a desire for revenge – wanting to see him humiliated – morphs into a desire for him to apologize and atone, his apology stemming from a genuine recognition of the real significance of what he has done to her, and the effect it has had on her life. But it does not stop there. As their week in South Africa progresses, and she learns more of worldwide attitudes to rape through the impressive Cape Town victim support centre in that they both visit, she sees her rape in a significantly different light, developing a sense of gratitude that she at least lives in a society that takes rape seriously; that views it as something extraordinary rather than mundane; and that recognizes victims as deserving of sympathy and support rather than shame and ostracism. She also learns more of that terrible incident's effects on Tom – the guilt that Tom has come to feel as the realization of the horror of what he had done grows has significantly damaged his own life. Whereas once news of his suffering would have been precisely what Thordis wanted, the shift towards the end of the memoir is in both parties wanting to work to get something good to come out of this terrible ordeal (their joint book, and its consciousness-raising about rape and its after-effects, being an attempt in this direction).

My point here is not to defend any particular position on the spectrum of Thordis's shifting attitudes. It is simply to note *that the content of an attitude of hope in a multi-year experience of trying to reach forgiveness cannot be nailed down in advance with even the slightest degree of precision.* In other words, it is not 'something particular' in the allegedly problematic sense. The most precise we can be of Thordis, once she has got beyond her thirst for revenge, is that she wants Tom to repent and atone (whatever that would come to mean) and for some good to come out of her ordeal (whatever that would come to mean). In this way, it echoes what Lear says of Plenty Coups' interpretation of the dream vision that is crucial to his insight: 'if they followed the wisdom of the chickadee (whatever that would come to mean) they would survive (whatever that would come to mean) and hold on to their lands (whatever that would come to mean)'.[71] This is not to say that *any* eventuality could constitute the hope being fulfilled[72] – simply that our expectations of how the good is manifested are often extremely flexible.

Moreover, in some instances of forgiveness, the open-endedness of this hope is far more explicit right from the start. Marina Cantacuzino's exhibition and subsequent book *The Forgiveness Project*[73] includes one example that illustrates this particularly well. Katy Hutchison's husband Bob was beaten to death while checking on a rowdy party being thrown by her next-door neighbour's son. In the small Canadian town in which they lived, a wall of silence grew up around the murder, and it was four years before Ryan Aldridge admitted to having been responsible for the fatal blow. What is striking about Katy's near-immediate reaction, in telling her two small children that fateful night what had happened to their father, is her observation that 'I promised them and I promised myself that underneath the horror of what had just happened *we would find a gift*.'[74]

(Her story also contains a powerful example of *normative hope*: when Aldridge was arrested, Katy made a video urging him to 'dig down deep to find the words to say, "I did this".' Aldridge did so, writing a letter of apology within an hour of being arrested. He asked to meet her, breaking down in tears at the encounter. Through the work of a victim–perpetrator reconciliation programme, Katy reports having found the ability to forgive Aldridge. 'Forgiveness became an opportunity to create a new and hopeful beginning', she writes.[75] Aldridge describes Katy's forgiveness as 'the most incredible thing that anyone has ever given me. It changed my life'.[76])

'In this we will find a gift.' That, I submit, is a statement of radical hope – a kind of expectancy – in the context of a situation of serious wrongdoing and subsequent forgiveness. In its non-specificity, it illustrates Lear's claim of how the goodness of the world 'transcends our finite powers to grasp it'.[77] Lear argues that it would be unfitting, for finite creatures like us, to think that 'what is good about the world is exhausted by our current understanding of it'.[78] That is part of what radical hope expresses, and forgiveness is a context in which it has a vital place.

A second objection that some Kierkegaardians will raise is that my use of Pettit's non-theistic account of hope in terms of cognitive resolve is prevented from being a helpful illustration of Kierkegaardian hope because it does not take into account Kierkegaard's distinction between 'mundane', 'earthly' or 'temporal' hope on the one hand, and 'authentic', 'eschatological' or 'eternal' hope on the other.[79] Doesn't Pettit's substantial hope fall on the 'earthly' or 'temporal' side of this divide?

While for Kierkegaard there is of course a specifically Christian hope – and this, for him, is what matters most – it does not follow from this that (even for him) hope that is not specifically Christian is without value. Even after having qualified hope in terms of 'the eternal', Kierkegaard's specific examples of hope in its dialogue with despair are in terms of 'victories' that transpire in the 'earthly' or 'temporal' realm: the return of 'prodigal sons'; re-established friendships; rekindled romantic love.[80] But my main response to this second objection depends in part on my answer to the first: such hope as I am commending here is not 'something particular' in the sense to which Kierkegaard objects. Let's unpack this in stages. The object of *earthly* hope is said to be something realizable in the temporal world, but that can easily be lost. Like temporality itself, it cannot be thought of as permanent.[81] In *Works of Love*, Kierkegaard glosses the object of such hope ('a hope that is not hope at all') as follows: 'a wish, a longing, a longing expectation now of one thing, now of another, in short, an expectant person's relationship to the possibility of multiplicity'.[82] But this kind of fickle wish – now one thing, now another – is a long way removed from Katy Hutchison's 'In this we will find a gift'. The latter is not 'lost in multiplicity' as described here. The question is whether there is, in the kind of hope I see in Katy Hutchison, as well as in Prejean, an element of 'the eternal', which Kierkegaard takes to be the object of 'eschatological' hope. (Clearly, as a Catholic nun, we can expect Prejean's view of hope to have a dimension that may be absent from that of Katy Hutchison, about whose religious views, or lack thereof, I know nothing.) My answer is yes. I follow John Davenport here in taking 'eschatological' to be about the vindication of the good in a broader sense than specifically Christian forms of eschatology ('victory' as glossed in 'The Expectancy of Faith').[83] The target of such eschatological hope is 'the good as such, not reducible to any particular temporal end'.[84] When Kierkegaard says that 'the whole of one's life should be the time of hope',[85] it is such hope that he has in mind. But in a key *Works of Love* passage in which he seeks to distinguish 'true', authentic hope from what passes for it 'in ordinary speech',[86] he claims: 'as soon as the choice [to hope] is made, the possible is changed, because the possibility of the good is the eternal . . . by the decision to choose hope, one decides infinitely more than it seems, because it is an eternal decision'.[87] What makes this more than just a pro-attitude towards an abstraction ('the good') is that, as Mark Bernier puts it, '[t]he possibility of the good is a second order possibility that we relate to only through other possibilities'[88] – the possibilities inherent in the specific challenges of our lives. In this sense, authentic hope involves a synthesis between the temporal and the eternal.[89] The end to which it relates is not reducible to temporality but nevertheless contains temporal commitments.[90] 'Hope's task in the form of eternity', Kierkegaard claims, 'is to *hope all things*, and in the form of temporality *to hope always*'.[91] But Katy Hutchison's 'In this we will find a gift' seems to be an expression of such a hope: to hope all things (in the sense that nobody, even her husband's killer, is beyond the scope of her hope) and to 'hope always'. Note that this would not be destroyed even by the backsliding of a repentant wrongdoer. This contrasts with 'mundane' hope, in which 'the self receives its meaning from a worldly good, which can be taken away; and with the accumulation of loss, the self can become more and more wounded, until finally it cannot bring itself to hope for worldly goods any longer'.[92] It is quite clear that Hutchison's hope is not like this. 'Hoping always' does not mean a conscious choice made every second of every day, but rather that one must regularly renew 'one's commitment to hope, renewing the expectation for the possibility of the good – to never give in to despair, to always remain open to the good'.[93] This is the sense in which our whole lives are to be 'the time of hope'. Such hoping, Kierkegaard insists, must be done in *love*: we cannot expect the good unless we love. To lovingly hope for others is to remain open to the possibility of the good in their lives; never to despair over them.[94] It is this that we see in Prejean's attitude towards the Death Row inmates, and this that 'In this we will find a gift' expresses.[95]

Notes

A version of this chapter has previously been published as chapter 8 of my book *Love's Forgiveness: Kierkegaard, Resentment, Humility, and Hope* (Oxford: Oxford University Press, 2020). This material is reproduced with the kind permission of the Licensor through PLSclear.

1 Søren Kierkegaard, *Fear and Trembling*, ed. C. Stephen Evans and Sylvia Walsh; trans. Sylvia Walsh (Cambridge: Cambridge University Press), 37 / SKS 4, 138.

2 Ibid., 30 / SKS 4, 132.
3 Kierkegaard, *Repetition*, trans. Howard V. Hong and Edna H. Hong (Princeton: Princeton University Press, 1983), 132 / SKS 4, 10.
4 'The Expectancy of Faith' is one of the *Two Upbuilding Discourses* published earlier in 1843, five months prior to *Fear and Trembling* and *Repetition*.
5 Kierkegaard, *Works of Love*, trans. Howard V. Hong and Edna H. Hong (Princeton, NJ: Princeton University Press, 1995), 251 / SKS 9, 250. This 'slime' emerges from 'cook[ing] over the slow or the merely earthly blazing fire of passions' a combination of attitudes that Kierkegaard associates with living without the eternal: 'habit, sagacity, aping, experience, custom and usage' (ibid.).
6 'The eternal' in Kierkegaard is a notoriously broad-reaching category, which depending on context can refer to God; the *telos* of the self; one's eternal blessedness; or any combination thereof.
7 Kierkegaard, *Works of Love*, 251 / SKS 9, 251, my emphasis.
8 Ibid., 250 / SKS 9, 250.
9 On this point, see Robert C. Roberts, 'The Virtue of Hope in *Eighteen Upbuilding Discourses*', in *International Kierkegaard Commentary: Eighteen Upbuilding Discourses*, ed. Robert L. Perkins (Macon, GA: Mercer University Press, 2003), 189.
10 Kierkegaard, *Repetition*, 132 / SKS 4, 10.
11 See Mark Bernier, *The Task of Hope in Kierkegaard* (Oxford: Oxford University Press, 2015). Bernier's valuable book – which includes a detailed discussion of the relationship between hope and despair – is the only book-length study in English on Kierkegaard's view of hope.
12 This is the view that Pettit challenges: on this point, see Philip Pettit, 'Hope and Its Place in Mind', *Annals of the American Academy of Political and Social Science*, 592 (2004): 152–65 (154).
13 Margaret Urban Walker, *Moral Repair: Reconstructing Moral Relations after Wrongdoing* (Cambridge: Cambridge University Press, 2006), 46.
14 Ibid., 50. Some recent writers on hope – such as Adrienne Martin – have claimed that a mark of hope is *reliance* on a hoped-for outcome (Adrienne M. Martin, *How We Hope: A Moral Psychology* (Princeton, NJ: Princeton University Press, 2014), 21). But in many cases, surely 'reliance' is too strong a term. Martin complains that Walker's account doesn't pin down how hope surpasses *attraction*. But in merely finding an outcome attractive, one doesn't necessarily engage in 'plans'. I might fantasise about what I would do if I won the lottery – perhaps in some detail – but it would be misleading to describe these fantasies as 'plans'.
15 For a discussion of hope that gives a central place to *Shawshank*, see Luc Bovens, 'The Value of Hope', *Philosophy and Phenomenological Research*, 59 (1999): 667–81.
16 For more on this, see Bernier, *The Task of Hope in Kierkegaard*.

17 Søren Kierkegaard, *Upbuilding Discourses in Various Spirits*, trans. Howard V. Hong and Edna H. Hong (Princeton, NJ: Princeton University Press, 1993), 280 / SKS 8, 376.
18 On this point, see R. S. Kemp and Michael Mullaney, 'Kierkegaard on the (Un)happiness of Faith', *British Journal of the History of Philosophy* 26, no. 3 (2018): 475–97 (481).
19 Søren Kierkegaard, *Eighteen Upbuilding Discourses*, trans. Howard V. Hong and Edna H. Hong (Princeton, NJ: Princeton University Press, 1990), 17 / SKS 5, 26.
20 New International Version. The Hongs translate this as 'all things must serve for good those who love God'. While this is a perfectly reasonable translation of Kierkegaard's *alle Ting maae tjene dem til Gode, der elske Gode* (*Eighteen Upbuilding Discourses*, 19 / SKS 5, 28), if – as the Hongs suggest – this is indeed a reference to this passage in Romans, I find the meaning of the NIV translation clearer.
21 Ibid., 27 / SKS 5, 35.
22 Ibid., 21 / SKS 5, 30.
23 Ibid., 219 / SKS 5, 213.
24 Pettit, 'Hope and Its Place in Mind', 161.
25 Kierkegaard, *Works of Love*, 249 / SKS 9, 249.
26 Pettit, 'Hope and Its Place in Mind', 157.
27 Ibid.
28 Ibid.
29 Ibid.
30 Ibid., 160.
31 Ibid., 160–1.
32 Ibid., 161.
33 For discussions of this, see Jerome Groopman, *The Anatomy of Hope: How People Prevail in the Face of Illness* (New York: Random House, 2004) and Stan van Hooft, *Hope* (Durham: Acumen, 2011), chapter 3.
34 Walker, *Moral Repair*, 42.
35 Pettit, 'Hope and Its Place in Mind', 159. So this is a sort of *pragmatic* confidence; an acting 'as if'.
36 Nancy Sherman, *Afterwar: Healing the Moral Wounds of Our Soldiers* (New York: Oxford University Press, 2015), 139.
37 While Kierkegaard's use of the term *Klogskab* is typically negative, there are exceptions: sometimes that use is more neutral. See for instance his discussion of virtue as 'the highest sagacity' (*Eighteen Upbuilding Discourses*, 380 / SKS 5, 363).
38 Pettit, 'Hope and Its Place in Mind', 160.
39 Kierkegaard, *Eighteen Upbuilding Discourses*, 22–3 / SKS 5, 29–30.
40 One parallel here is with Kant, for whom moral agency and our practical commitments require us to commit to projects whose feasibility or probability of success cannot be known in advance, hence the need for hope. For a discussion of

Kant and Kierkegaard under this aspect, see Roe Fremstedal, 'Kierkegaard on Hope as Essential to Selfhood', in *The Moral Psychology of Hope*, ed. Claudia Blöser and Titus Stahl (Lanham, MD: Rowman and Littlefield, 2019), 75–92.
41 See William James, 'The Sentiment of Rationality', in *The Will to Believe and Other Essays* (New York: Longman, Green and Co., 1917), 96–7.
42 Pettit, 'Hope and Its Place in Mind', 160.
43 Ibid.
44 Ibid., 162.
45 Ibid.
46 Pettit further argues that it also cannot be dismissed as *evidentially* irrational, but I am more interested in the practical dimension.
47 Walker, *Moral Repair*, 60. This kind of hope has something in common with Václev Havel's connection between hope and the ability to make sense of one's world: 'Hope is not the conviction that something will turn out well but the certainty that something makes sense, regardless of how it turns out' (Václev Havel, *Disturbing the Peace: A Conversation with Karel Huizdala* (New York: Vintage, 1991), 181–2). I am grateful to Kamila Pacovská for reminding me of this passage.
48 For a Christian, this effectively takes the form of 'Lord, I believe; help thou my unbelief' (cf. Mark 9: 24).
49 Thordis Elva and Tom Stranger, *South of Forgiveness* (London: Scribe, 2017); Helen Prejean, *Dead Man Walking* (London: Fount, 1996). I discuss both memoirs in some detail in *Love's Forgiveness*. For why I hold that in some circumstances, third-party forgiveness is a legitimate kind of forgiveness, see Lippitt, *Love's Forgiveness*, 41–54.
50 Kierkegaard claims that hope for others and hope for oneself are inextricably linked: see *Works of Love*, 259–60 / SKS 9, 258–9.
51 *Works of Love*, 248 / SKS 9, 248.
52 See Martin, *How We Hope*, especially chapter 5.
53 This is Sherman's gloss on Martin's idea: see Sherman, *Afterwar*, 135.
54 Ibid., 137. For more on this, see my discussion of resentment as moral address in *Love's Forgiveness*, chapter 1.
55 I put it this way because of the following problem with applying Sherman's account to the Prejean case. In the case of moral address that is hopeful, Sherman thinks, the person in question is addressed in a way that is 'aspirational rather than binding', such that the person at whom this hope is directed might be praised if they succeed, but not blamed if they fail (ibid., 137). This is too weak to capture 'hope for repentance' cases. When someone who should repent fails to do so, we *do* blame them for this failure: indeed, we might think, their failure in this respect adds a second wrong to the first. For this reason, Sherman's suggestion that '[d]isappointment is not the same as reproach, even if it sometimes has that flavour' (ibid.) will not adequately capture such a case. Any disappointment we feel about such a failure to repent blurs into reproach and may, in fact, be an expression of it.

56 Sherman, *Afterwar*, 208.
57 Ibid., 139.
58 Nicholas Wolterstorff, *Justice in Love* (Grand Rapids, MI: Eerdmans, 2015). For further discussion, see Lippitt, *Love's Forgiveness*, chapter 4.
59 Genuine hope is that which 'relates essentially and eternally to the good' (*Works of Love*, 261 / SKS 9, 261).
60 Ibid., 255 / SKS 9, 255. This 'giving up on' is presented as a manifestation of despair: presumably, akin to what *The Sickness Unto Death* presents as the despair that 'lacks possibility' (Kierkegaard, *The Sickness Unto Death*, trans. Howard V. Hong and Edna H. Hong (Princeton, NJ: Princeton University Press, 1980), 37–42 / SKS 11, 153–7). And 'to despair over another person is to be in despair oneself' (*Works of Love*, 256 / SKS 9, 256) – one of the manifestations of 'eternity's like for like' (ibid.). Giving up hope for another person is later said to be a 'dishonor', which – unlike hope – puts a person 'to shame' (Ibid., 262 / SKS 9, 261).
61 For Kierkegaard's polemical attack on sagacity in this context, see *Works of Love*, 260–1 / SKS 9, 259–60. There is an interesting parallel here with Martin's account of 'secular faith', which she understands as a hope that targets 'a contingently unimaginable outcome' (Martin, *How We Hope*, 99). (The inspiration for this is Jonathan Lear's Plenty Coups, of whom more shortly.) Martin claims that such hope is 'immune to empirical disappointment ... Nothing in the hopeful person's experience need count as a reason to stop desiring the unimaginable outcome, or to stop seeing its chances as licencing a feeling of anticipation ... or to stop treating her desire as sufficient justification for this feeling and planning. That is to say, nothing in the hopeful person's experience need count as evidence that her hope is fruitless' (ibid., 101).
62 Kierkegaard, *Eighteen Upbuilding Discourses*, 23 (translation adjusted) / SKS 5, 32.
63 David J. Kangas, *Errant Affirmations: On the Philosophical Meaning of Kierkegaard's Religious Discourses* (London: Bloomsbury, 2017), 22.
64 Because forgiveness has the recognition that a wrong has been done built into it, which condonation and excuse typically do not.
65 Kierkegaard, *Eighteen Upbuilding Discourses*, 23 / SKS 5, 32.
66 Kangas, *Errant Affirmations*, 16.
67 Bernier, *The Task of Hope in Kierkegaard*, 129.
68 Jonathan Lear, *Radical Hope: Ethics in the Face of Cultural Devastation* (Cambridge, MA: Harvard University Press, 2006), 103. I have sketched elsewhere how Lear's notion of radical hope sheds illuminating light on the conception of faith to be found in *Fear and Trembling*: see my 'Learning to Hope: The Role of Hope in *Fear and Trembling*', in *Kierkegaard's Fear and Trembling: A Critical Guide*, ed. Daniel Conway (Cambridge: Cambridge University Press, 2015).
69 Elva and Stranger, *South of Forgiveness*, 11.
70 Lear, *Radical Hope*, 105.

71 Ibid., 141. The 'wisdom of the chickadee' is presented in a dream vision, from which Plenty Coups learns that it is 'the mind that leads a man to power, not strength of body' (ibid., 70–1).
72 Despite what Kemp (in Kemp and Mullaney, 'Kierkegaard and the (Un)happiness of Faith', 484–5) unconvincingly alleges. Mullaney's position is both more subtle, and – as he acknowledges – closer to my own: he sees himself as filling in something that my account allegedly 'leaves underdeveloped' (ibid., 488n13).
73 Marina Cantacuzino, *The Forgiveness Project: Stories for a Vengeful Age* (London: Jessica Kingsley, 2015), 109–13. The book consists of multiple forgiveness narratives, often including dialogues of change resulting from interactions between victims and perpetrators.
74 Ibid., 110.
75 Ibid., 112.
76 Ibid.
77 Lear, *Radical Hope*, 121.
78 Ibid., 122.
79 On this terminology, see Bernier, *The Task of Hope in Kierkegaard*, 104ff.
80 Kierkegaard, *Works of Love*, 254 / SKS 9, 253–4.
81 Bernier, *The Task of Hope in Kierkegaard*, 105.
82 Kierkegaard, *Works of Love*, 250 / SKS 9, 250.
83 See John J. Davenport, 'Faith as Eschatological Trust in *Fear and Trembling*', in *Ethics, Love, and Faith in Kierkegaard*, ed. Edward F. Mooney (Bloomington, IN: Indiana University Press, 2008).
84 Bernier, *The Task of Hope in Kierkegaard*, 122.
85 Kierkegaard, *Works of Love*, 251, 252 / SKS 9, 251.
86 Ibid., 250 / SKS 9, 250.
87 Ibid., 249–50 / SKS 9, 249.
88 Bernier, *The Task of Hope in Kierkegaard*, 131.
89 Kierkegaard, *Works of Love*, 249 / SKS 9, 249.
90 Cf. Bernier, *The Task of Hope in Kierkegaard*, 126.
91 Kierkegaard, *Works of Love*, 249 / SKS 9, 249, my emphases.
92 Bernier, *The Task of Hope in Kierkegaard*, 105.
93 Ibid., 127. I say 'regularly' rather than 'constantly' (Bernier's term), as the latter seems insufficiently distinct from 'every second of every day'.
94 Kierkegaard, *Works of Love*, 254 / SKS 9, 254.
95 More tentatively, I also suspect that there is this same element of 'the eternal' in Thordis, despite her resolutely secular approach to forgiveness. Her years of emailing Tom, and commitment to the meeting in South Africa, itself serves as an example of never giving up on hope for another, and her at least tacit recognition that hope for herself is inextricably linked with hope for another.

Bibliography

Kierkegaard (primary)

Multi-volume works

Kierkegaard, Søren. *Journals and Notebooks*, 11 vols. Edited by Niels Jørgen Cappelørn, Alistair Hannay, David Kangas, Bruce H. Kirmmse, George Pattison, Vanessa Rumble and K. Brian Söderquist. Princeton, NJ: Princeton University Press, 2007–2020.

Kierkegaard, Søren. *Papirer*, 16 vols. Edited by P. A. Heiberg, V. Kuhr and R. Torsting. Copenhagen: Gyldendal, 1909–48.

Kierkegaard, Søren. *Søren Kierkegaard's Journals and Papers*, 7 vols. Edited and translated Howard V. Hong and Edna H. Hong, assisted by Gregor Malantschuk. Bloomington, IN: Indiana University Press, 1967–78.

Kierkegaard, Søren. *Søren Kierkegaards Skrifter*, 28 vols. Edited by Niels Jørgen Cappelørn, Joakim Garff, Jette Knudsen, Johnny Kondrup, Alstair McKinnon, Tonny Aagaard Olesen and Steen Tullberg. Copenhagen: Gads, 1997–2013.

Single works

Kierkegaard, Søren. *Christian Discourses* and *The Crisis* and *A Crisis in the Life of an Actress*. Edited and translated by Howard V. Hong and Edna H. Hong. Princeton, NJ: Princeton University Press, 1997.

Kierkegaard, Søren. *The Concept of Anxiety*. Edited and translated Reidar Thomte in collaboration with Albert B. Anderson. Princeton, NJ: Princeton University Press, 1997.

Kierkegaard, Søren. *Concept of Irony*. Edited and translated by Howard V. Hong and Edna H. Hong. Princeton, NJ: Princeton University Press, 1989.

Kierkegaard, Søren. *Concluding Unscientific Postscript to* Philosophical Fragments, 2 vols. Edited and translated by Howard V. Hong and Edna H. Hong. Princeton, NJ: Princeton University Press, 1992.

Kierkegaard, Søren. *Early Polemical Writing*. Edited and translated by Julia Watkin. Princeton, NJ: Princeton University Press, 1990.

Kierkegaard, Søren. *Eighteen Upbuilding Discourses*. Edited and translated by Howard V. Hong and Edna H. Hong. Princeton, NJ: Princeton University Press, 1992.

Kierkegaard, Søren. *Either/Or*, vol. 1. Edited and translated by Howard V. Hong and Edna H. Hong. Princeton, NJ: Princeton University Press, 1987.

Kierkegaard, Søren. *Either/Or*, vol. 2. Edited and translated by Howard V. Hong and Edna H. Hong. Princeton, NJ: Princeton University Press, 1988.

Kierkegaard, Søren. *Fear and Trembling* and *Repetition*. Edited and translated by Howard V. Hong and Edna H. Hong. Princeton, NJ: Princeton University Press, 1983.

Kierkegaard, Søren. *For Self-Examination* and *Judge for Yourself*. Edited and translated by Howard V. Hong and Edna H. Hong. Princeton, NJ: Princeton University Press, 1990.

Kierkegaard, Søren. *Philosophical Fragments* and *Johannes Climacus*. Edited and translated by Howard V. Hong and Edna H. Hong. Princeton, NJ: Princeton University Press, 1985.

Kierkegaard, Søren. *The Point of View for My Work as an Author*. Edited and translated by Howard V. Hong and Edna H. Hong. Princeton, NJ: Princeton University Press, 1998.

Kierkegaard, Søren. *Practice in Christianity*. Edited and translated by Howard V. Hong and Edna H. Hong. Princeton, NJ: Princeton University Press, 1991.

Kierkegaard, Søren. *Repetition/Philosophical Crumbs*. Translated by M. G. Piety. Oxford: Oxford University Press, 2009.

Kierkegaard, Søren. *The Sickness Unto Death*. Translated by Alastair Hannay. London: Penguin Books, 1989.

Kierkegaard, Søren. *Sickness Unto Death: A Christian Psychological Exposition for Upbuilding and Awakening*. Edited and translated by Howard V. Hong and Edna H. Hong. Princeton, NJ: Princeton University Press, 1980.

Kierkegaard, Søren. *Stages on Life's Way: Studies by Various Persons*. Edited and translated by Howard V. Hong and Edna H. Hong. Princeton, NJ: Princeton University Press, 1988.

Kierkegaard, Søren. *Two Ages: The Age of Revolution and the Present Age: A Literary Review*. Edited and translated by Howard V. Hong and Edna H. Hong. Princeton, NJ: Princeton University Press, 1978.

Kierkegaard, Søren. *Upbuilding Discourses in Various Spirits*. Edited and translated by Howard V. Hong and Edna H. Hong. Princeton, NJ: Princeton University Press, 2009.

Kierkegaard, Søren. *Without Authority*. Edited and translated by Howard V. Hong and Edna H. Hong. Princeton, NJ: Princeton University Press, 1997.

Kierkegaard, Søren. *Works of Love*. Edited and translated by Howard V. Hong and Edna H. Hong. Princeton, NJ: Princeton University Press, 1995.

Kierkegaard (secondary)

Abbagnano, Nicola. 'Kierkegaard e il sentiero della possibilità'. In *Studi Kierkegardiani*, edited by Cornelio Fabro, 11–28. Brescia: Morcelliana, 1957.

Assiter, Alison. *Kierkegaard, Eve and Metaphors of Birth*. London: Rowman and Littlefield, 2015.
Ballard, Bruce W. 'Macintyre and the Limits of Kierkegaardian Rationality'. *Faith and Philosophy, Journal of the Society of Christian Philosophers* 12, no. 1 (1995): 126–32.
Barnett, Christopher B. *From Despair to Faith. The Spirituality of Søren Kierkegaard*. Minneapolis, MN: Fortress Press, 2014.
Barrett, Lee C. 'Vigilius Haufniensis: Psychological Sleuth, Anxious Author, and Inadvertent Evangelist'. In *Kierkegaard's Pseudonyms. Kierkegaard Research: Sources, Recourses, Reception*, vol. 17, edited by Katalin Nun and Jon Stewart, 259–80. London and New York: Routledge, 2015.
Beabout, Gregrory R. *Freedom and Its Misuses: Kierkegaard on Anxiety and Despair*. Milwaukee: Marquette University Press, 1996.
Becker-Lindenthal, Hjördis. 'Kierkegaard's Reception of German Vernacular Mysticism: Johann Tauler's Sermon on the Feast of the Exaltation of the Cross and Practice *in Christianity*'. *International Journal of Philosophy and Theology* 80, nos. 4–5 (2019): 443–64.
Becker-Lindenthal, Hjördis. 'Mirroring God. Reflections of Meister Eckhart's Thought in Kierkegaard's Authorship'. *Kierkegaard Studies Yearbook* 17 (2012): 3–24.
Becker-Lindenthal, Hjördis and Ruby S. Guyatt. 'Kierkegaard on Existential Kenosis and the Power of the Image: *Fear and Trembling* and *Practice in Christianity*'. *Modern Theology* 35, no. 4 (2019): 706–27.
Bernier, Mark. *The Task of Hope in Kierkegaard*. Oxford: Oxford University Press, 2015.
Burgess, Andrew J. 'Kierkegaard, Moravian Missions, and Martyrdom'. In *International Kierkegaard Commentary* vol. 18 (*Without Authority*), edited by Robert L. Perkins, 177–201. Macon, GA: Mercer. University Press, 2006.
Carlisle, Clare. 'How to Be a Human Being in the World: Kierkegaard's Question of Existence'. In *Kierkegaard's Existential Approach*, edited by Arne Grøn, René Rosfort and K. Brian Söderquist, 113–30. Berlin: Walter de Gruyter, 2017.
Carlisle, Clare. 'Humble Courage. Kierkegaard on Abraham and Mary'. *Literature & Theology* 30, no. 3 (2016): 278–92.
Carlisle, Clare. *Kierkegaard's Philosophy of Becoming: Movements and Positions*. Albany, NY: State University New York Press, 2005.
Come, Arnold. *Trendelenburg's Influence on Kierkegaard's Modal Categories*. Montreal: Inter Editions, 1991.
Das, Saitya Brata. *The Political Theology of Kierkegaard*. Edinburgh: Edinburgh University Press, 2020.
Davenport, John D. 'Faith as Eschatological Trust in *Fear and Trembling*'. In *Ethics, Love, and Faith in Kierkegaard*, edited by Edward F. Mooney, 196–233. Bloomington, IN: Indiana University Press, 2008.
Elrod, John W. *Being and Existence in Kierkegaard's Pseudonymous Works*. Princeton, NJ: Princeton University Press, 1975.

Emmanuel, Steven M. 'Actuality'. In *Kierkegaard's Concepts*. Tome I: Absolute to Church. *Kierkegaard Research: Sources, Recourses, Reception*, vol. 15, edited by Steven M. Emmanuel, William McDonald and Jon Stewart. London and New York: Routledge, 2013.

Evans, C. Stephen. 'Does Kierkegaard Think Beliefs Can Be Directly Willed?'. *International Journal for Philosophy of Religion* 26, no. 3 (December 1989): 173–84.

Fabro, Cornelio. 'Actuality (Reality)'. In *Concepts and Alternatives in Kierkegaard*. *Bibliotheca Kierkegaardiana*, vol. 16, edited by Niels Thulstrup and Marie Mikulová Thulstrup, 111–13. Copenhagen: C.A. Reitzels Forlag, 1980.

Fabro, Cornelio. 'Analogy'. In *Theological Concepts in Kierkegaard*. *Bibliotheca Kierkegaardiana*, vol. 5, edited by Niels Thulstrup and Marie Milkulová Thulstrup, 96–8. Copenhagen: C.A. Reitzels Forlag, 1980.

Fabro, Cornelio. 'Edification'. In *Some of Kierkegaard's Main Categories*. *Bibliotheca Kierkegaardiana*, vol. 16, edited by Niels Thulstrup and Marie Mikulová Thulstrup, 154–63. Copenhagen: C.A. Reitzels Forlag, 1988.

Fabro, Cornelio. 'Kierkegaard e il Cattolicesimo'. *Divus Thomas* 59 (1956): 67–70.

Fabro, Cornelio. *The Selected Works of Cornelio Fabro* vol 2: *Selected Articles on Søren Kierkegaard*. Edited by Nathaniel Dreyer and translated by J. B. Mondin. Chillum, MD: IVE Press, 2020.

Ferreira, Gabriel. 'Contingency'. In *Kierkegaard's Concepts*. Tome II: Classicism to Enthusiasm. *Kierkegaard Research: Sources, Recourses, Reception*, vol. 15, edited by Steven M. Emmanuel, William McDonald and Jon Stewart. London and New York: Routledge, 2014.

Ferreira, Gabriel. 'De Dicto and De Re: A Brandomian Experiment on Kierkegaard'. *Revista de Filosofia Moderna e Contemporânea*, [S. l.] 7, no. 2 (2019): 221–38.

Ferreira, Gabriel. 'Kierkegaard Descends to the Underworld: Some Remarks on the Kierkegaardian Appropriation of an Argument by F. A. Trendelenburg'. *Cognitio* 14, no. 2 (2014): 235–46.

Ferreira, Gabriel. '"O que nosso tempo mais precisa": Kierkegaard e o problema das categorias na filosofia do século XIX'. *Kriterion: Revista de Filosofia* 58, no. 137 (2017): 333–50.

Ferreira, Gabriel. '"The Philosophical Thesis of the Identity of Thinking and Being is Just the Opposite of What it seems to be": Kierkegaard on the Relations between Being and Thought'. *Kierkegaard Studies Yearbook* 20 (2015): 13–30.

Ferreira, M. Jamie. *Transforming Vision: Imagination and Will in Kierkegaardian Faith*. Oxford: Clarendon Press, 1991.

Furnal, J. R. *Catholic Theology after Kierkegaard*. Oxford: Oxford University Press, 2016.

Furnal, J. R. 'Introduction'. In *Selected Works of Cornelio Fabro* vol 2. *Selected Articles on Søren Kierkegaard*, edited by Nathaniel Dreyer. Chillum: IVE Press, 2020.

Furtak, Rick Anthony. 'Varieties of Existential Uncertainty'. In *The Kierkegaardian Mind*, edited by Adam Buben, Eleanor Helms and Patrick Stokes, 376–85. London: Routledge, 2019.

Garff, Joakim. 'Formation and the Critique of Culture'. In *The Oxford Handbook of Kierkegaard*, edited by John Lippitt and George Pattison, 252-72. Oxford: Oxford University Press, 2013.

Garff, Joakim. 'Kierkegaards billeddannelsesroman – Om at mime det sublime'. In *Geni og Apostel. Litteratur og teologi*, edited by David Bugge, 11-27. Copenhagen: Anis Forlag, 2006.

Gauvin, Mitchell J. 'Can Isaac Forgive Abraham?'. *Journal of Religious Ethics* 45, no. 1 (2017): 83-103.

González, Dario. 'Trendelenburg: An Ally against Speculation'. In *Kierkegaard and His German Contemporaries: Philosophy*, vol. 6, edited by Jon Stewart, 309-34. Aldershot: Ashgate, 1997.

Gouwens, David J. 'Kierkegaard on the Ethical Imagination'. *The Journal of Religious Ethics* 10, no. 2 (1982): 204-20.

Gouwens, David J. *Kierkegaard's Dialectic of Imagination*. New York et al.: Peter Lang, 1988.

Green, Ronald. *Kierkegaard and Kant: The Hidden Debt*. Albany, NY: State University of New York Press, 1992.

Gregor, Brian. 'Thinking Through Kierkegaard's Anti-Climacus: Art, Imagination, and Imitation'. *The Heythrop Journal* 50, no. 3 (2009): 448-65.

Hanson, Jeffrey. 'After Actuality: Ideality and the Promise of a Purified Religious Vision in Frater Taciturnus'. *History of European Ideas* 47 no. 3 (2021): 514-27.

Hanson, Jeffrey. 'Imagination, Suffering, and Perfection: A Kierkegaardian Reflection on Meaning in Life'. *History of Philosophy Quarterly* 38, no. 4 (forthcoming).

Hanson, Jeffrey. *Kierkegaard and the Life of Faith: The Aesthetic, the Ethical, and the Religious in* Fear and Trembling. Bloomington, IN: Indiana University Press, 2017.

Hanson, Jeffrey. 'Returning (to) the Gift of Death: Violence and History in Derrida and Levinas'. *International Journal for Philosophy of Religion*, 67, no. 1 (2010): 1-15.

Harnow Klausen, Søren. *Søren Kierkegaard: Educating for Authenticity*. Cham: Springer, 2018.

Jackson, Timothy P. 'Is Isaac Kierkegaard's Neighbor? Fear and Trembling in Light of William Blake and Works of Love'. *The Annual of the Society of Christian Ethics* 17 (1997): 97-119.

Jacquier, Francisco. *Institutiones Philosophicae ad Studia Theologica Potissimum Accommodotae*, Tomus II. Matriti: Ex Officina Ildephonsi a Lopez, 1787.

Kaftanski, Wojciech. 'Kierkegaard and Existential Mimesis'. In *The Kierkegaardian Mind*, edited by Adam Buben, Eleanor Helms and Patrick Stokes, 191-202. Abingdon, Oxon: Routledge, 2017.

Kaftanski, Wojciech. *Kierkegaard, Mimesis, and Modernity: A Study of Imitation, Existence, and Affect*. London: Routledge, 2022.

Kaftanski, Wojciech. 'Mimesis in Kierkegaard's "Does a Human Being Have the Right to Let Himself Be Put to Death for the Truth?" Remarks on the Formation of the Self'. *Kierkegaard Studies Yearbook* 58 (2011): 195-220.

Kaftanski, Wojciech. 'The *Socratic* Dimension of Kierkegaard's Imitation'. *The Heythrop Journal* 58, no. 4 (2017): 599–611.

Kangas, David J. *Errant Affirmations: On the Philosophical Meaning of Kierkegaard's Religious Discourses*. London: Bloomsbury, 2017.

Kangas, David J. *Kierkegaard's Instant: On Beginnings*. Bloomington, IN: Indiana University Press, 2007.

Kemp, Ryan S. and Michael Mullaney. 'Kierkegaard on the (Un)happiness of Faith'. *British Journal of the History of Philosophy* 26, no. 3 (2018): 475–97.

Kemp, Ryan S. and Michael Mullaney. 'The Role of Imagination in Kierkegaard's Account of Ethical Transformation'. *Archiv für Geschichte der Philosophie* 100, no. 2 (2018): 202–31.

Khawaja, Noreen. 'Heidegger's Kierkegaard: Philosophy and Religion in the Tracks of a Failed Interpretation'. *The Journal of Religion* 95, no. 3 (2015): 295–317.

Kjær, Grethe. 'The Role of Folk and Fairy Tales in Kierkegaard's Authorship'. In *Kierkegaard on Art and Communication*, edited by George Pattison, 78–87. Berlin: Springer Verlag, 1992.

Kosch, Michelle. *Freedom and Reason in Kant, Schelling and Kierkegaard*. Oxford: Oxford University Press, 2006.

Krishek, Sharon. *Kierkegaard on Faith and Love*. Cambridge: Cambridge University Press, 2009.

Languilli, Nino. 'Kierkegaard'. In *Possibility, Necessity, and Existence: Abbagnano and His Predecessors*, 88–100. Philadelphia, PA: Temple University Press, 1992.

Law, David R. *Kierkegaard's Kenotic Christology*. Oxford: Oxford University Press, 2013.

Lippitt, John. 'Learning to Hope: The Role of Hope in *Fear and Trembling*'. In *Kierkegaard's Fear and Trembling: A Critical Guide*, edited by Daniel Conway. Cambridge: Cambridge University Press, 2015.

Lippitt, John. *Love's Forgiveness: Kierkegaard, Resentment, Humility, and Hope*. Oxford: Oxford University Press, 2020.

Llewelyn, John. *Margins of Religion: Between Kierkegaard and Derrida*. Bloomington, IN: Indiana University Press, 2009.

Løgstrup, K. E. *Kierkegaard's and Heidegger's Analysis of Existence and Its Relation to Proclamation*. Translated by Robert Stern. Oxford: Oxford University Press, 2020.

Marek, Jakub. 'Anti-Climacus: Kierkegaard's "servant of the word"'. In *Kierkegaard's Pseudonyms*. Kierkegaard Research: Sources, Reception and Resources, vol. 17, edited by Jon Stewart and Katalin Nun, 39–51. Farnham: Ashgate Publishing, 2015.

Marek, Jakub. 'Contradiction'. In *Kierkegaard's Concepts*. Tome II: Classicism to Enthusiasm. Kierkegaard Research: Sources, Recourses, Reception, vol. 15, edited by Steven M. Emmanuel, Steven M., William McDonald and Jon Stewart, 73–80. London and New York: Routledge, 2014.

Masi, Guiseppe. *Disperazione e Speranza. Saggio sulle categorie Kierkegaardiane*. Padua: Gregoriana, 1971.

Masi, Guiseppe. *La determinazione della possibilità dell'esistenza in Kierkegaard.* Bologna: Zuffi, 1949.

Maughan-Brown, Frances. 'Imagination'. In *Kierkegaard's Concepts, Tome III: Envy to Incognito*. Kierkegaard Research: Sources, Reception and Resources, vol. 15, edited by Steven M. Emmanuel, William McDonnald and Jon Stewart, 195–207. Farnham: Ashgate, 2014.

Maughan-Brown, Frances. 'Kissing the Image: An Allegory of Imagination in "The Seducer's Diary"'. *History of European Ideas* 47, no. 3 (2021): 528–42.

Maughan-Brown, Frances. *The Lily's Tongue.* Albany, NY: State University of New York Press, 2019.

McCarthy, Vincent A. 'Schelling and Kierkegaard on Freedom and Fall'. In *International Kierkegaard Commentary: The Concept of Anxiety*, edited by Robert L. Perkins, 89–109. Macon, GA: Mercer University Press, 1985.

Melendo Millán, Irene. 'Kierkegaard and Metaphysics'. *Rivista di Filosofia Neo-Scolastica* 110, no. 3 (2018): 625–40.

Mikulová Thulstrup, Marie. 'The Significance of Mortification and Dying away (to)'. In *The Sources and Depths of Faith in Kierkegaard*, edited by Marie Mikulová Thulstrup, 160–97. Copenhagen: C.A. Reitzel, 1978.

Mjaaland, Marius Timmann. *Autopsia: Self, Death and God after Kierkegaard and Derrida.* Berlin: Walter de Gruyter, 2008.

Mooney, Edward F. 'Abraham and Dilemma. Kierkegaard's Ethical Suspension Revisited'. *International Journal for Philosophy of Religion* 19 (1986): 23–41.

Mulhall, Stephen. *Inheritance and Originality: Wittgenstein, Heidegger, Kierkegaard.* Oxford: Oxford University Press, 2001.

Newmark, Kevin. 'Modernity Interrupted: Kierkegaard's Antigone'. In *Irony on Occasion: From Schlegel and Kierkegaard to Derrida and de Man*, 66–96. New York: Fordham University Press, 2012.

Nørager, Troels, 'Kierkegaard, Love, and Sacrifice: Is There A Solution To Abraham's Dilemma?' *Neue Zeitschrift für Systematicsche Theologie Und Religionsphilosophie* 50, nos. 3–4 (2008): 267–83.

Pattison, George. 'Art in an Age of Reflection'. In *The Cambridge Companion to Kierkegaard*, edited by. Alastair Hannay and Gordon D. Marino, 76–100. Cambridge: Cambridge University Press, 1998.

Pattison, George. *God and Being: An Enquiry.* Oxford: Oxford University Press, 2011.

Pattison, George (ed.). *Kierkegaard on Art and Communication.* Berlin: Springer, 1992.

Pattison, George. *Kierkegaard's Upbuilding Discourses. Philosophy, Literature and Theology.* London and New York: Routledge.

Paulsen, Anna. 'Education'. In *Kierkegaard and Human Values. Bibliotheca Kierkegaardiana*, vol. 7, edited by Niels Thulstrup and Marie Mikulová Thulstrup, 42–3. Copenhagen: C.A. Reitzels Forlag, 1980.

Piety, M. G. 'The Stillness of History: Kierkegaard and German Mysticism'. *Konturen* 7 (2015): 42–63.

Podmore, Simon. *Struggling with God: Kierkegaard and the Temptation of Spiritual Trial*. Cambridge: James Clarke & Co, 2013.

Purkarthofer, Richard. 'Origineity and Recognisability: On Kierkegaard's Ontology'. *Rivista di Filosofia Neo-Scolastica* 105, nos. 3–4 (2013): 805–21.

Purkarthofer, Richard. 'Trendelenburg: Traces of a Profound and Sober Thinker in Kierkegaard's *Postscript*'. *Kierkegaard Studies Yearbook* 10 (2005): 192–207.

Rasmussen, Joel D. S. *Between Irony and Witness. Kierkegaard's Poetics of Faith, Hope, and Love*. New York and London: T&T Clark, 2005.

Roberts, Robert C. 'The Virtue of Hope in *Eighteen Upbuilding Discourses*'. In *International Kierkegaard Commentary: Eighteen Upbuilding Discourses*, edited by Robert L. Perkins. Macon, GA: Mercer University Press, 2003.

Rocca, Ettore. 'Kierkegaard's Second Aesthetics'. *Kierkegaard Studies Yearbook* 4 (1999): 278–92.

Rosfort, René. 'Kierkegaard in Nature: The Fragility of Existing with Naturalism'. *Kierkegaard Studies Yearbook* 19 (2014): 79–108.

Rossatti, Gabriel Guedes. 'Culture/Education'. In *Kierkegaard's Concepts. Tome II: Classicism to Enthusiasm. Kierkegaard Research: Sources, Recourses, Reception*, vol. 15, edited by Steven M. Emmanuel, William McDonald and Jon Stewart, 115–20. London and New York: Routledge, 2014.

Šajda, Peter. 'Meister Eckhart: The Patriarch of German Speculation Who was a Lebemeister: Meister Eckhart's Silent Way into Kierkegaard's Corpus'. In *Kierkegaard and the Patristic and Medieval Traditions*. Kierkegaard Research: Sources, Reception and Resources, vol. 4, edited by Jon Stewart, 237–64. Aldershot: Ashgate, 2008.

Šajda, Peter. 'Tauler: A Teacher in Spiritual Dietethics. Kierkegaard's Reception of Johannes Tauler'. In *Kierkegaard and the Patristic and Medieval Traditions*. Kierkegaard Research: Sources, Reception and Resources, vol. 4, edited by Jon Stewart, 265–87. Aldershot: Ashgate, 2008.

Shestov, Lev. *Kierkegaard and the Existential Philosophy*. Athens, OH: Ohio University Press, 1970.

Simmons, J. Aaron. 'What About Isaac? Rereading Fear and Trembling and Rethinking Kierkegaardian Ethic'. *The Journal of Religious Ethics* 35, no. 2 (2007): 319–45.

Stack, George J. 'The Concept of Human Possibility'. *The Southwestern Journal of Philosophy* 4, no. 2 (1973): 77–91.

Stack, George J.. 'Kierkegaard and Acosmism'. *Journal of Thought* 10, no. 3 (1975): 185–93.

Stack, George J.. 'Kierkegaard's Concept of Possibility'. *Journal of Thought* 5, no. 2 (1970): 80–92.

Stern, Robert. *Understanding Moral Obligation: Kant, Hegel, and Kierkegaard*. New York Cambridge University Press, 2012.

Stewart, Jon. *The Cultural Crisis of the Danish Golden Age: Heiberg, Martensen, and Kierkegaard*. Copenhagen: Museum Tusculanum Press, 2015.

Stewart, Jon (org). *Kierkegaard and His Contemporaries, the Culture of Golden Age*. Denmark, Berlin: Walter de Gruyter, 2003a.

Stewart, Jon. *Kierkegaard's Relations to Hegel Reconsidered*. New York: Cambridge University Press, 2003b.

Thomas, John Heywood. *The Legacy of Kierkegaard*. Eugene: Cascade Books, 2011.

Thulstrup, Niels. *Kierkegaard's Relation to Hegel*. Princeton, NJ: Princeton University Press, 1980.

Tolstrup, Christian Fink. 'Jakob Peter Mynster: A Guiding Thread in Kierkegaard's Authorship?' In *Kierkegaard and His Danish Contemporaries. Tome II: Theology*. Kierkegaard Research: Sources, Reception and Resources, vol. 1, edited by Jon Stewart, 267–87. London and New York: Routledge, 2009.

Wahl, Jean. *Études kierkegaardiennes*. Paris: Fernand Aubier, 1938.

Wahl, Jean. 'Heidegger et Kierkegaard: Recherche des éléments originaux de la philosophie de Heidegger'. *Recherches Philosophiques* 2 (1932–33): 349–70.

Wahl, Jean. *Kierkegaard: L'Un devant l'Autre*. Edited by Vincent Delecroix and Frédéric Worms. Paris: Hachette Littératures, 1998.

Watts, Daniel. 'The Paradox of Beginning: Hegel, Kierkegaard and Philosophical Inquiry'. *Inquiry* 50, no. 1 (2007): 5–33.

Westphal, Merold. *Becoming A Self*. West Lafayette, IN: Purdue University Press, 1996.

Wyschogrod, Michael. *Kierkegaard and Heidegger: The Ontology of Existence*. London: Routledge & Kegan Paul Ltd, 1954.

Other works cited in this volume:

Adams, Robert M. 'Theories of Actuality'. In *The Possible and the Actual: Readings in the Metaphysics of Modality*, edited by Michael J. Loux, 190–209. Ithaca, NY: Cornell University Press, 1979.

Alluntis, Felix. 'Demonstrability and Demonstration of the Existence of God'. In *John Duns Scotus 1265–1965*. Studies in Philosophy and the History of Philosophy 3, edited by John K. Ryan and Bernardine M. Bonansea. Washington, DC: The Catholic University of America Press, 1965.

Aquinas, Thomas. *On Being and Essence*. Translated by Armand Maurer. Toronto: Pontifical Institute of Medieval Studies, 1971.

Aquinas, Thomas. *Summa Theologica*. New York: Benzinger Bros, 1948.

Aristotle. *The 'Art' of Rhetoric*. Translated by John Henry Freese. Loeb Classical Library, no. 193. London: William Heineman, 1967.

Aristotle. *Metaphysics*. Translated by Hugh Tredennick. Cambridge, MA: Harvard University Press, 1961–2.

Beiser, Frederick C. *After Hegel - German Philosophy 1840–1900*. Princeton, NJ and Oxford: Princeton University Press, 2014.

Bencin, Rok. "*Sans Cause*': Affect and Truth in Marcel Proust". *Filozofski Vestnik* 38, no. 3 (2017): 53–66.
Benjamin, Walter. 'Critique of Violence'. In *Reflections*, translated by Edmund Jephcott, 277–300. New York: Schocken, 1986.
Benjamin, Walter. 'Theologico-Political Fragment'. In *Reflections*, translated by Edmund Jephcott, 312–13. New York: Schocken, 1986.
Benjamin, Walter. 'Theses on the Philosophy of History'. In *Illuminations*, translated by Harry Zohn, 253–64. New York: Schocken, 1968.
Bergson, Henri. 'The Possible and the Real'. In *The Creative Mind*, translated by Mabelle L. Andison. New York: Philosophical Library, 1946.
Blackburn, Simon. *Ruling Passions: A Theory of Practical Reason*. Oxford: Oxford University Press, 1998.
Bogue, Ronald. 'The Art of the Possible'. *Revue internationale de philosophie* 61, no. 241 (2007): 273–86.
Bogue, Ronald. 'Speranza, the Wandering Island'. *Deleuze Studies* 3, no. 1 (2009): 124–34.
Böhme, Gernot. *The Aesthetics of Atmospheres*. Edited by Jean-Paul Thibaud. London: Routledge, 2017.
Bonsiepen, Wolfgang, 'Einleitung'. In G. W. F. Hegel, *Phänomenologie des Geistes*. Hamburg: Felix Meiner Verlag, 1988.
Bornemann, Johann Alfred. 'Review of Martensen's *De autonomia conscientiae*'. In *Mynster's "Rationalism, Supernaturalism" and the Debate about Mediation*, edited and translated by Jon Stewart, 57–92. Copenhagen: Museum Tusculanum Press, 2009.
Boundas, Constantin V. 'Foreclosure of the Other: From Sartre to Deleuze'. *Journal of the British Society for Phenomenology* 24, no. 1 (1993): 32–43.
Bovens, Luc. 'The Value of Hope'. *Philosophy and Phenomenological Research* 59 (1999): 667–81.
Bowie, Malcolm. *Freud, Proust and Lacan: Theory as Fiction*. Cambridge: Cambridge University Press, 1987.
Cantacuzino, Marina. *The Forgiveness Project: Stories for a Vengeful Age*. London: Jessica Kingsley, 2015.
Colombetti, Giovanna. *The Feeling Body: Affective Science Meets the Enactive Mind*. Cambridge, MA: MIT Press, 2014.
Cullmann, Oscar. *Christ and Time: The Primitive Christian Conception of Time*. Translated by Floyd V. Filson. Westminster: John Knox Press, 1964.
Defoe, Daniel. *Robinson Crusoe*. Oxford: Oxford University Press, 2007.
Deleuze, Gilles. *Cinema 1*. Translated by Hugh Tomlinson and Barbara Habberjam. London: Athlone Press, 1986.
Deleuze, Gilles. *Difference and Repetition*. Translated by Paul Patton. London: Athlone, 1994.
Deleuze, Gilles. 'Immanence: A Life'. In *Pure Immanence: Essays on a Life*, translated by Anne Boyman, 25–34. New York: Zone Books, 2001.

Deleuze, Gilles. *The Logic of Sense*. Translated by Mark Lester with Charles Stivale and edited by Constantine Boundas. London: Athlone, 1990.

Deleuze, Gilles. 'We Invented the Ritornello'. In *Two Regimes of Madness*, translated by Ames Hodges and Mike Taormina, 377–81. London: MIT Press, 2006.

Deleuze, Gilles. *What is Grounding?*. Translated by Arjen Kleinherenbrink. Grand Rapids, MI: &&& Publishing, 2015.

Deleuze, Gilles and Félix Guattari. *What is Philosophy?*. Translated by Hugh Tomlinson and Graham Burchell. New York: Columbia University Press, 1994.

Derrida, Jacques. *The Gift of Death*. Translated by David Wills, 68–72. Chicago: The University of Chicago, 1996. Print.

Diego Bubbio, Paolo. 'Christ as Symbol in Kant's Religion'. In *God and Self in Hegel*, 13–30. New York: SUNY Press, 2018.

Diogenes Laertius. *Lives of Eminent Philosophers* I, II. Loeb Classical Library, nos. 184, 185. Translated by R. D. Hicks. London: William Heineman, 1925.

Duns Scotus, John. *The De Primo Principio of John Duns Scotus: A Revised Text and Translation*. Translated by Evan Roche. St. Bonaventure, NY: The Franciscan Institute, 1949.

Engelhard, Kristina Christian, J. Feldbacher-Escamilla, Alexander Gebharter and Ansgar Seide. 'Inductive Metaphysics'. *Grazer Philosophische Studien* 98, no. 1 (2021): 1–26.

Frankfurt, Harry G. *The Importance of What We Care About: Philosophical Essays*. Cambridge: Cambridge University Press, 1988.

Freuler, Leo. *La Crise de la Philosophie au XIXe Siècle*. Paris: Vrin, 1997.

Friedman, Michael. *A Parting of Ways – Carnap, Cassirer, and Heidegger*. Chicago and La Salle: Open Court, 2000.

Furtak, Rick Anthony. *Knowing Emotions: Truthfulness and Recognition in Affective Experience*. Oxford: Oxford University Press, 2018.

Gabriel, Jörg. *Rückkehr zu Gott. Die Predigten Johannes Taulers in ihrem zeit- und geistesgeschichtlichen Kontext. Zugleich eine Geschichte hochmittelalterlicher Spiritualität und Theologie*, 413–27. Würzburg: Echter Verlag, 2013.

Gammon, Martin. 'Exemplary Originality: Kant on Genius and Imitation'. *Journal of the History of Philosophy* 35, no. 4 (1997): 563–92.

Gilson, Étienne. *Being and Some Philosophers*, 2nd edn. Toronto: Pontifical Institute of Medieval Studies, 1952.

Gordon, Robert M. *The Structure of Emotions: Investigations in Cognitive Philosophy*. Cambridge: Cambridge University Press, 1987.

Groopman, Jerome. *The Anatomy of Hope: How People Prevail in the Face of Illness*. New York: Random House, 2004.

Gumbrecht, Hans Ulrich. *Atmosphere, Mood, Stimmung*. Translated by Erik Butler. Stanford, CA: Stanford University Press, 2012.

Halbertal, Moshe. *On Sacrifice*. Princeton, NJ: Princeton University Press, 2012.

Hegel, G. W. F. *Encyclopaedia of the Philosophical Sciences in Basic Outline, Part 1, Science of Logic*. New York: Cambridge University Press, 2010.

Hegel, G. W. F. *Hegel's Philosophy of Nature*. Edited and translated by M. J. Petry. London: Allen and Unwin Ltd, 1970.

Hegel, G. W. F. *Lectures on the History of Philosophy* vol. 3 *Medieval and Modern Philosophy*. Berkeley, CA: University of Central Punjab, 1990.

Hegel, G. W. F.. *Phänomenologie des Geistes*. Hamburg: Felix Meiner Verlag, 1988.

Hegel, G. W. F.. *Phenomenology of Spirit*. Translated by A. V. Miller. Oxford: Oxford University Press, 1977.

Heiberg, Johan Ludvig. 'Review of Dr. Rothe's *Doctrine of the Trinity and Reconciliation*'. In *Heiberg's Perseus and Other Texts*, edited and translated by Jon Stewart, 85–149. Copenhagen: Museum Tusculanum Press, 2011.

Heidegger, Martin. *The Basic Problems of Phenomenology*. Translated by Albert Hofstadter. Bloomington, IN: Indiana University Press, 1988.

Heidegger, Martin. *Being and Time*. Translated by Joan Stambaugh. New York: State University New York Press, 1996.

Heidegger, Martin. *The Fundamental Concepts of Metaphysics: World, Finitude, Solitude*. Translated by William McNeill and Nicholas Walker. Bloomington, IN: Indiana University Press, 1995.

Heidegger, Martin. 'The Origin of the Work of Art'. In *Basic Writings*, edited by David Krell, 139–213. San Francisco, CA: Harper, 1993.

Heidegger, Martin. *Sein und Zeit*. Frankfurt am Main: Vittorio Klostermann, 1977.

Heidegger, Martin. *Zollikon Seminars*. Translated by Franz Mayr and Richard Askay. Evanston, IL: Northwestern University Press, 2001.

Hölderlin, Friedrich. 'Becoming in Dissolution'. In *Essays and Letters on Theory*, translated by Thomas Pfau, 96–100. Albany, NY: State University New York Press, 1988.

Husserl, Edmund. *Analyses Concerning Passive and Active Synthesis*. Translated by Anthony J. Steinbock. Boston, MA: Kluwer Academic Publishers, 2001.

Husserl, Edmund. *Ideas II*. Translated by Richard Rojcewicz and André Schuwer. Dordrecht: Kluwer Academic Publishers, 1989.

James, William. 'On Some Hegelisms'. In *The Will to Believe and Other Essays in Popular Philosophy*, 263–98. London: Longmans Green and Co, 1912.

Jaspers, Karl. *Existenzphilosophie*, 4th edn. Berlin: De Gruyter, 1974.

Jaspers, Karl. 'The Sentiment of Rationality'. In *The Will to Believe and Other Essays*, 96–7. New York: Longman, Green and Co, 1912.

Jephcott, E. F. N. *Proust and Rilke: The Literature of Expanded Consciousness*. London: Chatto & Windus, 1972.

Kant, Immanuel. *Critique of Judgment*. Translated by Werner S. Pluhar. Cambridge: Hackett Publishing Company, 1987.

Kant, Immanuel. *Critique of Practical Reason*. Edited and translated by Mary Gregor. Cambridge: Cambridge University Press, 1997.

Kant, Immanuel. *The Critique of Pure Reason*. Translated by Norman Kemp Smith. New York: St. Martin's Press, 1965.

Kant, Immanuel. *Kritik der Urteilskraft* vol. 10 of *Werkausgabe*. Edited by Wilhelm Weischedel. Frankfurt am Main: Suhrkamp, 1978.

Kant, Immanuel. *Lectures on Metaphysics*. Translated and Edited by Karl Ameriks and Steve Naragon. Cambridge: Cambridge University Press, 1997.

Kant, Immanuel. *Religion Within the Bounds of Bare Reason*. Translated by Werner Pluhar. Cambridge: Hackett, 2009.

Kojève, Alexandre. *Introduction to the Reading of Hegel: Lectures on the Phenomenology of Spirit*, edited by Alan Bloom. Ithaca, NY: Cornell University Press, 1980.

Kreines, James. 'Hegel's Critique of Pure Mechanism and the Philosophical Appeal of the Logic Project'. *European Journal of Philosophy* 12, no. 1 (2004): 38–74.

Landy, Joshua. *Philosophy as Fiction: Self, Deception, and Knowledge in Proust*. Oxford: Oxford University Press, 2004.

Lear, Jonathan. *Radical Hope: Ethics in the Face of Cultural Devastation*. Cambridge MA: Harvard University Press, 2006.

Leibniz, Gottfried Wilhelm. *Theodicy*. Translated by E. M. Huggard. New Haven, CT: Yale University Press, 1952.

Levin, David Michael. *The Body's Recollection of Being: Phenomenological Psychology and the Deconstruction of Nihilism*. London: Routledge and Kegan Paul, 1985.

Lewis, David K. *Counterfactuals*. Cambridge, MA: Harvard University Press, 1973.

Little, Margaret Olivia. 'Seeing and Caring: The Role of Affect in Feminist Epistemology'. *Hypatia* 10, no. 3 (1995): 117–37.

Longuenesse, Béatrice. *Hegel et la critique de la métaphysique. Étude sur la doctrine de l'essence*. Paris: Vrin, 1981.

Lotze, Hermann. *Microcosmus*. Edinburgh: T&T Clark, 1885.

Löwith, Karl. *From Hegel to Nietzsche: The Revolution in Nineteenth-Century Thought*. New York: Columbia University Press, 1964.

Löwith, Karl, *The Meaning in History: The Theological Implication of the Philosophy of History*. Chicago, IL: Chicago University Press, 1957.

Łukasiewicz, Jan. *Aristotle's Syllogistic from the Standpoint of Modern Formal Logic*, 2nd edn. Oxford: Clarendon Press, 1957.

Macintyre, Alasdair. *After Virtue*. Notre Dame: University of Notre Dame Press, 1981.

Martensen, Hans Lassen. 'Martensen's "Rationalism, Supernaturalism" and the *principium exclusi Medii*'. In *Kierkegaard Studies Yearbook*, vol. 9, translated by Jon Stewart, 583–94. Berlin: DeGruyter, 2004.

Martin, Adrienne M. *How We Hope: A Moral Psychology*. Princeton, NJ: Princeton University Press, 2014.

Mauss, Marcel. *The Gift: Forms and Functions of Exchange in Archaic Societies*. London: Cohen & West, 1966.

Meister Eckhart. 'Daz buoch der göttlichen trœstunge'. In *Meister Eckhart. Die deutschen Werke*, 5 vols, edited by Josef Quint et al., vol. 5, 1–136. Stuttgart, W. Kohlhammer, 1936–2003.

Merleau-Ponty, Maurice. 'Eye and Mind'. In *Primacy of Perception*, edited by James M. Edie, 159–92. Indianapolis, IN: Northwestern University Press, 1964.

Merleau-Ponty, Maurice. *Phenomenology of Perception*. Translated by Donald A. Landes. London: Routledge, 2012.

Merleau-Ponty, Maurice. *The Visible and the Invisible*. Translated by Alphonso Lingis. Evanston, IL: Northwestern University Press, 1968.

Miller, J. Hillis. *On Literature*. London: Routledge, 2002.

Moltmann, Jürgen. *Theology of Hope*. Translated by James W. Leitch. Minneapolis, MN: Fortress Press, 1993.

Nehamas, Alexander. *Only a Promise of Happiness*. Princeton, NJ: Princeton University Press, 2007.

Nietzsche, Friedrich. 'On Truth and Lies in a Nonmoral Sense'. In *Philosophy and Truth: Selections from Nietzsche's Notebooks of the Early 1870's*, edited and translated by Daniel Breazeale, 79–97. Atlantic Highlands, NJ: Humanities Press, 1979.

Nietzsche, Friedrich. *The Will to Power*. Translated by Walter Kaufmann and R. J. Hollingdale. New York: Vintage Books, 1968.

Nussbaum, Martha C. *Love's Knowledge: Essays on Philosophy and Literature*. Oxford: Oxford University Press, 1990.

Patočka, Jan. *Heretical Essays in the Philosophy of History*. Translated by Erazim Kohák. Chicago, IL: Carus Publishing Company, 1996.

Petit, Susan, *Michel Tournier's Metaphysical Fictions*. Philadelphia, PA: John Benjamins Publishing Company, 1991.

Pettit, Philip. 'Hope and its Place in Mind'. *Annals of the American Academy of Political and Social Science* 592 (2004): 152–65.

Proust, Marcel. *À la Recherche du Temps Perdu*, 3 vols. Edited by Pierre Clarac and André Ferré. Paris: Gallimard, 1954.

Proust, Marcel. *Remembrance of Things Past*, 3 vols. Translated by C. K. Scott Moncrieff and Terence Kilmartin. New York: Vintage Books, 1982.

Ratcliffe, Matthew. *Experiences of Depression*. Oxford: Oxford University Press, 2015.

Ratcliffe, Matthew. *Feelings of Being: Phenomenology, Psychiatry, and the Sense of Reality*. Oxford: Oxford University Press, 2008.

Redding, Paul. *The Logic of Affect*. Ithaca, NY: Cornell University Press, 1999.

Rescher, Nicholas. 'The Ontology of the Possible'. In *The Possible and the Actual: Readings in the Metaphysics of Modality*, edited by Michael J. Loux, 166–81. Ithaca, NY: Cornell University Press, 1979.

Rosenzweig, Franz. *The Star of Redemption*. Translated by Barbara E. Galli. Madison, WI: Wisconsin University Press, 2005.

Sartre, Jean-Paul. *Being and Nothingness*. Translated by Hazel E. Barnes. New York: Pocket Books, 1978.

Sartre, Jean-Paul. *The Imagination*. Translated by Kenneth Williford and David Rudrauf. London: Routledge, 2012.

Scheler, Max. 'Ordo Amoris'. In *Selected Philosophical Essays*, translated by David Lachterman, 98–135. Evanston, IL: Northwestern University Press, 1973.

Schelling, Friedrich W. J. *Philosophical Investigations into the Essence pf Human Freedom*. Translated by Jeff Love and Johannes Schmidt. New York: State University of New York Press, 2006.

Schnädelbach, Herbert. *Philosophie in Deutschland – 1831–1933*. Frankfurt am Main: Surkamp, 1983.

Schnieder, Benjamin. 'Mere Possibilities: Bolzano's Account of Non-actual Objects'. *Journal of the History of Philosophy* 45, no. 4 (2007): 525–50.

Schrag, Calvin O. *Existence and Freedom*. Evanston, IL: Northwestern University Press, 1961.

Taubes, Jacob. *The Political Theology of Paul*. Translated by Dana Hollander. Stanford, CA: Stanford University Press, 2003.

Tauler, Johannes. *Die Predigten Taulers: Aus der Engelberger und der Freiburger Handschrift sowie aus Schmidts Abschriften der ehemaligen Straßburger Handschriften*. Edited by Ferdinand Vetter. Berlin: Weidmann, 1910.

Tauler, Johannes. *Johann Tauler's Predigten auf alle Sonn- und Festtage im Jhr. Zur Beförderung eines christlichen und gottseligen Wandels*, 3 vols. [on the basis of the editions of Johann Arndt and Philipp Jacob Spener]. Edited by Edudard Kuntze and Johann Heinrich Raphael Biesenthal. Berlin: August Hirschwald, 1841–1842.

Tauler, Johannes. *Sermon*. Translated by Maria Shrady. Mahwah, NJ: Paulist Press, 1985.

Thoreau, Henry David. 'Autumnal Tints'. In *Collected Essays and Poems*, edited by Elizabeth H. Witherell, 367–95. New York: Library of America, 2001.

Tournier, Michel. *Friday*. Translated by Norman Denny. Baltimore, MD: Johns Hopkins University Press, 1997.

Trendelenburg, Adolf. *Die logische Frage in Hegel's System. Zwei Streitschriften*. Leipzig: F. A. Brockhaus, 1843.

Ventura, David. 'The inTensive Other: Deleuze and Levinas on the Ethical Status of the Other'. *The Southern Journal of Philosophy* 58, no. 2 (2020): 327–50.

Vilkko, Risto. 'The Logic Question during the First Half of the Nineteenth Century'. In *The Development of Modern Logic*, edited by Leila Haaparanta, 203–21. New York: Oxford University Press, 2009.

Walker, Margaret Urban. *Moral Repair: Reconstructing Moral Relations after Wrongdoing*. Cambridge: Cambridge University Press, 2006.

Windelband, Wilhelm. 'History and Natural Science'. *Theory and Psychology* 8, no. 1 (1998): 5–22.

Wolff, Christian. *Gesammelte werke* vol. 3. *Philosophia prima sive ontologia*. Hildesheim: Georg Olms, 1962.

Wolterstorff, Nicholas. *Justice in Love*. Grand Rapids, MI: Eerdmans, 2015.

Zahavi, Dan. *Self-Awareness and Alterity: A Phenomenological Investigation*. Evanston, IL: Northwestern University Press, 1999.

Index

actuality   1–5, 8–19, 17 n.18, 19 n.50, 23–34, 37, 42–3, 47, 52–5, 66, 97 n.32, 100–1, 109, 126–8, 136, 173, 175, 177 n.4
  Virkelighed   42–3, 52–6, 126
aesthetic, the/aesthetics/aesthete   36–8, 70, 89, 91, 93, 97 n.32, 98 n.42, 141 n.21
  possibility   10–15, 30–5, 63, 65, 127, 188
  religious   15, 33–7, 84, 87, 93
affect, *see* attunement; mood
anxiety   1, 9, 13, 15–16, 112–14, 147, 157, 173, 181 n.22, 184
  education   125–32, 135–9
  hope   208, 209
  'possibility of possibility'   9, 13, 15, 79, 113
Aristotle   2, 4, 6, 17 n.18, 24, 30, 33, 127
attunement   13, 71–2, 75 n.32, 187, 197

becoming   3, 14, 19 n.50, 53, 89, 108, 172, 173, 176
  coming into existence   3, 4, 9, 14, 17, 19 n.49, 50
  self   10, 33, 34, 77 n.56, 128, 187, 190, 200 n.39
beginning/origin   1, 3, 4, 8, 18 n.25, 26, 45, 55, 79, 85–6, 96 n.12, 97 n.23, 99–100, 108–10, 168, 171, 187, 203 n.80, 214
being   1–7, 13–16, 17 nn.7, 13, 25, 26, 45–56, 77 n.56, 99, 168, 172, 179 n.4, *see also* metaphysics; ontology
  esse   23–31, 33, 39 n.4, 49–50, 54
Bergson, Henri   102, 108–9, 114–15, 118 n.36 and   38, 119 n.42

calculation, *see* probability
Christ   173, 180 n.11, 186, 191–5
  possibility   125, 128, 169, 194
  prototype/*Forbillede*   35–6, 38, 81, 83, 87, 92, 93, 186, 191

Christianity   26, 72, 81, 125, 129, 131, 137, 138, 160, 163 n.30, 169–73, 176–7, 179 n.7, 180 n.13, 181 n.22, 182 n.25, 191–3, 195, 197, 200 n.39, 215, 219 n.48, *see also* God
  theology   6, 14, 24–6, 92, 169, 170, 172–5, 181, 186, 190–1
climate   15, 184–90, 195–7
consciousness   13, 108–9, 119 n.42, 120 n.59, 133–5, 143 n.44, 173
  natural (unhappy)   133–5
  others   65, 104, 113, 118 n.31
  sin   126, 128, 132
contingency   2–5, 8, 14, 67–8, 73, 77 n.59, 100–1, 105, 117 n.25

Deleuze, Gilles   13, 99, 101, 103–16, 118 nn.36, 37, 119 nn.42, 51, 120 n.59, 121 n.66
  transcendental field   103, 107–10, 113–15
Derrida, Jacques   8, 120 n.60, 145, 148–51, 153–4, 156–60, 162 n.15
despair   1, 12, 13, 16, 38, 77 n.60, 82, 103, 116 n.3, 134, 184, 191
  climate   184–90, 195–7
  despair of necessity/finitude   9–10, 187–90, 220 n.60
  despair of possibility   12, 187–8, 190
  hope   186, 193, 195, 197, 205, 207–8, 210, 211, 215, 216, 217 n.11, 220 n.60

esse, see being
essence   2–3, 5–6, 10, 16–17 nn.7, 13, 27, 29, 51, 52, 55, 99
eternity, the/eternal   2, 5, 10, 14, 18 n.34, 38, 53–4, 66, 72, 103, 109, 110, 132, 167–72, 174, 178, 179 n.10, 181 n.22, 183 n.34, 187, 195, 197, 200 n.39, 202 n.67, 205, 206, 215–16, 217 nn.5, 6, 220 nn.59, 60, 221 n.95

ethics/ethical, the   27, 30–4, 37, 55, 94, 98 n.42, 137, 145–60, 163 n.30, 180 n.10, 187–8, 195
existence   10, 13, 24, 29, 32, 47–9, 51–6, 116, 128, 135, 167, 180 n.13, 195
  modality   1–7, 14, 17 n.7, 19 nn.49, 50, 25, 27, 30, 34, 48, 51–3, 74 n.17, 127, 136
  self   9, 10, 14, 34, 173, 174
existentialism   6–8, 44

faith   15, 16, 32–4, 38, 49, 82–4, 86, 90, 131, 145–8, 150–3, 162 n.20, 174, 177, 189–90, 192, 195–7, 204–6, 212, 220 n.61
  anxiety   126, 130, 135, 137
  Fear and Trembling   145–8, 150–3, 156–9
  gift (Derrida)   155–9
finitude/finite, the   4, 5, 9, 11, 54, 72, 73, 126–7, 135–7, 139, 159, 173, 187, 196, 204, 214
freedom   1, 3, 5, 9, 14, 19 n.49, 23, 27, 82–3, 93, 113, 118 n.36, 125–8, 130, 131, 135–6, 167, 170–3, 175, 177, 180 n.13, 182 nn.22, 25

God   8, 11, 25–6, 31, 51, 53, 54, 56, 73, 88, 125, 128, 145–8, 150–60, 162 n.22, 169, 171–3, 177–8, 179 n.7, 180 n.10, 181 n.22, 182 n.25, 187, 189–94, 196, 197, 201 n.63, 202 nn.64, 67, 204, 206, 217 n.6, *see also* Christianity
  divine   14, 73, 146, 149, 152, 157, 170–3, 175, 177, 178, 181 n.15, 186, 191, 193–5
guilt   82, 114, 120 n.60, 132, 137, 185, 196, 213

Hegel, Georg Wilhelm Friedrich   1–5, 8, 14, 17 n.18, 23–9, 34, 43–7, 55, 56, 126, 133–5, 138, 143 n.44, 168, 171, 174–8, 178 n.4, 179 n.10
  logic   1, 4–5, 25–31, 34, 45–6, 52–3, 99–101, 107, 114, 176, 182 n.25
Heidegger, Martin   6–8, 13, 15, 46, 52, 71, 95 n.5, 97 n.23, 136

hope   9, 10, 16, 49, 66, 137, 139, 162 n.20, 171, 181 n.22, 185–6, 189–91, 193–7, 204–16, 217 nn.11, 14, 219 nn.47, 50, 220 n.59–60, 221 n.95

idealism   2–3, 8, 45–7, 56, 182 n.25
imagination   1, 9, 11–15, 24, 30, 33–4, 37, 49, 67, 93, 95, 113, 186–90, 192–5, 197, 200 n.38, 205, 208
immanence   9, 14, 48, 100–2, 108, 111, 114, 150, 174–7, 180 n.13, 182 n.25
immediacy   33, 77 n.55, 86, 113–14, 132, 137, 150, 156, 168, 175
individual, the   31, 38, 49, 53, 54, 77 n.56, 82, 94, 100, 108, 109, 118 n.37, 121 n.66, 125, 127–8, 130–1, 134–9, 159, 162 n.23, 169, 172, 182 n.22, 188, *see also* self/selfhood
innocence   103, 110–16
instant, *see* moment

Kant, Immanuel   14, 17 n.13, 45, 48 nn.37, 40, 42, 106–7, 111, 180 n.10, 218 n.40
  Critique of Judgement   78, 80, 84–5, 87, 91–5, 98
  modalities   4, 25–6, 39 n.6, 52, 108

leap   48, 100, 114, 120 n.59, 145–6, 148, 150, 152, 155–8, 171, 173, 175–6, 179 n.10, 209
love   9–11, 35, 36, 38, 49, 63, 65–70, 72–3, 74 n.9, 77 n.57, 87, 98 n.42, 131, 139, 146–7, 153, 155–6, 158, 160, 162 n.18, 163 n.30, 168, 177–8, 187, 193, 199 n.17, 206, 210, 211, 215–16

metaphysics   3, 7, 13–14, 23, 25, 43–57, 67, 99, 175–7, *see also* being; ontology
  modality   1, 6, 7, 16, 42–3, 47, 52, 54, 56, 180 n.13
moment, instant   8, 131, 161 n.13, 174–6, 178, 179 n.10, 181 n.22, 203 n.80
mood   3, 7, 13, 14, 68, 70–2, 77 n.55, 109–10, 132, 139, 187, *see also* attunement
  affect   3, 10, 14, 65, 69–72, 75 n.35, 76 n.45, 77 n.55

necessity/necessary, the   1, 4–5, 9–10, 12, 14, 17 n.17, 19 nn.39, 49, 50, 25, 28, 42, 45, 47, 99, 100, 105, 107, 167, 177, 187, 188, 190, 195, 200 n.39

ontology   1–3, 5–10, 13–14, 16, 17 n.13, 25, 40 n.12, 42–5, 47–51, 53–6, 60 n.56, 67, 111, 125, 127–8, 126, 172, *see also* being; metaphysics
other, the   31, 35, 36, 38, 64–6, 70, 72, 77 n.57, 101, 103–13, 115, 116, 117 n.25, 118 n.31, 119 n.48–51, 121 n.66, 145, 146, 151–60, 162 n.17, 168, 211

phenomenology   6, 8, 10, 13–14, 58 n.12, 56 n.77, 67, 72, 104–7, 110–12, 119 nn.42, 48, 126, 132–3, 138, 178, *see also* Heidegger, Martin
Merleau-Ponty, Maurice   77 n.57, 100, 104–6, 110–12, 119 n.48
Sartre, Jean-Paul   7, 74 n.9, 75 n.32, 104–5, 108, 119 n.42
poet/poetic/poetry   30, 32–3, 35, 37, 49, 64, 109, 127, 131, *see also* aesthetic, the/aesthete
possibility, possible, the   1–16, 19 n.40, 23–5, 27–39, 39 nn.2, 4, 6, 42, 47, 52–5, 63–70, 72, 74 nn.9, 10, 17, 23, 75 nn.32, 35, 76 nn.41, 60, 99–101, 103, 104–9, 110, 113–16, 117 n.3, 118 nn.31, 38, 125–30, 133, 135–7, 139–40, 145, 150, 152–3, 157, 159–60, 167–75, 180 n.10, 181 n.15, 182 n.22, 191, 200 n.39, 201 n.63, 211, 220 n.60
God as possibility   8, 73, 152, 177–8, 189–90, 193–4, 196, 201 n.63, 204
good   10, 194–7, 204–9, 212, 216
moment/instant   178, 203 n.80
pattern   78–9, 81, 83–4, 86–7, 92–3
posse   23–31, 33, 39 n.4
possible worlds   65, 67, 73, 104, 106
probability/probable, the   9–11, 15, 84, 169–75, 179 n.7, 189–94, 196–7, 205–9, 218 n.40
calculation   8–10, 108, 150, 152, 155, 158–60, 161 n.13, 162 n.15, 173, 175, 189–94, 207, 209

economy/economic, the   11, 103, 108, 149–50, 158, 160, 161 n.13, 172
sagacity   10, 168, 191–3, 195–7, 204, 208, 211, 217 n.5

repetition   8–10, 74 n.17, 78, 82–90, 92–5, 96 n.14, 109, 116, 181 n.21, 203 n.80
representation   100–3, 106–12, 114–16, 119 n.51, 128, 132–3, 212

self/selfhood   1, 4–5, 7, 9–15, 19 n.40, 23, 24, 27, 29, 34, 35, 38, 77 n.56, 107, 109, 113, 127, 131, 132, 138, 154, 156, 158–9, 173, 186–95, 200 n.39, 201 n.63, 208, 216, 217 n.6, *see also* individual, the; spirit; subjectivity
sin   32, 35–6, 38, 113–15, 120 n.53, 126–7, 131–2, 139, 141 n.21, 181 n.22, 190, 196
singularity   68, 81, 82, 84, 94, 108–9, 118 n.37, 121 n.66, 146, 148, 152–5, 157, 159–60, 161 n.4, 163 n.30, 167, 172, 177–8, *see also* individual, the; subjectivity
single individual   30, 94, 126, 130, 134, 137–9
spirit   11, 12, 27–8, 114, 128, 132, 136, 137, 171, 177, 178 n.4, *see also* self
subjectivity   11, 13–14, 30, 37, 49, 54, 64, 69–72, 105, 107–15, 119 n.42, 121 n.66, 126, 134, 143 n.44, 146, 154–9, 163 n.30, *see also* self/selfhood

temporality   1, 2, 5, 53–4, 79, 102, 107–11, 115, 135–6, 168, 170–2, 174, 176, 177, 179 n.10, 181 n.22, 189 n.2, 185, 187, 195, 197, 200 n.39, 203 n.80, 215–16
transition   1, 5, 48–9, 100, 105–6, 112–16, 168, 171, 174–6
movement/motion   1–3, 5, 6, 9, 23, 25, 52, 107, 113, 139, 171, 176–7
Trendelenburg, Adolf   17 n.18, 42–8

uncertainty   4, 15–16, 32, 34, 66, 72, 74 n.23, 75 n.29, 78, 81–4, 86, 88, 90–1, 136, 185
hope   66, 207–8

Pseudonymous authors
Anti-Climacus   12, 34, 128, 132,
    137, 140, 187–90, 192, 194
Climacus, Johannes   3–5, 24,
    30–4, 38, 52, 81–6, 129,
    131–2
Constantius, Constantin   205

de Silentio, Johannes   80–2, 84–6,
    146–7, 154, 204
Haufniensis, Vigilius   4–5, 9, 32, 88,
    125–32, 135–8, 140, 141 n.21
Taciturnus, Frater   15, 24, 30–8
William, Judge   132

Kierkegaard's works
Concept of Anxiety, The   4–5, 9–10, 88,
    110, 125–33, 135–7, 139–40, 141
    n.21, 172, 173–4, 176, 177
Concluding Unscientific Postscript   3, 24,
    30, 38, 42, 48, 51, 53, 125, 128
Either/Or   11, 13, 70, 87–92, 128
Fear and Trembling   78, 80–2, 94, 145–60,
    162 n.18, 204, 220 n.68
Philosophical Fragments   3, 5, 14, 16 n.7,
    17 n.17, 19 nn.49, 50, 33, 51, 78, 81,
    82, 85, 86

Practice in Christianity   12, 34, 191–3
Repetition   48, 70, 75 n.27, 96 n.14, 204–5
Sickness unto Death, The   8–10, 12, 16,
    79, 137, 140, 152, 187, 201 n.63,
    220 n.60
Stages on Life's Way   24, 37
Upbuilding Discourses   125–6, 128–30,
    139, 178, 191–3, 199 n.18,
    202 n.69
Works of Love   10, 73, 146, 204, 211, 215,
    217 n.5

www.ingramcontent.com/pod-product-compliance
Lightning Source LLC
Chambersburg PA
CBHW071824300426
44116CB00009B/1430